OXFORD MONOGRAPHS ON MUSIC

English Bowed Instruments

from Anglo-Saxon to
Tudor Times

English Bowed Instruments

from Anglo-Saxon to Tudor Times

MARY REMNANT

CLARENDON PRESS · OXFORD
1986

Oxford University Press, Walton Street, Oxford OX2 6DP
Oxford New York Toronto
Dehli Bombay Calcutta Madras Karachi
Petaling Jaya Singapore Hong Kong Tokyo
Nairobi Dar es Salaam Cape Town
Melbourne Auckland
and associated companies in
Beirut Berlin Ibadan Nicosia

OXFORD is a trade mark of Oxford University Press

Published in the United States
by Oxford University Press, New York

British Library Cataloguing in Publication Data
Remnant, Mary
English bowed instruments from
Anglo-Saxon to Tudor times.
1. Stringed instruments, Bowed
— History   2. Musical instruments,
English — History
I.   Title
787'.012'0942   ML750
ISBN 0–19–816134–4

Library of Congress Cataloging in Publication Data
Remnant, Mary.
English bowed instruments from Anglo-Saxon to Tudor times.
(Oxford monographs on music)
Bibliography: p.
Includes index.
1. Stringed instruments, Bowed.   2. Musical
instruments — England.   I. Title.   II. Series.
ML760.A2R45   1986   787'.01'0942   85–32034
ISBN 0–19–816134–4

Typeset by Latimer Trend & Company Ltd, Plymouth
Printed in Great Britain by
Butler & Tanner Ltd
Frome, Somerset

A.M.D.G.

To all my friends
who have helped with this
book

Contents

❧

Illustrations and
Acknowledgements

❧

THE author is most grateful to the various owners and institutions who have kindly given permission for the use of their photographic material.

Titles of Manuscripts and Seals

THE following list gives the shelf-marks of those manuscripts and seals which are well known by particular titles and are described by them in the text. When one title can apply to more than one manuscript, it is followed by the name of the town where the relevant volume is kept, e.g. Canterbury Psalter (Oxford).

Alfonso Psalter	London, British Library, Additional MS 24686.
Amesbury Psalter	Oxford, All Souls College, MS 6.
Apocalypse of St. Sever	Paris, Bibliothèque Nationale, MS Latin 8878.
Bible of Charles the Bald	Paris, Bibliothèque Nationale, MS Latin I.
Bird Psalter	Cambridge, Fitzwilliam Museum, MS 2–1954.
Bohun Psalter (London)	London, British Library, MS Egerton 3277.
Bohun Psalter (Oxford)	Oxford, Exeter College, MS Coxe 47.
Brailes Psalter	Cambridge, Fitzwilliam Museum, MS 330.
Bromholm Psalter	Oxford, Bodleian Library, MS Ashmole 1523.
Canterbury Psalter (Oxford)	Oxford, Bodleian Library, MS Ashmole 1525.
Cantigas de Santa Maria	Escorial, Monastery of San Lorenzo, MS j. b. 2.
Christina Psalter	Copenhagen, Royal Library, MS G. K. S. 1606.
Douce Apocalypse	Oxford, Bodleian Library, MS Douce 180.
Dublin Apocalypse	Dublin, Trinity College, MS K. 4. 31.
Evesham Psalter	London, British Library, Additional MS 44874.
Glazier Psalter	New York, Pierpont Morgan Library, MS Glazier 25.
Gorleston Psalter	London, British Library, Additional MS 49622.
Grandison Psalter	London, British Library, Additional MS 21926.
Great Canterbury Psalter	Paris, Bibliothèque Nationale, MS Lat. 8846.
Henry VIII's Manuscript	London, British Library, Additional MS 31922.
Hours of Elizabeth the Queen	London, British Library, Additional MS 50001.
Howard Psalter	London, British Library, MS Arundel 83, ff. 1–116.
Huth Psalter	London, British Library, Additional MS 38116.
Iona Psalter	Edinburgh, National Library of Scotland, MS Accession 3141.
Lambeth Apocalypse	London, Lambeth Palace Library, MS 209.
Lambeth Bible	London, Lambeth Palace Library, MS 3.

Lindesey Psalter	London, Society of Antiquaries Library, MS 59.
Lisle Psalter	London, British Library, MS Arundel 83, ff. 117–35.
Litlyngton Missal	London, Westminster Abbey Library, MS 37.
Lunel Psalter	Lunel, Bibliothèque Municipale, MS I.
Luttrell Psalter	London, British Library, Additional MS 42130.
Old Hall Manuscript	London, British Library, Additional MS 59790.
Ormesby Psalter	Oxford, Bodleian Library, MS Douce 366.
Peterborough Psalter	Brussels, Bibliothèque Royale, MS 9961–2.
Queen Mary Psalter	London, British Library, MS Royal 2 B. vii.
Robertsbridge Fragment	London, British Library, Additional MS 28550.
Romance of Alexander	Oxford, Bodleian Library, MS Bodley 264.
St. Albans Psalter	Hildesheim, Church of St. Godehard.
St. Louis Psalter	Leiden, Bibliotheek der Rijksuniversiteit, MS Lat. 76A.
St. Martial Troper	Paris, Bibliothèque Nationale, MS Latin 1118.
St. Neots Psalter	London, Lambeth Palace Library, MS 563.
Shaftesbury Psalter	London, British Library, MS Lansdowne 383.
Sherborne Missal	Alnwick Castle, Northumberland.
Smithfield Decretals	London, British Library, MS Royal 10. E. iv.
Theodore Psalter	London, British Library, MS 19352.
Tiberius Psalter	London, British Library, MS Cotton Tiberius C. vi.
Tickhill Psalter	New York, Public Library, MS Spencer 26.
Trinity College Apocalypse	Cambridge, Trinity College, MS R. 16. 2.
Utrecht Psalter	Utrecht University Library, MS Script. eccles. 484.
Vaux Psalter	London, Lambeth Palace Library, MS 233.
Velislav Bible	Prague University Library, MS 412.
Venice Psalter	Venice, Biblioteca Nazionale Marciana, MS Latina I. 77.
Vespasian Psalter	London, British Library, Cotton MS Vespasian A. i.
Winchcombe Bible	Dublin Trinity College, MS 53.
Winchcombe Psalter	Cambridge, University Library, MS Ff. i. 23.
Winchester Psalter	London, British Library, MS Cotton Nero C. iv.
Worms Bible	London, British Library, MS Harley 2804.
York Psalter	Glasgow University Library, MS Hunter 229 (*olim* U.3.2.).
Seal of Roger Wade the Crowder	London, British Library, Seal lxxxvii. 44.
Seal of Walter le Vyelur	London, Public Record Office, Seal P.832.

Abbreviations

AEMR	*Ancient Engleish Metrical Romanceës* (ed. Joseph Ritson)
AIM	American Institute of Musicology
AMl	*Acta Musicologica*
BL	British Library
Bodl.	Bodleian Library
CEKM	*Corpus of Early Keyboard Music*
CMM	*Corpus Mensurabilis Musicae* (AIM)
CSM	*Corpus Scriptorum de Musica* (AIM)
CSP:OS	*Camden Society Publications: Original Series*
EEH	*Early English Harmony*, i, ed. H. E. Wooldridge
EETS:OS	*Early English Text Society: Original Series*
EETS:ES	*Early English Text Society: Extra Series*
EETS:SS	*Early English Text Society: Supplementary Series*
EM	*Early Music*
FoMRHI	Fellowship of Makers and Restorers of Historical Instruments
Grove 6	*The New Grove Dictionary of Music and Musicians*
GSJ	*Galpin Society Journal*
HAM	*Historical Anthology of Music* (ed. Archibald T. Davison and Willi Apel)
HMS	*History of Music in Sound*
IMS	*International Musicological Society*
JVdGSA	*Journal of the Viola da Gamba Society of America*
L & P	*Letters and Papers* (ed. J. Brewer)
LU	*Liber Usualis*
M & L	*Music and Letters*
MMS	*Monumenta Musicae Sacrae*
MSD	*Musicological Studies and Documents*
NOHM	*New Oxford History of Music*
PMMS	Plainsong and Mediaeval Music Society
PRMA	*Proceedings of the Royal Musical Association*
PRO	Public Record Office (London)
PSP	Percy Society Publications
RS	*Rolls Series*
SMIBI	*A Survey of Manuscripts Illuminated in the British Isles* (ed. J. J. E. Alexander)

Note to the Reader

THE period covered by this book stretches from the early eleventh century to the death of Henry VIII in 1547. The illustrations are set in approximately chronological order, so as to show the gradual appearance of new instruments and the development of others, and the groups in which they were played at different times.

Towns and villages quoted in the main text are not normally accompanied there by their county, which can be found, if necessary, in Appendix C.

Certain manuscripts are referred to by a particular title, for example Ormesby Psalter, and full details of these are given in the list on pp. xvii–xviii.

Wherever possible, manuscripts from before the mid-thirteenth century are dated here according to *A Survey of Manuscripts Illuminated in the British Isles* edited by J. J. G. Alexander (London, 1975–   ). Future volumes of the series will cover the later period.

When quotations are taken from certain publications, their spelling is as it appears in the works concerned. However, when a minstrel's name and description are known only in Latin, they are generally given in the nominative case, even if the source is, for instance, in the dative. The exception to this is in the actual quotation of sources.

It is inevitable that the book should quote from mediaeval English literature. However, much of this had already evolved through different periods and in different countries, so the names of the instruments quoted here are not necessarily given in their original forms; the versions used have been chosen for their relevance to the present text.

The terminology of certain plucked instruments has for long been under question, particularly since the appearance of Laurence Wright's article 'The Medieval Gittern and Citole: A case of mistaken identity'. The instruments concerned will be given their traditional names here, followed in brackets by those suggested by Wright, for example 'gittern (citole)' or 'mandora (gittern)'.

When the names of notes are quoted in the text, the following customs have been adhered to:

(a) Roman capital letters indicate no particular pitch,

     e.g. C, D, G.

(b) Italics indicate the specific pitch shown below:

Introduction

❧

IF there was a particular moment at which this book originated, it was a small and unexpected incident in May 1953, when, as a student at the Royal College of Music, I had just had an audition at London's County Hall for that vital grant which would cover my fees and maintenance over the next three years. Feeling worried about the outcome, I walked back across Westminster Bridge and was happily distracted by the arrival of the Queen and other members of the Royal Family for a Coronation rehearsal in Westminster Abbey. While I was standing in the crowd, there came out of the Abbey an old friend of my father's, Mr R. P. Howgrave-Graham, who worked there in the Muniment Room. He stopped to talk for a short time before moving on, and a few days later sent me a postcard of one of the musical angels in the roof of Gloucester Cathedral, saying that he hoped the audition had gone better than I thought, and that the angel would give me some inspiration. Fortunately the result was good after all, and the angel stimulated a lifetime's work which combined the musical interests of my mother with the architectural and archaeological interests of my father.

That angel was playing an instrument which looked rather like a violin (plate 96), but it was not one—so what was it? At the time I was too much involved with Flesch scales and Kreutzer studies to give it much thought, but about the time of leaving college in 1956 I decided to list and photograph (where possible) all the mediaeval representations of instruments that my path happened to cross. Inevitably further studies followed, this time at Oxford, and when a subject was needed for a D.Phil. thesis it was easy to choose 'Bowed Instruments in England up to the Reformation', which was completed in 1972.

This book is the revision of that thesis, extended throughout the reign of Henry VIII, and the long gap between the completion of the one and the publication of the other has meant that it could profit by many new discoveries, of which the most exciting was certainly the excavation, in 1981–2, of two fiddles on Henry VIII's sunken warship, the *Mary Rose* (plates 150–1).

When I began to study mediaeval instruments there were very few people making them, either in this country or abroad, but since then there has been a great surge of interest in the subject. Now it is even possible to go into a shop and buy a rebec or a fiddle straight away. However, the craft of making such instruments still has a very long way to go, if only because of their great variety during the Middle Ages. The unending designs shown by mediaeval and early Renaissance artists (a notable exception being Hans Memling in Flanders) show quite clearly that makers of that period made a point of designing nearly every instrument differently. To do this they must have experimented, not only in the designs themselves, but also in playing on the results, to see if they would work. It would therefore have been essential for a maker to be able to play adequately on any bowed instrument before he attempted to sell it, a situation which, unfortunately, is not always understood by the makers of today.

At this point it should be made clear that I am not an instrument maker myself, so I have purposely not become too technical on this matter in the chapters which follow. I am, however, including as many pictures as the publisher will allow, in the hope that they will give ideas for new designs to contemporary fiddle-makers. They are only a small proportion of the pictures and carvings which have been consulted, and they are, of course, subject to the considerations about artistic licence and error which are mentioned in Chapter I. Each picture has been mentioned in the text for one or more different reasons, but they are not all accurate in every detail, and only the most reliable should be used as models.

Much has been written about mediaeval bowed instruments, and different names have been used for them by different authors. Perhaps the safest method is to use the generic word *fiddle* to cover them all, but I have preferred to give a different name to each basic type which emerges from the hundreds of pictures and carvings on which this book is based. These types are more distinct in English than in continental sources, and there is less overlap between the plucked and bowed instruments than there is abroad. Each family of instruments will have a chapter to itself, but a brief introductory definition of each can be given as follows:

Rebec: a pear-shaped instrument with tapering sides and generally with a vaulted back.

Crowd: a bowed instrument of the lyre family, characterized by a yoke bridging the two arms which rise from the soundbox.

Mediaeval Viol: an early form of fiddle, often large, with some indentation of the sides, and normally played down in the lap.

Fiddle: an instrument with very varying characteristics, of which the most usual are a flat back and/or a clear distinction between the body and the neck.

Renaissance Viol: an instrument with indented sides, nearly always with frets on the fingerboard, and generally with six strings; after the early stages it was made in specific different sizes for consort playing.

Trumpet Marine: a long, narrow instrument on which, at least on the Continent, the one or more strings were touched lightly by the thumb in order to produce harmonics.

Table 1 shows the approximate appearance of these instruments in English mediaeval art.

Several folk instruments of today are survivals of mediaeval ones, but they are not played traditionally in England, and those that are still played abroad are only referred to here for historical or comparative reasons. There is no space to include photographs of them all, so I have chosen to illustrate the Yugoslav *gusle*, which happens to be mentioned most often.

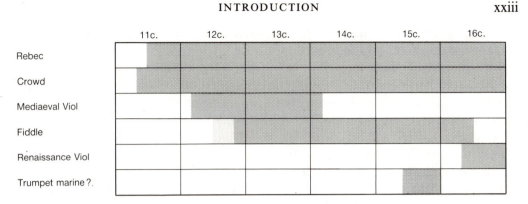

Table 1. *The Approximate Appearance of Bowed Instruments in English Art*

Several works have been particularly helpful to the preparation of this book. Firstly there is Dr Werner Bachmann's *The Origins of Bowing*, which is by far the most comprehensive publication on the subject, extending to the early fourteenth century; I was privileged to hear his latest views at the 'Fiddle Happening' arranged by Utrecht University in 1981 (p. 123 n. 1). Secondly there is Professor John Stevens's *Music and Poetry at the Early Tudor Court*, which has been a considerable help for details about instrumentalists of the Tudor period. Various theses, unpublished while the present work was being written, have also been invaluable. Dr Richard Rastall's 'Secular Musicians in Late Mediaeval England' is a mine of information about English minstrels during the Middle Ages, while J. Marshall Bevil's 'The Welsh Crwth' is essential for any study of the English crowd which features in Chapter IV. Dr Ian Woodfield's 'The Origins of the Viol' has answered many questions concerning the appearance and development of the viol during the Renaissance period, and in its published form *The Early History of the Viol* (1984) has provided further details about that instrument in England. Peter Holman has unearthed very valuable information about Henry VIII's viol-players who came from Italy, showing that they played instruments of the violin family in England not later than 1545; he has kindly allowed me to refer to his paper 'The English Royal Violin Consort in the 16th Century' before its publication by the Royal Musical Association. Dr Bernard Ravenel's thesis 'Vièles à Archets et Rebecs en Europe, au Moyen Age (Fin X^e siecle, début XVIe siecle)' is to a certain extent complementary to the present work, as the author is himself an instrument maker, and makes welcome observations on the instruments in the light of reconstructions. Unfortunately I have not yet had the opportunity to see 'The Rebec: an Orthographic and Iconographic Study' by Dr Margaret Downie, nor 'Swyddogaeth a Chelfyddyd y Crythor' (The Role and Art of the Crowther) by Bethan Miles.

The other people who have helped towards this book are numerous, and space allows me to mention only a small number, although the many librarians, curators, vicars, and vergers are not forgotten. Professional musicians and other specialists who have told me of a particular item of interest connected to their own work are acknowledged in footnotes to the relevant texts.

Other individual names must start at Oxford, where the thesis was presented; here my thanks go particularly to Dr Frederick Sternfeld, who supervised the work for nearly seven years, besides being very helpful over many different aspects of music. I am also grateful to the two Principals of St. Anne's College during my time there, Lady Mary Ogilvie and her successor Mrs Nancy Trenamen, besides Dr Annie Barnes, the late Dr Ruth Harvey, Dr Marjorie Reeves, and the late Lady Isobel Richmond. Many of my fellow students told me of minstrels in church carvings and literary quotations, but the one who has continued ever since to provide just the right word at the right moment is Dr Margaret Gibson, now of Liverpool University. The late Professor Sir Jack Westrup kindly allowed me to stay for five years at the Faculty of Music, where the librarian Mrs Valerie Elliott-Leach has ever since exercised considerable patience besides being extremely helpful, together with her assistants, particularly Miss Sarah Cobbold. Many members of the Bodleian Library staff should be remembered, especially the late Dr Richard Hunt and Dr W. O. Hassall, whose card index of subjects represented in Bodleian manuscripts has been of immense value; his assistants Miss Maureen Pemberton and Miss Elizabeth Arkell also deserve a special mention for their willing co-operation over many years. In Duke Humphrey's Library my special gratitude goes to Dr A. de La Mare, and to Dr J. J. G. Alexander before his translation to work further afield.

Many other people have helped, although for reasons of space all that they have done for me cannot be described; it is, however, greatly appreciated. Listed alphabetically, they are Dr Anthony Baines, Dr Anthea Baird, Sr José María Ballesteros, Mr Michael Boardman, the staff of the British Library, the late Mr Antonio Brosa, Dr Maurice Byrne, the late Comtesse Geneviève de Chambure, Mrs Julie Champeney, the staff of Chelsea Colour Laboratories, Dr Nicola Coldstream, the staff of the Council for the Care of Churches, the staff of the Courtauld Institute, Miss Elizabeth Creed, Mr Alan Crumpler, Dr Richard Gem, Professor Franco Gianturco and Dr Carolyn Gianturco, the late Dr Rose Graham, Foto Guitian, the late Mr Eric Halfpenny, Major and Mrs Guy Hamilton, Professor John Hancock, Mrs Peggy Hand, Dr Margaret Harvey, the late Dom René-Jean Hesbert, OSB, Mr Henry Holst, the late Mr R. P. Howgrave-Graham, Miss Anna Hulbert, Miss Jill Ker, Miss Joy Kilkenny, Mr David King, Mr Dennis King, Mrs Myrtle Lane, Miss Monica Langham, Major-General Anthony Lascelles of the Winston Churchill Memorial Trust, Dr Graeme Lawson, Professor the Revd José Lopez-Calo, SJ, Mrs Helen Lovegrove, the Revd Germain Marc'hadour, the late Mr L. Russell Muirhead, the staff of the National Monuments Record, Professor and Madame Claude Nicolet, Dr David O'Connor, Mrs Frances Palmer, Dr Isabel Pope, Captain John Powell, RN, Professor Gilbert Reaney, Mr George Remnant, Mr Ronald Roberts, Dr John Martin Robinson, the late Miss Violet Meredith Roberts, Dr Margaret Rule, Mr Miguel Sabater, Mr D. Roy Saer, Mr Ian Stewart, the Revd Anthony Stott, the late Dr and Mrs Laurence Tanner, the Triangle Audio-Visual Partnership, Mr Derek H.

Turner, Miss Marylin Wailes, Miss Narcissa Williamson, Dr Margaret Wood, and Professor George Zarnecki. The help of all these people has been entirely constructive, and any defects in the text are entirely my own. The actual production of the book could not have been possible without the kind and patient co-operation of Mr Bruce Phillips, Mrs Mary Worthington, and Mrs Carol Cumming of Oxford University Press, and Mr Bruce Hunter of David Higham Associates, to whom I am very grateful indeed, as also to Dr Christopher Page who has read the text and made very valuable suggestions, particularly regarding the literary sources.

We have already seen that the subject of this book combines the interests of my parents, the late Mr Eustace Remnant and Mrs Joan Remnant, and without their encouragement it might never have come to fruition. My father taught me not only to appreciate mediaeval architecture, but also to use his photographic equipment, which has been indispensable for this study. My mother not only gave me a love for music in the first place, but has sustained me throughout the years when the book often seemed to be nearly finished, yet was held up by the checking of many small but important details which tended to become magnified as time went on. The debt to my parents is infinite.

Finally, there are the cats. The subject of the cat and fiddle appears several times in the following text, as indeed it should. There have, however, been four real cats whose calm presence has helped considerably while the text was being prepared, and who have provided necessary distractions in moments of tension. Firstly there was the unforgettable Tobias Augustus (Toby), who, while he thoroughly approved of quiet work, could not tolerate fiddling on any instrument, and tore up the carpet when it happened in his presence. His successors, Matilda and her children Tinkerbell and Marmaduke, are not so distrustful of the actual sounds, although Marmaduke, when he has the opportunity, eats gut fiddle strings. To those who would see a symbolism at Beverley, Fawsley, Hereford, Northleach, and Wells—what have we here?

Chelsea, 1986   MARY REMNANT

CHAPTER I

The Sources

❦

SURVIVING INSTRUMENTS

Her wes fiðoelinge and song: her wes harpinge imong.
pipen & bemen: murie þer sungen.

FIDDLING was one of the most important musical crafts of the Middle Ages, to judge by this description from a banquet scene in Layamon's *Brut* (*c*.1200–25),[1] by numerous other literary sources, and by hundreds of fiddlers, human and otherwise, who decorate our ancient churches and can be found in most branches of the visual arts.

Unfortunately, very few bowed instruments actually survive from the Middle Ages, and until 1981 no substantial remains were known from mediaeval or early Renaissance England. However, before this book was finished there came the good news that two fiddles had been discovered on Henry VIII's sunken flagship the *Mary Rose*. Both are badly damaged and incomplete, but it is hoped that such objects as bridges, tailpieces, and pegs may eventually emerge from among the numerous artefacts still waiting to be investigated. When further knowledge is available it will be published in detail by Dr Graeme Lawson, but a preliminary description of the fiddles and other instruments can be seen in Frances Palmer's article 'Musical Instruments from the *Mary Rose*'.

Bowed instruments remaining from the Continent of Europe are for the most part listed in Frederick Crane's *Extant Medieval Musical Instruments* (pp. 15–17) under the generic title 'Fiddles'. They include four incomplete instruments excavated at Novgorod in levels dating from 1055–76, 1177–97, before 1368, and 1369–82. The most complete is that from a house burnt down in 1368. Its body is made of fir, and its basic shape is that of the rebec family; there are three pegholes, but no pegs remain.[2]

Also listed by Crane among the fiddles is a small north Italian instrument of hybrid shape which shows a certain resemblance to the rebec and dates from *c*.1400.[3] This is made of boxwood, with a large carved rose in the belly and grooves for five strings; it is elaborately carved and the scroll is surmounted by the figure of a woman playing a mandora (gittern). Until recently it was in the Irwin Untermyer Collection, but it can now be seen in the Metropolitan Museum, New York, where, when the present writer last saw it, it was labelled 'Mandora'. This description is not unreasonable, as no bow has survived with the instrument, and in certain cases the only distinguishing factor between the mandora (gittern) and the rebec was the plucking of the former and the bowing of the latter. Another very small and elaborately carved hybrid is to be found in the Kunsthistorisches Museum, Vienna.[4] Its general outline is somewhat like that of the rebec played by an angel in Fra Angelico's painting *The Coronation of the Virgin* at the Louvre, Paris.[5] Again there is no bow, and only the body of the instrument has survived.

Perhaps the most complete mediaeval or early Renaissance bowed instrument extant is a fiddle of very unusual shape, which is said to have belonged to St. Caterina de' Vigri who became Abbess of the Convent of Corpus Domini, Bologna, in 1456.[6] Together with its bow it has been preserved at the present convent with other relics of the saint, who apparently called it a 'violeta'. In the mediaeval tradition its back, sides, and sickle-shaped pegbox are all carved from the same piece of wood (in this case maple), but the body consists of two sections, each with its own soundboard, and these are at different levels. The soundboard at the upper end is made of maple reinforced below by a bar, and contains a carved rose, while that at the lower end has two c-shaped holes and is of spruce.[7] There are four strings, but their age is unknown. The bow is short, has a fixed nut under which the hairs are stuck to the stick at its lower end, and a cap to hold them in place at the point.

The instrument described above has no lateral drone strings; in Italy such fiddles developed into the Renaissance *viola da braccio*, of which a few examples still exist today, notably one dating from *c*.1535–50 at the Kunsthistorisches Museum, Vienna.[8] Here the most pronounced difference from the viola of the violin family is in the presence of c-shaped soundholes, which were a frequent, although not an essential characteristic. Although its neck and scroll-type pegbox are not original, the scroll can be seen clearly on a similar instrument painted *c*.1510 by either Ludovico Mazzolino or Michele Coltellini in the apse vault of the Church of Santa Maria della Consolazione at Ferrara.[9] However, not even the scroll was essential, and many examples had flat pegboxes. (The expression *viola da braccio* was also applied over a long period to various different bowed instruments, including the violin, but in this book it will be used only for the type of instrument just described.)

The fiddle with one lateral drone string culminated in the Italian *lira da braccio*, which had five strings over the fingerboard and two lateral drones, and preserved the old pegbox with an inverted cup shape as described on p. 21. Surviving examples of this instrument include one by Giovanni d'Andrea of Verona, dated 1511 and kept at the Kunsthistorisches Museum, Vienna,[10] and another by Giovanni Maria (dalla Corna) of Brescia, made later in the century and now preserved at the Ashmolean Museum, Oxford.[11] Although they are important for comparative reasons, the *viola da braccio* and *lira da braccio* of Italy do not seem to have become established on the English musical scene, but they may, however, have been played by some of the musicians from Italy who worked at the Tudor Court (pp. 73, 85).

A mediaeval viol has yet to be discovered, but due to the early period at which this instrument flourished (*c*.1080–*c*.1320) the chances of such a find are remote, although not impossible.

Many Renaissance viols are still extant, but most of them date from later than the time span covered here. Two examples can, however, give an idea of the great contrast among the shapes which were used in the sixteenth century. A smoothly outlined figure-of-eight shape can be seen in a treble viol of uncertain date by Giovanni Maria of Brescia in the Ashmolean Museum,[12] while a wide body with distinct corners are characteristics of the tenor viol by Francesco Linarol of Venice, dating from c.1540. This is now in the Kunsthistorisches Museum, Vienna.[13]

No bowed lyre has survived which resembles the English crowd, although the instrument which came to light at Danzig in 1949 has been described by Ernst Emsheimer as a 'Streichleier'.[14] Its shape is more akin to those of some of the Scandinavian folk instruments described by Otto Andersson in *The Bowed Harp*. However, surviving examples of the Welsh *crwth* are important relatives, one of the best being that made by Richard Evans in 1742, and now kept in the National Museum of Wales at St. Fagan's Castle near Cardiff (plate 154).

REPRESENTATIONS IN THE VISUAL ARTS

A. Reliability and Artistic Licence

Because there are so few bowed instruments left from the Middle Ages, and particularly from mediaeval England, it becomes necessary to search for them in the visual arts. This in itself is an absorbing occupation, but one which is full of hazards, particularly as the lack of standardization among mediaeval instruments allowed for numerous variations within one basic type. To get a general idea of the situation it is not sufficient to look at only a few examples; anyone who takes the subject at all seriously should examine literally hundreds of pictures and carvings. It is necessary to search in as many different media as possible, because by chance certain instruments appear more in one than in another. Two examples can illustrate this point. There are so few rebecs in thirteenth-century English church sculpture that the organologist who only looked for them in churches would tend to think that they had gone out of fashion at that period; however, there are plenty of them in contemporary manuscript illustrations, as can be seen from Appendix C. Similarly, there are very few fiddles to be found in fifteenth-century manuscripts produced in England. This is because at that time the English artists preferred to decorate their margins with artificial foliage, instead of the general assortment of musicians and other characters who filled them in the previous century, and still did in France. It seems that the best media for producing representations of fifteenth-century English fiddles are roof angels and stained glass, particularly the glass associated with the schools of Norwich and York.

When only a few pictures and carvings have been observed, it becomes apparent that many artists did not attempt to be accurate over details, and thus portrayed instruments which could not possibly be made to work. Such an example is in the Smithfield Decretals, fo. 71, where a fiddle has no strings or any means of attaching them (plate 85). In other cases, however, the basic ingredients are there, but they are not properly connected. In the Ormesby Psalter, fo. 9^v, for instance, the strings do not meet the tailpiece as they should, simply because the artist miscalculated their direction (plate 72). However, a slight mistake such as this should not cause the whole picture to be treated as worthless. (The apparent lack of a bridge on this instrument can be explained by the use of a combined bridge and tailpiece, as described on p. 24.)

If a possibly dubious characteristic appears in a good many unrelated works of art, this gives reason to suppose that it did sometimes exist, even if it were unusual. Fretted rebecs are a typical example. Although various authors, including Martin Agricola (who called them 'kleine Geigen one bünde'),[15] have asserted that the rebec had no frets, there are enough of them in continental sources to show that they must have been known, albeit not universally used.[16]

An instrument may appear to be basically correct in itself, but played in an unlikely position for reasons of artistic convenience and effect. This occurs particularly in those churches where large musical angels decorate a late mediaeval roof. These angels have to slant their instruments downwards to a certain extent, as if they did not, all that would be seen from below would be a small part of the back of the instrument, with the rest of it hidden by the angel's elbow—not a very satisfying sight. Such an example of the adapted playing position of a rebec can be seen in St. John's Church, Stamford, where the only odd detail of construction—the rather strange angle of the pegbox—is apparently due to the instrument being pressed against the body of the player, just where the pegbox should be (plate 128).

The playing position is also modified when the instrument could otherwise easily get broken off. At St. Mary's Church, Beverley, the arm-rests in the fifteenth-century stalls show angels leaning backwards slightly, in order to suit the structure of the seats, and the rebec-player accordingly holds his rebec flat against himself (plate 120). Quite apart from the possibility of the instrument getting broken, many clerical garments could have been torn by it projecting in such a place. The same applies to misericords (a typical case being that with an angel playing a crowd in Worcester Cathedral, as seen in plate 108), which were made to be tipped up so that the clergy could lean against them while standing in the stalls during the liturgical Office.

A great many pictures show an instrument being held up at the shoulder, but presented in a 'full face' view with the soundboard facing outwards, as in the Peterborough Psalter, fo. 57 (plate 57). This position, in which a good performance is virtually impossible, has clearly been adopted by the artist to give the best view of the instrument.

One other point concerning the playing position is when the performer is left-handed, holding the instrument in his right hand and the bow in his left. This could be due to the artist's absent-mindedness, or else to his desire for symmetry, in which a left-handed player happened to suit the picture better than one who was right-handed. However, it should be pointed out that even today, when the violin family has on the whole become so standardized, there are still some left-handed players around, and instruments have to be built especially for them with the strings set in the opposite way from usual.[17]

When an instrument is not being played at all there can be difficulties of classification. This occurs particularly in illustrations of the Apocalypse, where the twenty-four Elders are each holding a vase of incense in one hand and an instrument in the other. The Vulgate refers to these instruments in Latin as 'citharae', and one of the relevant passages, as translated in the Jerusalem Bible, reads

The Lamb came forward to take the scroll from the right hand of the One sitting on the throne, and when he took it, the four animals prostrated themselves before him and with them the twenty-four elders; each one of them was holding a harp and had a golden bowl full of incense made of the prayers of the saints.[18]

Mediaeval artists created very different interpretations of these Apocalyptic 'citharae'. Up to the twelfth century the continental sources normally showed them as stringed instruments, whether all without bows as in the Apocalypse of St. Sever, ff. 121^v–122, with bows as in the west doorway of Oloron Cathedral, or a mixture of both as at the church of San Lorenzo at Carboeiro in Galicia. By the time that the whole Apocalypse was being illustrated in England, in the thirteenth century,[19] the instruments had become more varied, and it was not unusual, from that time onwards, to find the Elders playing or holding the supposed instruments of the Psalms. This occurs, for instance, in the late fourteenth-century Cambridge, Trinity College MS B. 10. 2, fo. 4^v, where strings are joined by the trumpet, organ, and cymbals (p. 50 and plate 106).

Now comes the problem of classification. If an Elder is holding a normally bowed instrument in one hand and a vase of incense in the other, he cannot possibly be playing as well, so the artist generally leaves out the bow altogether. This can result in some confusion as to whether the instrument should in fact be plucked or bowed, especially in continental sources where the dividing line is often very difficult to find. At Santiago at least one of the instruments is ambiguous in this way, but others are clearly mediaeval viols or fiddles, even though they have no bows.[20] At Oloron, however, the designer has been most considerate to the twentieth-century organologist, while having a good joke himself. When an Elder is holding both vase and instrument, the bow is hanging up on the wall behind,[21] and if he is actually playing, the vase is hanging up. The real humour breaks through when it is seen that one Elder is holding two instruments, with a bow on his lap, while his neighbour holds two vases of incense and the 'missing' bow hangs on the wall behind him. At Hardham in Sussex, where a rare English Romanesque collection of painted Elders includes both rebecs and fiddles besides vases of incense, there are again no bows to be seen in the clearer parts of the much worn design.[22] However, there is little doubt that they would have been used, as in England the plucking of such instruments seems to have been very rare indeed (p. 38).

The Oloron sculptor found his own way of relieving the potential monotony of carving twenty-four musicians in a doorway, but at least he did not have to illustrate the whole Apocalypse. Illustrators of the complete text, however, had to show these Elders with their instruments not once but several times, so it is small wonder that they became downright careless. They also devised a method of setting six Elders in each of four panels, in such a way that only the front two of the six need to have instruments at all, thus drastically reducing the number of instruments from twenty-four to eight, as can be seen in the Cambridge, Trinity College MS B. 10. 2, fo. 4^v (plate 106). It may well be true to say that when there is uncertainty over the bowing or plucking of an instrument, or even an uncertainty over just what type of instrument the artist intended, that confusion is most likely to appear in manuscript illustrations of the Apocalypse.

So far we have considered artistic licence with regard to the construction, playing position, and classification of the instruments. Another important aspect is the context in which they were used. Scenes from mediaeval life were naturally enough illustrated with mediaeval instruments when they were needed, but so were scenes from the past, as the mediaeval artist normally made little or no attempt to distinguish between the instruments of different historical epochs.[23] Thus Herod's feast is frequently shown with a fiddler playing while Salome dances, although the bow itself was invented several hundred years after Herod's own time. Such pictures in fact tell us more about music for mediaeval feasts and dances than they do about music for biblical ones. With regard to performance practice, sacred art tends to become less realistic as the number of musicians increases. David and his minstrels, who generally number up to about eight, are usually shown in rather stylized settings, but nevertheless they often play instruments which could have sounded well together. The twenty-four Elders of the Apocalypse, as we have already observed, are often to be found in church doorways on the Continent, and particularly on the pilgrimage routes to Santiago de Compostela.[24] There are no such doorways in England (although figures which may be Elders can be found in a now incomplete arch at Brinsop in Herefordshire where, according to Professor Zarnecki, the sculptor was influenced by carvings which he had seen on his own pilgrimage to Santiago[25]), but the twenty-four Elders do occur with their instruments in the early twelfth-century wall-paintings at Hardham; from the thirteenth century onwards they can be seen in rectangular painted panels, or clustered together on a roof boss or some other decorated part of a church or cloister. They, and the large collections of performing angels which adorn Lincoln and Gloucester Cathedrals and Tewkesbury Abbey, are unlikely to represent actual mediaeval orchestras, but symbolize heavenly music to the glory of God.[26]

Angel groups do become more realistic when there are fewer instruments involved, particularly two or three. Nevertheless, there is a school of thought in musicological opinion which holds that because angels are not part of the earthly scene, their pictorial music-making can tell us little or nothing about performance practice. Yet if we examine duos or trios of angel musicians, we see the same combinations of instruments being played again and again, and these same combinations also appear in the hands of ordinary human minstrels. After all, what is more natural for the artist than to depict an instrumental grouping with which he is familiar? One of the most usual involving a bowed instrument is that of the fiddle and gittern (citole) which are played by angels in the Ormesby Psalter, fo. 9^v and the Lisle Psalter, fo. 134^v, in each case above the Coronation of the Virgin. The same instruments can be seen in the hands of human beings on a roof boss at Norwich Cathedral (plate 65) and in an initial from a Book of Hours (plate 44), to name but two of the English sources, and also in many continental scenes.[27] It is not, however, only angels who are subject to the suspicion mentioned above, but also animals, grotesques, and devils, although devils are seldom to be seen with bowed instruments, and that at Canterbury is a rare case (plate 13). While naturally accepting that such performers *could* be unreliable witnesses, we must clearly keep an open mind and judge each case on its merits. (In the last few years there has been such a revival in the art of making mediaeval instruments that it should be comparatively easy for their players to experiment with the different groupings as shown in pictures, and to find out what are the possible sound effects. Even so, it should be remembered that due to the lack of standardization in the Middle Ages there must have been a very great variety of sound available between instruments of the same basic type.)[28]

Another point to be considered about unorthodox musicians is that quite often they actually represent ordinary people dressed up, or at least are based on them. There is considerable evidence for the dressing up as angels, particularly in Mystery Plays and civic ceremonial occasions (pp. 92, 95). Glynne Wickham has drawn attention to an entry in the Pageant accounts of the Bridge House Rentals for the year 1464, showing that 1s. 9d. was spent on 900 peacocks' feathers for making angels' wings.[29] Fifteenth-century pictures and carvings show numerous feathered angels which are apparently based on people dressed in this way, and many of them, notably those at Warwick (plates 122–4) and of the Norwich school of stained glass (plate 131) are playing instruments.[30] M. D. Anderson has shown that actual scenes from the lost Norwich Mystery Plays are portrayed in the early sixteenth-century roof bosses of the north transept in Norwich Cathedral,[31] and at least two of these involve musicians.

A very human musical angel from an earlier period can be seen in the BL MS Stowe 17, fo. 188, a Flemish Book of Hours dating from *c.*1300 (plate 52). Here the angelic fiddler is in a great hurry. He is moving with long strides, if not actually running, and he plays his fiddle at the same time. What concerns us here is that this angel is moving by means of his feet rather than his wings. What real angel, in such a hurry, would run if he could fly?

As people dressed up as angels, so they dressed up as animals, or in costumes which showed them to be partly animal and partly human. When Edward III spent Christmas 1348 at Otford, the Wardrobe supplied:

12 men's heads, each surmounted with a lion's head
12 men's heads, each surmounted with an elephant's head
12 men's heads, with bats' wings
12 wildmen's heads
17 girls' heads[32]

and for the following feast of the Epiphany at Merton, a new order included:

13 dragons'-head masks, 13 masks of crowned men,
black buckram and English linen cloth.[33]

In the light of such descriptions we can try to assess which pictures are based on real life and which are purely due to the artist's sense of humour. Sometimes it is obvious that a player is meant to be a man dressed up, but that the artist, in his enthusiasm, got the proportions muddled. However much a man were disguised, his own knees, for instance, would still bend forwards, whereas if his lower half resembled a bear or a horse, they should really bend backwards (p. 101). Finally the artist leaves reality altogether and depicts a complete monstrosity. Just where the dividing line comes between fact and fantasy must depend on each individual case.

When animal musicians are not based on people dressed up, they can either be inspired by the artist's whim of the moment, or they can have a symbolic meaning, or some particular association with an instrument, such as the cat and fiddle. These matters will be considered further on pp. 85–6.

B. The Materials used, and their Chances of Survival

The destruction caused by the Reformation and the Commonwealth has left us with only a small proportion of the sources which would otherwise have been available for study. Of those that do remain, their general condition depends largely on where they are placed and on the materials from which they are made.

Among the most vulnerable sources are movable carvings. Anything which could be knocked over naturally stands a greater chance of being destroyed than something which is fixed and out of reach, such as a roof boss. Low-level carvings such as poppyheads and misericords can even today be accidentally damaged, and in the past have been wilfully destroyed. The different types of stone employed can determine how long certain sculptures will last, particularly if they are on the outside of a building. Soft stone which is easy to carve will not last as long as hard stone, but hard stone in itself discourages carving. Numerous mediaeval carvings were painted, but though in many cases the original colouring has almost or completely disappeared, the basic shape remains.

Paintings on a flat surface have the disadvantage that once the colour has worn off, there is no more to be seen. In other cases they were painted over, either to avoid destruction in times of danger, or else to make room for more up-to-date works of art. Gradually more and more of these pictures are coming to light, and sometimes they contain musicians; such an example is at Longthorpe Tower near Peterborough, where six minstrels including a fiddler were among the fourteenth-century wall-paintings discovered in 1945.[34]

The chances of details surviving in embroidery depend largely on the type of thread to be used and the stitches involved. If we accept as a general rule that the stitches which were sewn on last will be the first to wear off through constant rubbing (unless they are made of especially durable thread), then the more important details will disappear before their background. This was particularly apparent at the exhibition of *Opus Anglicanum* held at the Victoria and Albert Museum in 1963.[35] In the Bologna Cope the strings and pegs of the bowed instruments were very worn indeed (plate 77),[36] while the Lateran Cope had fared even worse, and some of its instruments can be identified only by their shapes against the differently-coloured background. In this latter case black-and-white photographs are of little help.[37]

Perhaps the best-preserved sources are the illustrations in surviving manuscripts, when these are not damaged by fire, floods, reformers, mice, or other unexpected agents. The very closing of a book can contribute towards its preservation, and the parchment used in the Middle Ages should last longer than any modern paper intended for regular use. As with other flat-surfaced media there is the disadvantage of not seeing the instruments in three dimensions, but at least the colouring normally remains intact, except in the case of tarnishing silver paint.[38]

C. Restoration and Renovation

With most of the visual arts there comes a time when repairs are needed, and in past years great damage has been done by well-meaning 'restorers'. Manuscripts have perhaps been the least affected, but carvings, wall-paintings, and other media have been subjected to much alteration, and must be treated with great caution. It may be that an original carving has been repainted, as has happened to numerous corbels and roof bosses, such as those of St. Mary's Church, Beverley and Norwich Cathedral (plates 144 and 65). Here the original basic shape remains, even though it may sometimes have been repaired, but the colouring is new. If the first paint has practically disappeared it is up to the renovator to decide what to do, and in many cases he has used his imagination in such a way that it has completely altered the original design. At Tewkesbury Abbey plaster casts have been made of the roof bosses, and although these do not show the original colouring, they do at least give valuable information about the shapes of the instruments involved (plate 97).

Plaster casts, however, cannot be made of paintings on flat surfaces, and in these cases the original design is in even greater danger of being drastically altered. In the thirteenth-century painted roof of Peterborough Cathedral there are several musicians, including two with bowed instruments (plate 31). They have been 'restored' at least twice, the first known occasion being between 1740 and 1750, and the second shortly before 1835. According to a letter by Gov. Pownall, the first restoration was done carefully, and he quotes the Bishop of Peterborough as telling him in August 1773 that

He heard that the man, who about thirty years ago was employed to repair the cieling, was still living. He sent for him, and learnt from him that the whole was repainted in oil. He told his lordship that several of the figures were intirely encrusted with dirt, but that upon applying a sponge they became clear and bright, whence he concludes that the last coat was of oil. He was altogether of the same opinion with what I had suggested, that the body of the painting (under what he supposed to be the coat of oil) was in distemper: parts came clear off from the wainscot. He assured his Lordship that he only retraced the figures, except in one instance the third or fourth compartment from the West door, where the whole figure peeled off: in this single instance he followed his own fancy, having nothing else to trust to, and even here he endeavoured to imitate the style of the rest. The Bishop said, he had no doubt of his veracity.[39]

In the restoration of 1835, however, the artists responsible paid little attention to the existing shapes of the bowed instruments, and turned them into the violins which they themselves knew. The other instruments, being in the then less familiar shapes of the psaltery, symphony, and others, fared better, as the artist was apparently content to follow the existing outlines rather than to exert his imagination too far.

At Beverley Minster we come up against a different, though related problem. In the late nineteenth century John Baker and his son restored many of the musical carvings, particularly those of the north aisle. He took such trouble to make the instruments seem authentic that it is often difficult to see where the original ends and his own work begins. When he inserted a completely new instrument, however, he generally inscribed his name or initials on the back.[40]

In recent years the situation has begun to improve. Although some 'restorers' of paint devise a colour scheme entirely their own, there are others who first go to great trouble to find out just what mediaeval paint does survive. They then fill in the places where the colouring has worn away, using the same colours in the type of pigment that was used during the Middle Ages, before finally leaving a written report of what they have done, together with photographs taken during different stages of the work.

D. The Possible Influence of Foreign Art on English Instruments

Although continental music, and particularly that of France, was known and performed in England during the Middle Ages (p. 113), English compositions retained certain insular characteristics which were not upset by influence from abroad.[41] In general the same seems to have been true with regard to instruments. Thirteenth-century England had none of the variety to be found in the illustrations of the *Cantigas de Santa Maria* manuscripts belonging to King Alfonso X 'The Wise' of Castile,[42] although the marriage of Edward I to Eleanor of Castile in 1254 may have been responsible for the introduction of certain instruments to this country. On the whole, however, throughout the period covered by this book, English musical craftsmen do seem to have been less adventurous than their continental counterparts.

We can never know to what extent, if at all, the development of English instruments was influenced by the importation of foreign works of art. Objects such as the Flemish-made Braunche brass at St. Margaret's Church, King's Lynn, contain a good many instruments (plate 101), but none of them were new to England when it arrived in 1364. (A similar Flemish brass can be found in the Church of St. Mary Magdalene, Newark, commemorating Alan Fleming who died in 1363.) On the other hand, there were certainly some sources around which contained pictures of instruments that were apparently unknown here. One such is the Bodleian Library's copy of the 'Romance of Alexander' (MS Bodley 264). Illuminated by Jehan de Grise in Flanders between 1338 and 1344, it contains pictures of about 300 musicians among the numerous illustrations. Their instruments include several examples of the transverse flute, which is virtually non-existent in English art dating from before the reign of Henry VIII. This manuscript apparently did nothing to promote its use here, although the book was owned by the type of people who would often have employed minstrels, if they did not actually have regular ones in attendance. It is thought to have belonged to Thomas, Duke of Gloucester, who died in 1397, and in 1466 it was bought in London by Richard Wydevill, Lord Rivers.[43] Meanwhile the traffic continued. Foreign artists worked in England, and English artists worked abroad. Works of art were dispatched by order from one country to another, and decorated articles must have been brought back by Crusaders and pilgrims from the Holy Land, by those other pilgrims who had taken the various routes to Rome and Santiago de Compostela, and by the adventurers who just liked travelling. Nevertheless, the negative results do suggest that unusual instruments in these sources were generally regarded as outlandish. Continental instruments either came to England slowly, or else they never came at all, preferring to remain south of the English Channel, if not south of the Alps and the Pyrenees.

REFERENCES FROM LITERARY SOURCES

As with the visual arts, literary references must be treated with great caution. A single word might be used for hundreds of years, but during that time its meaning could cover several different instruments. On the other hand one instrument might, in varying places and times, be given many different names.[44]

Specialized mediaeval treatises on bowed instruments are unfortunately very rare, and at present there is a lack of known contemporary authorities from England. We therefore have to rely on continental sources, such as Jerome of Moravia's information as to the tuning of the 'rubeba' and the 'viella'. This Moravian by birth lived for some time in Paris during the second half of the thirteenth century, and if his various tunings represent Parisian practice, they may also have been used in England, where contacts with France were strong at that time. However, the very existence of at least three different contemporary tunings for the 'viella' shows that there must have been great freedom in this respect, and it must also be remembered that Jerome was only referring to fiddles with five strings, and not to those with two, three, and four, which also abound in the visual arts. Writers such as Johannes de Grocheo (Grocheio) give us useful information about the performing possibilities of bowed instruments, but, with the possible exception of the fourteenth-century treatise by Jean Vaillant, it is not until the fifteenth century that we find further definite details about their tuning, given this time by the Fleming Johannes Tinctoris (1445–1511), who worked in Naples. By 1540 several relevant continental treatises had appeared, including Sebastian Virdung's *Musica Getutscht* (1511), Martin Agricola's *Musica Instrumentalis Deudsch* (1528), and Hans Gerle's *Musica Teusch* (1532), and thanks to the invention of printing all these have survived.

Some help is provided by labelled illustrations, although here again continental sources are more fruitful than English ones. Prominent are two pictures of rebecs, one of them described as 'lyra' in a thirteenth-century manuscript from the monastery of St. Blasius,[45] and the other as 'lira' in the twelfth-century *Hortus Deliciarum* of the Abbess Herrad von Hohenbourg (Herrad of Landsberg).[46] Although both of these are Germanic sources, the fact that the labels are in Latin does allow for the use of the words in this context in England. (However, it should not be forgotten, as shown on p. 13, that Higden's 'lyra' was translated by John of Trevisa as 'harpe', and that in the Anglo-Saxon period the 'hearpe' of *Beowulf* had almost certainly been a Another useful source is the BL MS Sloane 3983, fo. 13, of fourteenth-century Flemish origin (plate 63); this labels a fiddle as 'viola' and its bow as 'arcus viole', thereby indicating that 'viola' was not only used for the mediaeval viol, as has sometimes been thought. Unfortunately most of the illustrated references to instruments as such come in glosses to the Psalms, or in the forged letter from 'Jerome to Dardanus', or in *De Proprietatibus Rerum* by Bartholomaeus Anglicus, and as these are based on the fourth-century Vulgate translation by St. Jerome, they do not normally refer to bowed instruments. However, in pictures which illustrate the instruments of the Psalms in general, the 'chordae' are sometimes represented by fiddles and the 'chorus' by a crowd, as in the Cambridge, Trinity College MS B. 10. 2, fo. 4ᵛ (plate 106).

Closely related to labelled pictures are dictionaries and word lists, and these are often no more accurate than their modern counterparts. Perhaps the earliest English one to deal with bowed instruments is the Glossary of Aelfric, Abbot of Eynsham, who lived from *c*.950 to *c*.1020. Among musical terms he lists 'fiðelere' and 'fiðelestre', meaning male and female fiddlers respectively.[48] If the instruments played by these musicians really did have bows, they would have been of the rebec or crowd types, as no others are known in English art until after 1100. However, variants of the word *fiddle* have not always implied the use of a bow. The ninth-century poet Otfrid von Weissenburg referred in his *Evangelienbuch* (*c*.870) to a 'fidula' which is assumed to have been plucked, as there is as yet no definite evidence of the bow being known in Europe at that time.[49] Aelfric's fiddlers, being over a century later, might just have used bows, as the earliest known English pictures of them, playing a rebec and a crowd, date from about thirty years, or less, after his death (plates 2, 1).

The *Dictionarius* of John de Garlande gives us information about the instruments used in Paris in the early years of the thirteenth century, and an almost contemporary version of his work adds further details, including the French names of the instruments concerned:

Giga est instrumentum musicum et dicitur Gallice *gigue* . . .
Vidulatores dicuntur a vidula -e; Gallice *viele*.[50]

(The 'giga' is a musical instrument and in French is called *gigue* . . .
'Vidulatores' are named from the 'vidula, -e'; in French *viele*.)

These statements are recorded here as John de Garlande was English, and studied at Oxford before living for many years in France and working at the University of Paris.

From the fifteenth century there survive several relevant dictionaries and word lists, notably the *Promptorium Parvulorum* (*c.* 1440), the *Catholicon Anglicum* (1483), and two anonymous *nominalia*, one in the BL MS Royal 17 C. xvii, fo. 43ᵛ, and one which formerly belonged to Joseph Mayer of Liverpool. (These will henceforth be referred to as *Nominale A* and *Nominale B* respectively.) Between them they list many bowed instruments and their accessories, but the discrepancies are noteworthy, as can be seen in Appendix B. For instance, 'fidis' denotes a harp string in the *Catholicon* and a fiddler in *Nominale A*, while 'fidicen' is a harper in the former manuscript and a fiddler in the *Promptorium*. The word 'viella', which is normally taken to mean a fiddle (or occasionally an instrument of the symphony family), appears also in the *Promptorium* as a lute.

John Palsgrave's *Lesclarissement de la Langue Francoyse* (1530) only adds to the confusion by calling every bowed instrument a rebec:

Croude an instrument	*robecq*
Croudar	*ieuevrde [joueur] de rebecq*
Fyddell	*rebeq*
Fydlar or croudar	*rebecquet*
Rebecke an instrument of musyke	*rebec*
	(from 'The Table of Substantyves')

I fyddell	*Ie ieoue du rebecq*
Can you fydell and playe upon	*Scauez vous iouer du rebecq*
a tabouret to	*et sus le tabouryn aussi*
	(from 'The Table of Verbes')

Translations by mediaeval writers are also inclined to be somewhat vague, and some of their references to instruments may even have depended on dictionaries such as those mentioned above. Higden's description of instruments used at Welsh feasts and funerals, which originally runs

> Choro, lyra et tibiis
> Utuntur in conviviis
> Sed elatis funeribus
> Clangunt caprinis cornibus

is rendered by John of Trevisa as

> They haueþ in greet mangerie
> Harpe, tabor, and pype for mynstralcie.
> They bereþ forþ cors wiþ sorwe grete;
> Þey bloweþ lowde hornes of geete

and by the anonymous fifteenth-century translator in the BL MS Harley 2261, fo. 57, as

Men of that cuntre vse in theire festes a crowde, an harpe, and trumpes. But at the dethe of a man thei crye lyke to wylde bestes in exaltenge the bloode of Troy, of whom thei toke begynnenge.[51]

Similar variations are seen in the translations of Higden's contrast between the instruments used by the Welsh and the Scots.[52] In both cases, as far as musical instruments are concerned, the version in the Harley manuscript is somewhat more accurate than that of Trevisa. Ranulph Higden, who was a monk at the Abbey of St. Werburgh at Chester during the fourteenth century, based parts of his Chronicle on that of Giraldus Cambrensis (*c.*1146–*c.*1220), whose own reference to Welsh instruments was 'Tribus autem utuntur instrumentis; cithara, tibiis, et choro'.[53] Perhaps a suitable warning of the dangers of trusting to chronicles can be seen in Trevisa's translation of Higden's paraphrase of Giraldus's comments on the opinions of Solinus, Isidorus, and Bede about Ireland, without, in this case, any reference to music or instruments:

[Solinus and Isidorus wryten that Irlond hath no bees; netheles it were better wryten that Irlond hath bees and no vyneyerdes.] Also Beda seiþ þat þere is grete huntynge of roobukkes, and it is i-knowe þat roobukkes beeþ noon þere. It is no wonder of Beda; for Beda knewe neuere þat ilond wiþ his eyȝe; bot som tale tellere tolde hym suche tales.[54]

Instruments of the Bible have always been a challenge to translators. During the Middle Ages it was customary to give them the names of contemporary instruments, just as it was to show them in pictures of biblical scenes. Thus we find that 'David ordeyned . . . instrumentes . . . organs and harpes . . . Symbals and Sawtres, Kroudes and tympans, Trumpettes and tabours'.[55] In the 81st, 149th, and 150th Psalms the word 'chorus' is sometimes interpreted as a crowd, although this instrument seems not to have appeared in England until the eleventh century AD (p. 46). This lack of scholarly translation, however, would have made the Psalms more realistic to ordinary people, who perhaps were more likely to respond to the exhortation 'loue thai his name in croude: in taburn and in psautere synge thai til him',[56] than to a list of Hebrew instruments of which they had never heard.

In the same way, many writers had no scruples when describing the events of more recent times. In *The Story of England* Robert Manning of Brunne gives a vivid picture of minstrelsy at the court of King Arthur, but the instruments that he mentioned were certainly those that he himself knew, rather than those of an earlier age:

> Iogelours were þere ynowe,
> þat þer queyntise forþ drowe;
> Many mynestrales þorow out þe toun,
> Som blewe trompe & clarioun,
> Harpes, pypes, & tabours,
> ffyþeles, sitoles, sautreours,
> Belles, chymbes, & symfan
> & oþere y-nowe, þat nemne y ne can;
> Gestours, singers, þat merye sang,
> So gret murþe was, þat ouer al rang.[57]

Straight poetry or prose on contemporary subjects is less likely to be anachronistic, as the writer must have had some knowledge of the instruments of his time, and sometimes his references to them contain further information about playing and technical aspects. References in foreign sources can of course throw extra light on a subject when it would have corresponded to English practice.

While certain literary works can help to co-ordinate pictures with the names of instruments, there are other cases where the matter is not quite so straightforward. Such an example is the generic use of the word *fiddle* in John Lydgate's *Pilgrimage of the Life of Man*, where 'ffedle' in the text is illustrated in the adjacent picture by a distinct rebec (BL MS Cott. Tiberius A. vii, fo. 79ᵛ).

From expense accounts we learn of the people who employed minstrels, of the minstrels themselves, of the money they earned, and of those who accompanied their masters abroad or went abroad on their own to study (see Chapters IX and X). Further details come to light about the cost of instruments and their repair (although very little of this evidence concerns bowed instruments before the sixteenth century), and about which instruments were played on certain occasions. The most noteworthy English musical event of which documents have survived was the Feast of Westminster in 1306, where a vast concourse of minstrels included 'gigatores', 'vidulatores', and 'crouderes'.

Too often a minstrel is referred to only by his Christian name, and this can inevitably cause confusion. In 1332, for instance, a 'vidulator' called Richard accompanied the Princess Eleanor to Holland on her journey to marry the Count of Guelders. A 'Ricard le Vieler' went abroad with Edward II in 1325/6,[58] and in 1306 'Mons. Ricard Le Vilour Rounlo' played an important part in the Feast of Westminster. Although the apparent surname Rounlo does not appear in other references, Constance Bullock-Davies has pieced together the career of this minstrel, and believes that he was employed by the court from 1290 onwards, and was the same Richard who followed Edward II abroad in 1325/6.[59] Another possible surname occurs in a list of payments made by Bishop Richard de Swinfield in the year 1289–90. This is to one 'Bennett', a 'violator', who played to the Bishop in London and was rewarded with three shillings.[60] However, although 'Bennett' is a surname today, during the Middle Ages it could have been a form of the Christian name 'Benet', which itself is taken from 'Benedict'.

Inventories and wills from the sixteenth century onwards provide much information about bowed instruments, but very little, if any, before the reign of Henry VIII. Outstanding is the inventory made after his death in 1547, where twenty-five 'vialles' are included with organs, regals, crumhorns, 'instruments of soundrie kindes', and the 'Instrumente that goethe with a whele without playinge uppon . . .'[61]

Having considered the main type of source available, and having seen some of the many difficulties which they can produce, we must now proceed warily, and use them with discretion.

CHAPTER II

The Ingredients of Bowed Instruments

❧

ALTHOUGH bowed instruments can be classified broadly into different types according to shape, many of their essential ingredients are interchangeable. To avoid too much repetition, therefore, these ingredients will be discussed first here, and any differences with regard to particular instruments will be found in the appropriate chapters.

THE BOW

Whether or not the bow was derived from the hunting bow, as Werner Bachmann and others have suggested,[1] it certainly had the same name early in its history. Three important word lists and dictionaries from fifteenth-century England list it as follows:

Promptorium Parvulorum		
Bowe	Arcus	
Nominale A		
Fydylstyk	Arculus	
Catholicon Anglicum		
Fidylle stik	Arculus	(Appendix A)

while the fourteenth-century Flemish source, BL MS Sloane 3983, fo. 13, shows a picture of a bow with the caption 'arcus viole' (plate 63).

The bow is traditionally made of wood, and the types of wood must have varied from one country to another according to the available trees and plants. We can see, for instance, that bamboo was sometimes used in southern countries, as it is plainly depicted in the *Cantigas de Santa Maria*, fo. 118. (The instruments concerned are two-stringed rebecs almost identical to the Moroccan *rabāb* of today, which very often has a bow made of bamboo.) Such detail is rare, however, and English sources do not usually give enough detail for the wood to be identified.

During the Middle Ages the bow was normally strung with horsehair, and evidence of this practice is provided by several continental writers, including the Fleming Johannes Tinctoris in his *De Inventione et Usu Musicae*: 'arculus quom chorda ejus pilis equinis confecta' ('the bow, which is strung with horsehair . . .').[2] Just as today some bows are strung with white hairs and some with black, so it was during the Middle Ages, according to the paintings of the period. Among English sources, examples of white hairs can be seen in the Peterborough Psalter, fo. 57, and black ones in the Ormesby Psalter, fo. 9ᵛ (plates 57, 72). In many cases the whole drawing has been outlined in black, so it is difficult to guess at what colour, if any, the artist had in mind. Sometimes he only had a few colours available, so to obtain a suitable balance he sacrificed reality, with results such as the red bow hairs which decorate the Winchcombe Bible, fo. 151 (plate 16), but cannot, unfortunately, be seen from a black-and-white photograph.

It is believed that mediaeval bows had far fewer hairs than modern ones, and although it is difficult to guess at their number from most illustrations, there are a few, notably that mentioned above in the Winchcombe Bible, where a small number of hairs seems to be implied. Continental literature is more forthcoming than that of England on this as on many related subjects, an important source being a treatise in Turkish by Aḥmed-oghlu Shükrullāh (c.1400), who says that 'the horsehair should be attached to the bow like bowstrings, the number of hairs being nine. And if they be more than nine, it is no matter; but let them not exceed forty'.[3]

Artistic representations show a great variety of shapes among mediaeval bows. The early ones are generally curved to a greater or lesser extent, thus recalling their probable origin; this basic shape continued throughout the Middle Ages, appearing for instance with a rebec in the twelfth-century York Psalter and a fiddle in fifteenth-century stained glass from Norwich (plates 21, 131). From the late twelfth century onwards there was also a tendency for the distance between the stick and the hairs to get deeper towards the point of the bow, as witnessed by the Great Canterbury Psalter (plate 23). In contrast to these were the bows which were actually straight or nearly so, and are well represented by the Venice Psalter (plate 45). This and many others are long, but there was no set rule about length, and a representative short bow can be seen with a rebec at St. Mary's Church, Beverley (plate 144). Perhaps it is true to say that when bows are very short they are generally associated with rebecs, although rebecs themselves are often shown with long bows, particularly during the earlier period. However, from artistic evidence and the experience of playing, we can be certain that many bows were interchangeable from one type of instrument to another.

Some bows were fashioned from a cleft stick. One of the forks would be broken off, leaving the other as the bowstick, with the thicker part as the natural handle; when a small part of the broken fork remained, this formed a nut to which the hairs were attached. These two types are both represented in the twelfth-century St. Alban's Psalter, pp. 56, 417 (plates 10, 11), in conjunction with mediaeval viols, which, among all the bowed instruments of mediaeval England, tended to have the most elaborate and highly decorated bows. A trefoil, which is such a characteristic of mediaeval art in general, and is frequently used for soundholes and pegboxes, terminates the point of a bow in fourteenth-century stained glass at Audley End.

The manner of fastening the hairs to the bowstick is often far from clear, but certain basic methods can be deduced. Let us first take the point, or upper end of the bow. The simplest way is to wind the hairs round the stick as can be seen in the Luttrell Psalter, fo. 149 (plate 89), but this runs the risk of their slipping, unless they are held in position by grooves in the wood, or by glue. Other pictures, such as that from the BL MS Arundel 91, fo. 218ᵛ, show a knob which is presumably intended to secure them, and is balanced by a similar knob at the other end, both of which add character to the instrument (plate 6). Further examples show the point of the bow to be deflected in order to stop the hairs from slipping off, as in the BL MS Cott. Tiberius A. vii, fo. 77 (plate 118), while a further method involves passing the hairs through a hole in the stick and knotting them on top. This appears in the Winchcombe Psalter, fo. 4ᵛ (plate 1).

At the heel, or lower end of the bow, some of the same methods apply. It is rare to find the hairs attached at the extreme lower end, as occurs in the BL MS Arundel 91, fo. 218ᵛ, where they are secured by the knob mentioned above (plate 6). The Flemish source, BL MS Sloane 3983, fo. 13, shows them to pass through the stick and to be knotted above it (plate 63). When a bow is made from a cleft stick, or carved to resemble that shape, the hairs can either be attached to the handle as in the BL MS Cott. Tiberius A. vii, fo. 77 (plate 118), or to the nut, when there is one, as in the Smithfield Decretals, fo. 71 (plate 85). It must, however, be emphasized that in the great majority of illustrations it is quite impossible to see how the hairs are supposed to be fixed.[4]

According to the methods of attaching the hairs, it might or might not be possible to alter their tension, once they had been set. A knot, for instance, could be re-knotted, if it were not sealed until the next re-hairing. Two continental sources provide food for thought on other methods. One is a twelfth-century ivory relief from the Abbey of St. Bertin, on the back of the BL Add. MS 37768.[5] It shows David holding a bow in one hand and a lyre in the other, and both are quite unique. What concerns us here is not so much that the bow looks like some kind of exotic feather, but that at its lower end there are several notches which could be alternative receptacles for the angular device holding the ends of the hairs. If this is so, we have here a Romanesque forerunner of the notched violin bow of the seventeenth century,[6] but in fairness it should be admitted that other notches, less evenly spaced, continue up the rest of the bowstick, and are presumably intended as decoration. Although this example may be one of artistic fantasy, it should not be totally ignored.

The other example is from the 'arcus viole' of the BL MS Sloane 3983, fo. 13 (plate 63). Near the upper end of the bow a peg passes through the stick and hairs are attached to it underneath. In the Yugoslav *gusle* of today there is just such a device, which sometimes takes the form of an animal's ears, the face being the tip of the bow itself. By turning the ears to the right or left, the player can thus increase or diminish the tension of the hairs (plate 155). It is possible that the 'arcus viole' provides an important mediaeval parallel to this, but even if it does, it is not from an English source, and the author has yet to find a similar one that is.

Occasionally the player seems to be controlling the hairs with his fingers, as can be seen at St. Mary's Hall, Coventry (plate 110).

THE WOOD OF THE INSTRUMENT, AND ITS DECORATION

Centuries of experience have shown that a soft wood, such as fir or spruce, is suitable for the soundboard of a stringed instrument, while a stronger wood like sycamore or maple is needed for the back. This practice was described in *De vegetalibus* by Albertus Magnus (1206–1280), whose words served as the model for Konrad von Megenberg's fourteenth-century description in *Das Buch der Natur*:

Fir wood is unsuitable for the back of a stringed instrument, either fiddles, lyres or anything else, since wood of this sort lets the air through . . . And therefore it does not hold the air, from which the sound comes; but fir wood makes a good belly for such an instrument, for, when the air has pushed against the strong strings into the belly of the thing, it filters slowly through the soft top, making the sound sweeter.[7]

The author also says, in another context, that a rough fiddle speaks less well than one that is well polished.[8] An anonymous Turkish treatise of *c*.1440 describes how the resonator of some instruments was varnished with a mixture of powdered glass and glue.[9]

There are many continental references to inlaid instruments, and to others ornamented by jewels and other precious materials;[10] these are amply illustrated by pictures from the late Middle Ages and early Renaissance, notably in Italian and Flemish sources. In England, however, the decoration seems to have been comparatively simple. There are some instances of brightly coloured instruments, such as a green rebec in the BL MS Arundel 91, fo. 218[v], and a mauve one in the BL MS Arundel 157, fo. 71[v] (plates 6, 29), but in both cases these colours are predominant in the picture as such, and may have been used just for the sake of pictorial balance. More realistic, perhaps, are the red spots on a light brown rebec in the Vienna, Nationalbibliothek MS 1100, fo. 1 (plate 5), and the small dots which encircle the soundholes on a mediaeval viol in the St. Alban's Psalter, p. 417 (plate 11). These may represent shallow incisions in the wood, such as can be seen on the crowd on a Worcester Cathedral misericord (plate 108). Occasional elaborate carving on the body of English instruments is evidenced by the British Museum's gittern (citole), but this is rare, and that particular instrument may have been made for a noble amateur.[11] The professional minstrel who made his own instrument would have known just how far it could be adorned without this affecting the sound.[12] According to the visual arts, the most decorated parts of English bowed instruments were the pegbox, tailpiece, and fingerboard, which in themselves would make very little difference, if any, to the quality of sound produced, and also the soundholes, which made a considerable difference.

The early flat pegboxes were normally of a round or diamond-shaped outline, and these were joined by a trefoil design, as in the Bird Psalter, fo. 38[v] (plate 51) in the thirteenth century. After 1300 they became even more varied, with typical examples being the floral shape seen on the rebec of a Worcester Cathedral misericord (plate 109), and the carved head in the Smithfield Decretals, fo. 4 (plate 84). The crown shape in the Romanesque St. Alban's Psalter, p. 417 is extremely rare, and it is balanced at the other end of the instrument by an end projection of similar design (plate 11). The tailpiece could be carved in a special shape as in the Luttrell Psalter, fo. 149 (plate 89), or painted with a pattern as in the Trinity College Apocalypse, fo. 22 (plate 41). A decorated fingerboard appears on the stained-glass fiddle at Ringland (plate 74). Soundholes, which were built primarily for acoustic reasons, were also designed to the artistic advantage of the whole instrument.[13] Up to the thirteenth century the most usual types included round, c-shaped and narrow rectangular holes, and the first two continued throughout the Middle Ages. They were occasionally joined by more unusual forms such as the f-shaped pair in the Cambridge, Trinity College MS B. 11. 4, fo. 128, dating from c.1220–30 (plate 35), and the fourteenth-century cross-shaped ones on a corbel in Exeter Cathedral (plate 75). Carved roses became frequent in sources from the late fourteenth century onwards, such as the Litlyngton Missal, fo. 121 (plate 104), and the glass from Besthorpe (plate 126). A fifteenth-century rebec in the roof of All Saints' Church, North Street, York, has four soundholes of which two are trefoils and the other two quatrefoils (plate 121). However, as with many things in the history of instruments, several of these shapes had been anticipated earlier on the Continent, such as the roses in the *Cantigas de Santa Maria*, fo. 118,[14] of the thirteenth century.

THE STRINGS

Although silk strings were used a great deal in Asia, and were mentioned occasionally in European sources,[15] the material most used in England was gut. The English Franciscan Bartholomaeus Anglicus, in his *De Proprietatibus Rerum* of c.1230, says

... sicut chorde facte de intestinis luporum in vigella vel in cithara posite cum chordis factis de intestinis ouium eas destruunt et corrumpunt[16]

which was translated by John of Trevisa in 1398/9 as

strengis imade of guttes of wolues destroyeþ and fretiþ and corrumpiþ strengis imade of guttis of schiepe ʒif hit so be þat þey beþ so isette among them as in fethele or in harpe ...[17]

A method of making 'cordas lire' is described in the *Secretum Philosophorum* which survives in several fourteenth-century manuscripts.[18] The author describes how the intestines of sheep are washed, and then put into water or lye for at least half a day, until the flesh is separated from the sinews. The gut is then soaked in lye or red wine for two days, after which it is dried with a linen cloth, and two, three, or four lengths are twisted together, according to the thickness of the string required. After being laid out to dry, the strings should be put in a place which is neither too dry nor too humid, as in each of these extremes they are likely to break.[19]

THE FASTENING OF THE STRINGS AT THE UPPER END

A clear development can be seen in the manner of fastening the strings at each end of the instrument. In the early period (from the eleventh to thirteenth centuries inclusive) the pegholder at the upper end was generally flat, with the pegs inserted from above or below according to taste. The strings could be attached to the pegs in two ways, either being wound round them above the pegholder, or passing through holes at the end of the neck, and being attached to them underneath. When an instrument had a lateral drone string (known in Latin as *bordunus*), this passed through a hole in the side of the pegholder, which was made deep enough to contain it. The wood was carved out from behind, to create an open box like an inverted cup, a form which continued to be used on certain fiddles in Italy right up to the Renaissance period, when it became a characteristic of the *lira da braccio* of that country (p. 2).[20] Certain pegboxes were carved out even if they had no *bordunus*; in early examples their pegs were inserted from above or below, but from the fourteenth century onwards they often passed through the sides. From that period also, there appear sickle-shaped and right-angled pegboxes, due respectively to the influence of the mandora (gittern) and the lute, which had both recently arrived in this country.[21] The sickle could be relatively simple, or terminated by a carved head or a scroll. (It should be mentioned here that the scroll on the south aisle stained-glass fiddle in York Minster is not original, being due to a twentieth-century reassembly of glass, as seen in plate 113. Photographs of the window before and after 'restoration' can be seen in the *Friends of York Minster Annual Report* (1955), plate VII, which shows the earlier version of the fiddle to have had a more normal flat pegbox.) In some pictures the neck ends abruptly, with no indication as to the arrangement of pegs. This generally happens only when the front view of an instrument is depicted, as a pegbox which turns back at a right-angle would not therefore be seen. Two fiddles in the Peterborough Psalter, ff. 57, 74, dating from the early fourteenth century, could just have had this design (plates 57, 58), although most illustrations of English bowed instruments with right-angled pegboxes date from the fifteenth and sixteenth centuries.

Table 2 gives examples of some of the most usual types of pegbox, without trying to explain occasional irregularities of detail.

THE FASTENING OF STRINGS AT THE LOWER END

Some of the earliest known English pictures of bowed instruments show the strings to be attached at the lower end to a tailpiece which is not unlike that of the violin family. In fact, the one led without a break to the other, being used on many instruments throughout the Middle Ages and Renaissance. English sources show three chief devices for holding the tailpiece in position. These are (a) an end button as on the violin, (b) a downward and generally rounded projection from the body, as on the Yugoslav *gusle*, although this instrument itself does not have an actual tailpiece (plate 155), and (c) a hookbar consisting of a strip of wood covering the width of the rib and extending out to the front, as on many Renaissance and Baroque viols. In the first case the tailpiece was connected to the button by means of a piece of gut, or by some other strong but flexible substance. The end projection (which in pictures is often

Shape	Detail	Example	Date
1. Flat	strings attached above	BL MS Arundel 91, fo. 218ᵛ Rebec (plate 6)	12c.
	strings attached below	Cambridge, Trinity College, MS B. 11. 4, fo. 85. Mediaeval viol (plate 34)	13c.
2. Cup-shaped	flat part uppermost	Lincoln Cathedral, spandrel carving. Fiddle (plate 46)	13c.
	hollow part uppermost	Luttrell Psalter, fo. 149. Rebec (plate 89)	14c.
3. Decorative design, obscuring arrangement of pegs	crown	St. Alban's Psalter, p. 447. Mediaeval viol (plate 11)	12c.
	flower	Worcester Cathedral, misericord. Rebec (plate 109)	14c.
4. Curved, to form sickle-shape or scroll	sickle-shape	BL MS Cott. Tiberius A. vii, fo. 77. Rebec (plate 118)	15c.
	scroll	London, Victoria and Albert Museum, stained glass. Rebec (plate 112)	15c.
5. Right-angled	plain right-angle	Beverley, St. Mary's Church, corbel. Rebec (plate 144)	16c.
	right-angle with carved head	Hours of Elizabeth the Queen, fo. 7. Fiddle (plate 115)	15c.

Table 2. *The Development of the Pegbox*

indistinguishable from the button) was generally used in the same way, but sometimes the tailpiece would be shaped to fit right round it. The hookbar could similarly anchor an extended tailpiece, or else hold a loop of gut. However, in certain representations the tailpiece ends where the rib begins, and there is no indication as to how it should be fixed.

Sometimes there is no tailpiece at all. In such cases the strings could be attached either (a) directly to the end projection, as on the *gusle*, (b) to single pins, or (c) to a frontal stringholder in the form of a low bar, as on the lute. Single pins could be fixed into the rib or else inserted into the belly itself. This last method could not have been good for the soundboard, which, as mentioned on p. 19, was made of softer wood than the rest of the instrument. Although the frontal stringholder is suggested in a few early but indistinct pictures, it did not become usual in English sources until the late fourteenth century, and then probably due to the influence of the lute. Occasionally a bar of this type can be found, not on the belly of the instrument, but securing the strings onto its rib or, when there is no rib, to the rounded back.

Examples of these methods can be seen in tables 3a and b.

Attached to	Example	Date
end button	Lisle Psalter, fo. 134ᵛ. Fiddle (plate 87)	14c.
end projection	Great Malvern Priory, north transept glass. Fiddle (plate 139)	16c.
hookbar	Oakham Castle, sculpture. Mediaeval viol (plate 24)	12c.

Attached by	Example	Date
gut, or other suitable substance	Luttrell Psalter, fo. 149ᵛ. Rebec (plate 89)	14c.
tailpiece hooked round projection	St. Alban's Psalter, p. 56. Mediaeval viol (plate 10)	12c.
no visible means of attachment	Norwich, St. Peter Hungate, glass. Fiddle (plate 125)	15c.

Table 3b. *The Tailpiece and other Stringholders; no tailpiece*

Strings attached to	Example	Date
end projection	Litlyngton Missal, fo. 221ᵛ. Fiddle (plate 105)	14c.
single pins	Gorleston Psalter, fo. 35. Fiddle (plate 70)	14c.
frontal stringholder	Warwick, St. Mary's Church, Beauchamp Chapel glass. Rebecs (plate 122)	15c.
stringholder on rounded back	York Minister, tower sculpture (interior). Fiddle (plate 129)	15c.

Table 3a. *The Tailpiece and other Stringholders; the tailpiece*

THE BRIDGE, AND ITS COMBINATION WITH THE TAILPIECE

The bridge presents one of the chief problems of the present study, partly because its important details can seldom be seen to the best advantage. When an instrument is held parallel to the ground and facing outwards, as in the Peterborough Psalter, fo. 57 (plate 57), the only visible part of the bridge is a straight line. All that such a bridge can tell us is that it does exist as a separate entity, and where it stands in relation to the other ingredients.

In contrast to this, there are pictures where there is no bridge in evidence at all. It could be thought that the artist just forgot to put it in, but there must be a better reason, as the omission occurs frequently in sources from the eleventh-century BL MS Cott. Tiberius C. vi, fo. 30^v (plate 2), to the fifteenth-century stained glass in the south choir aisle of York Minster (plate 113), and beyond. Here again the reason for the problem is the angle from which the image is shown, namely the 'full face' view. Fortunately there are other examples, portrayed from different angles, which show that the tailpiece either has feet, or is sitting on the bridge, or is made in one piece with it, or else is placed right up against it. Such views can be seen in many continental sources, a notable one being Stefan Lochner's *Weltgerichtsaltar* at the Wallraf-Richartz Museum, Cologne.[22] There are not so many clear English examples, because the device appears mainly in large-scale paintings which have room to show such detail, and there are comparatively few of these surviving from mediaeval England. (Those large paintings that do remain here either have no instruments in them at all, such as the Wilton Diptych at the National Gallery, London, or else they do not show bowed instruments with this device, as is the case with the Chapter House wall-paintings in Westminster Abbey.) There are, however, a few English manuscripts which have it, such as the Bohun Psalter (London), fo. 24 (plate 99), the Queen Mary Psalter, fo. 193, and Bodl. MS Bodley 691, fo. 1 (plate 93), while relevant church carvings can be found at Beverley Minster and Cogges (plates 95, 94). In stained glass it appears in Kimberley Church and in the north transept of Lincoln Cathedral. One advantage of the combined or joined bridge and tailpiece is that the sounding length of each string is a good deal longer than it is when these items are separate from each other, and it consequently gives out a lower pitch. Modern makers of mediaeval instruments would do well to use this device instead of the anachronistic covered strings which are still being used today on far too many instruments.

Separate mediaeval bridges vary considerably in shape. The great majority appear to be quite flat, and quite low in comparison to that of the modern violin. They span most of the period covered by this book, with examples appearing on the twelfth-century mediaeval viol in Oakham Castle (plate 24), and on the fifteenth-century rebec in the stalls of St. Mary's Church, Beverley (plate 120). The musical result of a low flat bridge is that all the strings sound together, the melody being accompanied by permanent drones. The same normally applies with a taller bridge where the strings are all in the same plane, but here there is one advantage. If the bridge is sufficiently high to give the bow a good clearance from the sides of the instrument, then the two outer strings can each be sounded separately, should the performer wish it.

Curved bridges are less easy to find, although they do exist.[23] Examples include one on a five-stringed fiddle in the thirteenth-century Lambeth Apocalypse, fo. 3 (plate 39) and another on the Steeple Aston Cope (plate 76). One of the best appears on a fiddle played by an animal in Bodl. MS Douce 131, fo. 20 (plate 91). Unfortunately the picture as a whole is somewhat worn, but there is enough to show that the bridge is quite tall, and distinctly curved. Even more so is that of a fiddle in the fifteenth-century stained glass of All Saints' Church, North Street, York, but here the design is in general rather out of perspective.

When there is no separate bridge, its substitute is not always flat. In the Bohun Psalter (London), fo. 24, a tailpiece with feet is curved in such a way that the strings could be sounded separately (plate 99), and in the Cambridge, Trinity College MS B. 10. 2, fo. 30, a frontal stringholder also seems intended to be curved (plate 107); in this case, however, it is doubtful whether the bow would have sufficient clearance from the side of the instrument. (The completely inaccurate position of the player's left hand shows that the artist here was not too well aware of the necessary characteristics of fiddles and fiddling.)

More imagination can be seen in the illustration of bridges in continental sources, and even if the artist is not wholly accurate they are worth considering. One example comes from the Paris, Bibliothèque Nationale MS Fr. 962, fo. 17 (plate 98), a French manuscript of the fourteenth century. Here there are two rebecs leaning up against the side of a picture in which David plays a harp. The rebec on the left has three single strings and that on the right three double courses (pp. 1–2) although the latter may in fact be a plucked mandora (gittern). On both instruments the bridge extends across the whole width of the instrument, being curved upwards slightly towards the centre. The bridge of the rebec on the left, however, is crenellated, with the central string being placed across the highest point of the bridge, and the outer ones being let down into the cavities on each side. It is tempting to assume that this is a means for holding the strings at different heights so that they can be played separately, but if this is the case the artist has made the whole bridge slightly too low, as the bow would rub against the side of the instrument while trying to play on either of the outer two strings. An alternative reason for such a shape would be to drop any one or two strings down into a hole so that they need not be played upon at all; this is the case in many continental pictures, particularly of the fifteenth century, but if it was at all customary in England, evidence has yet to be forthcoming.

Two hypothetical questions may be considered concerning flat bridges. While accepting the fact that throughout the Middle Ages a great many of them did result in all the strings sounding together, it is possible that they were sometimes adapted in ways that would not be apparent from most representations. The first suggestion concerns the grooves into which the strings are set in a bridge, to prevent them from sliding around. It is possible that, on a flat bridge of sufficient height, these grooves were sometimes set at different depths so that each string could be held at a different level, and therefore touched separately by the bow.[24] This is a similar method to that in the first theory mentioned above concerning the Paris, Bibliothèque Nationale MS Fr. 962, fo. 17 (plate 98), but as the grooves would be so narrow the artist would not normally bother to represent them. However, on the Minstrels' Gallery in Exeter Cathedral (plate 86), an angel plays a fiddle on which this does seem to be indicated for the lateral *bordunus*, although the other strings appear to be set in one plane.

Related to this possibility is one which creates a comparison with the Yugoslav *gusle* (plate 155). On certain examples of this instrument the one string passes through a hole in the middle of the bridge rather than over its top, and in some *gusle* bridges there are actually three holes although only one is used. On the mediaeval flat bridges which were not too low, such an arrangement would have enabled each string to be sounded separately if the holes were placed at different levels.[25]

Alan Crumpler has suggested to the author that when the bridge and tailpiece are combined, small studs of different heights could be placed on the tailpiece beneath the strings. These could raise the strings to appropriate heights and thus enable them to be played upon separately. Although the theory started as a hypothesis, it may well be supported by the rebec in the BL MS Royal I C. vii, fo. 92 (plate 14), where just such an arrangement appears to be visible.

Bearing in mind these facts and hypotheses, we can now consider the implications of Johannes de Grocheo (*c*.1300) and Johannes Tinctoris (*c*.1487) concerning bridges, although neither writer specifically mentions them. Grocheo's statement that 'a good performer on the fiddle uses normally every cantus and cantilena and every musical form'[26] ('bonus autem artifex in viella omnem cantum et cantilenam et omnem formam musicalem generaliter introducit')[27] must mean that on many instruments it was possible to play completely free melodies without the restrictions of drones. Tinctoris declared that on the 'viola' 'the bow ... can touch any one string the player wills, leaving the others untouched' ('arculus ... unam tangens: juxta libitum sonitoris: alias relinquat inconcussas'),[28] thus implying that either a curved bridge or one of its substitutes would be used.

In the light of these problems over bridges it is clear that the subject is very complex, and needs a considerable amount of experimentation from instrument makers—far more than is happening at the time of going to press.

Experimentation is also urgently needed over the matter of instruments which have two bridges. The relevant illustrations show not only the normal bridge or its equivalent, but also a second one at the upper end of the body. In many cases, such as that of Lochner's *Weltgerichtsaltar*, this second bridge is lower in height than the usual one.

Paired bridges such as these are rare in English sources, but among clear examples are those of a rebec on a misericord in Worcester Cathedral (plate 109) and one from the Tickhill Psalter, fo. 17 (plate 61). On fiddles they can be seen without doubt on the BL Add. MS 47680, ff. 6, 9ᵛ, 16ᵛ, and 18ᵛ (plate 81). All these sources happen to date from the fourteenth century, but from the greater number of continental representations it is clear that the device extended over a much greater period of time. An earlier English example where it is suggested but not definite comes from the Florence, Biblioteca Medicea Laurenziana MS Pluteus XII.17, fo. 2ᵛ (plate 9).

While a small amount of speculation on the matter has appeared in print,[29] the device cannot be properly described until instrument makers have produced satisfactory working models. The only working solution seen so far by the author is on a gittern (citole) adapted by Crawford Young of Basel. His suggestion is that the second bridge causes the strings to sound slightly louder by the buzz that it creates, in a manner related to that of the bray pins on certain harps, or the loose foot of the bridge on the trumpet marine. This idea (which is also being advocated in lectures by Bernard Ravenel) certainly works, and now needs to be tried out on bowed instruments, if it has not already been done by the time that this book appears in print.

THE FINGERBOARD AND ITS ABSENCE, AND THE USE OF FRETS

On instruments of the violin family today, the neck is surmounted by a fingerboard against which the performer presses the strings in order to obtain the required notes. At its upper end there is a small notched bar known as the nut, which serves a triple purpose. Firstly, it holds the strings in position before they are deflected to be wound round the lateral pegs; secondly, it supports them at a suitable height to be clear of the fingerboard or the neck; and thirdly, it determines the upper end of the sounding length of the strings. Such a device appears on a fiddle in the Tickhill Psaltar, fo. 14 (plate 59). However, there are many cases, exemplified by that of the Lisle Psalter, fo. 134ᵛ (plate 87), where there is a fingerboard and no nut, and others where there is a nut and no fingerboard, but it should be noted that this applies mainly to mediaeval viols, such as that from the York Psalter, fo. 21ᵛ (plate 22). The rebec from the Luttrell Psalter, fo. 149 shows a nut fashioned from the actual rim of the rounded pegbox (plate 89). Some kind of nut or rim is implied by necessity when the strings pass through the neck to be attached to the pegs behind, as in the example from the Lisle Psalter mentioned above.

Whether or not there was a fingerboard depended to a great extent on the height of the bridge, as if that were low, or if it were replaced by a frontal stringholder, then the fingers could press the strings directly on to the neck of the instrument, and no fingerboard would be necessary. It is, however, possible to play on strings without pressing them down on to the surface below, as happens with the *gusle*. By pressing the strings more firmly than is needed to make harmonics, an adequate sound can be obtained.

When Jerome of Moravia listed the notes that could be played on the 'rubeba' and the 'viella' he took them only to the top of what we now call the first position. Most of the fingerboards depicted up to this time are quite short, and give no scope for climbing into higher positions. Others, however, are a good bit longer, and they do raise the question as to whether or not mediaeval performers ever used the second and third positions. The example from the Lisle Psalter, fo. 134ᵛ, for instance, has not only a neck which is long enough for the performer to change positions, but also a fingerboard which, like many others, extends some way along the soundboard (plate 87). These longer fingerboards seem to appear from the late thirteenth century onwards, and it is from this time also that frets begin to appear on bowed instruments.[30] These frets can help our knowledge of how the strings could have been tuned, and they can also give some clue as to the changing of positions.

First of all, let us consider the gittern (citole) or mediaeval guitar, from which the fiddle may have acquired its frets in the first place. Here the most usual number of frets is five, which, by reason of their being placed a semitone apart, would indicate the maximum distance of a perfect fourth playable on each string. In the early fourteenth-century Ormesby Psalter, fo. 9ᵛ, however, there are seven frets, which are spaced far enough apart to necessitate the changing of positions if the top available notes are to be reached (plate 72). Hence we know that changing position was not unheard of during the Middle Ages; indeed, it must have been practised as far back as the ninth century, judging by the very long-necked fretted instruments of the guitar family which can be seen in the Utrecht Psalter, fo. 81ᵛ.[31]

In pictures of fiddles the exact amount of frets is often obscured by the performer's hand, but their number can generally be guessed at. In the Bohun Psalter (London), fo. 29ᵛ and the Ormesby Psalter, fo. 9ᵛ (plates 102, 72) it can be assumed that there should be four, which would cover a major third on one string and suggest a tuning in fourths, probably with a third in the middle as on many other fretted instruments. Five frets, which may be intended on the embroidered Cope of the Virgin (now in the Cathedral of St. Bertrand de Comminges),[32] ensure the playing of up to a fourth on each string, although they do not necessarily imply a tuning in fifths. Seven frets, which can be assumed from the Steeple Aston Cope (plate 76), produce up to a perfect fifth on each string.

Now comes the question as to whether the performer ever changed position on the fretted fiddle in mediaeval England. It seems that he must have done so in France, because in the Paris, Bibliothèque Nationale MS Fr. 1951, fo. 9 ('Le Bestiaire de l'amour rimet', c.1300),[33] the presumed seven frets could not possibly have been reached without it. Here the frets are spread quite far apart, so each semitone would have been covered by one finger and each tone by two, as on the modern guitar and the (fretless) cello. Similar distances, however, occur in the Bohun (London) and Ormesby Psalters (plates 102, 72), although in these cases the four frets should lie more or less beneath the fingers, rendering any change of position unnecessary. It is possible that here the artist just spaced the frets too far apart. The opposite situation appears in the Steeple Aston Cope (plate 76), where the seven frets are spaced very closely together. If the designer of this cope was not in error, it would mean that one finger could cover two frets as on the Neapolitan mandolin of today, and the changing of positions would not have been needed. Although we must allow for a considerable amount of artistic error in this respect, it is reasonable to deduce that a certain amount of position changing was known in mediaeval England on fretted fiddles, and that the technique may have been transferred to unfretted ones, although how far it was done can never be known.

WAS THERE A SOUNDPOST?

The violin of today has its soundboard strengthened below by a strip of wood known as the bassbar, which also helps to disperse the vibrations. So does the soundpost, a small pillar of wood placed near the right foot of the bridge to support the soundboard and to carry the vibrations through more easily to the back. Whether or not these two items existed during the Middle Ages is one of the most tantalizing questions concerning mediaeval bowed instruments. No surviving example has them, but then there are so few that remain to tell the tale. Some folk instruments of the rebec family today do not have them, and neither do the few that are extant from the Middle Ages. Of the mediaeval viols there is as yet no survivor known to us. The later Welsh crwth had a soundpost which was the continuation of one leg of the bridge, but there is no certainty that this was the case with any of its mediaeval ancestors (p. 48). The Baroque viols had both bassbar and soundpost, but many of their Renaissance predecessors did not, as they were strengthened by transverse barring.[34]

There remains the fiddle. Those that survive from the *Mary Rose* are in a fragmentary state and show no clear signs of having had soundposts. The 'violeta' of St. Caterina de' Vigri contains a transverse bar beneath the rose, and no soundpost, but this is a very unusual instrument in several respects,[35] and cannot be considered representative of average fiddles. However, the possibility of a post for supporting the soundboard cannot be ruled out altogether from earlier examples, even if the device were not built for acoustical reasons. At Santiago Cathedral, when the main doors are opened and the sun lights up the *Pórtico de la Gloria*, it shines directly into the soundholes of the fiddle on the right. The lower hole, which is easily visible from below, shows an interior post on each side, one just to the right of the bridge, and the other just below the end of the tailpiece, which itself is supported on the belly of the instrument (plate 25). Such a sight is extremely rare, if not unique according to our present knowledge, but it does open up the possibility of the post being known to the fiddlers of mediaeval England.

CHAPTER III

The Rebec

❦

ACCORDING to the research of Dr Werner Bachmann, the bow may have appeared first in Central Asia, in the land around the River Oxus (Amu-Darya), where for many years craftsmen had been renowned for their making of bows and arrows.[1] This adaptation in the use of an article of hunting and war had apparently taken place by the ninth century AD, when the bow was producing new sounds on instruments which hitherto had normally been plucked, rubbed, or struck.

The invention spread rapidly. The Persian traveller Ibn Khurdādhbih, in writing to the Kalif al-Mu'tamid (d. 893) said that the five-stringed wooden *lūrā* of Byzantium was similar to the Arabic *rabāb*, although he did not say specifically that either of them was bowed.[2] However, in the first half of the tenth century the scholar al-Fārābī, in his *Kitāb al-mūsīqī al-kabīr*, made it quite clear that on certain instruments the strings were rubbed 'with other strings or some material resembling strings', and somewhat later Ibn Sina (Avicenna, 980–1037) wrote in the *Kitāb al-Shifā* that one of these instruments was the *rabāb*.[3]

Instruments known by the names *rabāb* and *lyra* are still played today in northern Africa and the Balkans, but both words cover very different types. Those that chiefly concern us here are the two-stringed *rabāb* of Morocco and the wider three-stringed *lyra* of Greece and Crete. What they have in common are a curved back, carved from one piece of wood, a gradually tapering outline so that there is no clear distinction between the body and the neck, and the fact that both are played with a bow. Instruments resembling these can be seen in European art as far back as the eleventh century, and it is from a fusion of the two types that there emerged the instrument now known as the *rebec*.

TERMINOLOGY

It will be seen from the following pages that during the mediaeval period the instrument underwent various changes, including that of its name. While different forms of the word *rebec* appear in literature from *c.*1300 onwards, they are not to be found in much earlier sources, and if Aelfric's fiddlers were rebec-players, their instruments must have been covered by the generic use of the word *fiddle*. Other early words for the rebec family include *lira* or *lyra*, and *gigue*. While the former variants appear with pictures of rebecs in continental sources of the twelfth and thirteenth centuries (pp. 11–12), such evidence for England seems to be lacking. (Indeed, the fifteenth-century *Promptorium Parvulorum* is one of several cases where 'lira' is equated with a harp, as seen in Appendix B.) 'Gigours' can be found in the thirteenth-century *Geste of Kyng Horn*,[4] and in the *Dictionarius* of John de Garlande the 'gigatores' of Paris clearly played different instruments from the 'vidulatores'. The three German 'gigatores' who performed at the Feast of Westminster in 1306 were listed separately from the 'vidulatores', not only then, but on several other occasions (p. 83). After this time, forms of the word *rebec* appear in English works, for instance in Chaucer's *Friar's Tale* where it is 'rebekke'. Meanwhile various derivatives of *rabāb* appeared, notably *ribible*, *rybybe*, *rebube*, *rubebe*, etc., and from their context in literature it would seem that they were also members of the rebec family. John Lydgate, in *Reson and Sensuallyte* (*c*.1407), lists both 'fythels' and 'rubibis' separately in one group of instruments,[5] and the poem 'Herkyn to my tale' (*c*.1500) also suggests that they were different: 'Tho fox fydylyd, tho raton rybybyd, tho larke noty with all'.[6] Nevertheless it will be seen from the contradictions in Appendix B that 'rybybe' = 'vitula' = 'viella' = 'fydyll', so a general caution must be observed on this matter, bearing in mind that the rebec belongs to the generic family of fiddles anyway. Lydgate's reminder of this has already been mentioned on p. 15. A further example can be seen in the Seal of Walter le Vyelur, dating from *c*.1256–7 (PRO Seal no. P832); this shows three instruments of the rebec family (plate 42), although Walter 'The Fiddler' is described on the seal as a painter. After 1500 there appeared the word *kit*, which was to last for 400 years, applying to small members of the rebec family and their descendants.[7] During the period covered by this book, however, it is unlikely to have meant anything other than the rebec as used in England at that time.

THE REBEC IN ENGLAND

Bachmann has shown that the bow was known in Spain, Sicily, and southern Italy during the tenth century, and that in the eleventh it was being used throughout most of Europe.[8] There are numerous pictures of bowed instruments in continental sources dating from before 1100, but very few from that period in England. Before their English appearance, however, there was the enigmatic reference to fiddlers in Aelfric's *Glossary*:

| fidicen | fiðelere |
| fidicina | fiðelestre[9] |

If their instruments were bowed rather than plucked, they would have been of the rebec or crowd families, or possibly of both. Aelfric died *c*.1020, and, as we have seen, the earliest known English picture of a rebec dates from *c*.1050, in an Anglo-Saxon manuscript, the Tiberius Psalter, fo. 30ᵛ (plate 2). Here it appears in the page before that of the initial B(eatus vir), played by Idithun while David plays a harp in the centre, and around him two other minstrels blow a horn and a long cylindrical wind instrument supported on a stick. Another man juggles with three knives and three balls. The rebec is of a wide pear shape, and played up at the shoulder, facing outwards so that only the front view can be seen. It has four strings, four pegs in a flat pegbox, and a tailpiece, and on each side of this there is a small round soundhole. There is no separate bridge, so the tailpiece must have been intended to have some means of support from below, as suggested on p. 24. In its general outline this instrument is not unlike the *lyra* of Greece and Crete today, although this latter instrument is played down on the lap. The bow in the manuscript is curved, but little detail can be seen.

Another English manuscript illustration of a rebec from the eleventh century is in a copy of St. Augustine's *Commentary on the Psalms (1–50)*, written at Christ Church, Canterbury, *c.*1070–1100, by monks brought from the Norman Abbey of Bec by Archbishop Lanfranc (Cambridge, Trinity College MS B. 5. 26, fo. 1).[10] Here it appears within the initial B(eatus vir), played by one of David's minstrels while his companion juggles with three knives and David himself plays the harp (plate 4). By a fortunate coincidence this rebec bears a certain similarity to the Moroccan *rabāb*, being narrow in outline and having only two strings. Like the previous example it is played up at the shoulder and facing the viewer, but it does not show much detail. There is no indication as to how the strings are attached at the lower end, nor are there any soundholes. The shape at the upper end is not clear; it almost suggests a sickle-shaped pegbox, but as this does not otherwise appear in English art until the fourteenth century, the question must remain open.

The third known English representation of a rebec from this period was dug up on 3 November 1983 by the archaeologist Ian Stewart, during an excavation of Gloucester Castle (plate 3). It is on one of a complete set of thirty backgammon counters which had been discarded, together with their incomplete board, in a rubbish pit. The pottery in the pit is of a type made in the eleventh century but not in the twelfth, so the counters are also believed to be of that date. They include figures from several well-known series of designs, such as the Signs of the Zodiac and the Occupations of the Months, and the presence of a crowned harpist and a juggler suggests that these, together with the rebec-player, represent King David and his minstrels, in just the same grouping as that of MS B. 5. 26.

The rebec itself is not unlike that of the Tiberius Psalter, with a wide body and a diamond-shaped flat pegbox. It also has four strings and apparently a combined bridge and tailpiece, but this device is hidden by the short bow. No soundholes are visible, but the soundboard is decorated around the edges by a series of pricks. By good fortune this figure is one of the best preserved in the complete set of tablesmen.

After 1100, English representations of the rebec became much more frequent. In addition to David's minstrels, its players were generally animals and grotesques, and on a well-known capital in the crypt of Canterbury Cathedral it is played by a devil (plate 13). The basic pear shape with flat pegbox was prevalent, with the body varying in width from one example to another. Already at this stage a great variety can be seen in the number of strings, ranging from one in the Winchcombe Bible and the Shaftesbury Psalter to five (albeit somewhat erratically drawn) in the York Psalter (plates 16, 15, 21). The instrument in the Lunel Psalter has four strings over the fingerboard besides a lateral drone or *bordunus* which could be touched by the bow or plucked by the left thumb as needed (Bachmann, *The Origins of Bowing*, plate 69).

This *bordunus* continued to be built into certain rebecs in the thirteenth century, being accompanied by three main strings in the Canterbury Psalter (Oxford) and the Venice Psalter (plates 30, 45). The former instrument has a very wide soundboard with no fingerboard, and an implied combination of bridge and tailpiece, while the latter has a fingerboard, a separate bridge, and a decorative line parallel to the outline of the instrument. This brings to mind the purfling on later viols and violins, but as it is not known that this practice definitely existed in thirteenth-century England, the line may have been intended solely for decoration. In both rebecs the strings pass through the end of the neck to be attached to the pegs below the pegbox, which has the flat top still customary at that time. Its outline, however, was becoming more varied, as indicated by the trefoil shape in the Bird Psalter (plate 51). The long straight bow of the Venice Psalter has already been noted on p. 17 (plate 45).

The *bordunus* was only to be found on a minority of rebecs, and by the fourteenth century it had gone out of fashion. A drone effect could, however, still be obtained on instruments where all the strings sounded together. The chief developments during this century concern the pegbox. The old flat shape can still be seen on a capital at Oakham Church with the strings attached to the pegs above it, and the bottom of at least one peg visible from below. In the Luttrell Psalter the pegbox is cup-shaped, with its two pegs inserted from the side (plate 89), instead of from above or below as had previously been usual. An early floral pegbox can be seen in the Peterborough Psalter (plate 58), and the later one from Worcester Cathedral has already been mentioned on p. 22 (plate 109). The most lasting development came with the introduction of the sickle shape, which appears in the Smithfield Decretals surmounted by an animal's head (plate 84), and in St. Mary's Hall, Coventry, where it is of a more simple design (plate 110). This was the shape which the rebec never completely abandoned, and finally passed to the violin when that instrument emerged *c.*1500.[11]

During the fifteenth century the basic width of the instrument continued to fluctuate, from narrow examples such as that in the stained glass at Warwick (plate 122), to wide ones as seen in the frieze to the north of the altar at Hillesden (plate 137). Certain continental sources show the outline to be interrupted by slight corners, but as they do not affect the gradual tapering of the neck or the curvature of the back, the instruments can still be regarded as rebecs, although somewhat hybrid ones. An English example of this type occurs in the stained glass of the church at Besthorpe, near Norwich (plate 126),[12] where a new development is the carved rose, in place of the smaller soundholes that were prevalent before. The sickle-shaped pegbox on this instrument is terminated by what appears to be a leaf. Other shapes of the pegbox at this period were a complete right-angled turn, seen at the church of Stow Maries in Essex, and a similar turn ending in a scroll, as in a stained glass roundel from Suffolk, now kept at the Victoria and Albert Museum (plate 112). While a good many instruments still had no fingerboard, there were more examples of it than before. Generally it followed the tapering outline of the instrument, being in effect a raised platform caused by the cutting away of the soundbox to leave the belly at a slightly lower level. This is clearly seen in two examples from Lydgate's *Pilgrimage of the Life of Man*, of which one is reproduced in plate 118. While a good many continental fingerboards had frets at this period,[13] they must have been extremely rare in England; the only possible English example known to the author is in the church at Castor, but here they are only suggested by the shape of the carving, which is now totally covered by gold paint. The frontal stringholder, which was already known on fiddles during the late fourteenth century, seems to have become established on English rebecs in the fifteenth, as witnessed by the glass at Warwick among other sources (plate 122). The bow, which hitherto had been of any length ranging from very long to very short, now appears in most cases to be short. An intriguing example occurs at Warwick, where it is made in the shape of a saw (plate 122). This could be intended just as a joke,[14] but the knowledge that such bows have existed for the later Flemish *bumbass* calls for further investigation.[15] Experiments with a notched stick show that when used on a rebec it can make a very exciting sound, certainly suitable for lively dances and bucolic activities. It would be good to know just what was in John Prudde's mind when he put it in the hand of an angel . . .

Rebecs of the early sixteenth century display the same characteristics as those of the late fifteenth, as witnessed by the two dating from *c*.1500 in St. Wendreda's Church at March. These have three strings, a frontal stringholder, and a right-angled pegbox. A five-stringed rebec appears on a corbel in the north chapel of St. Mary's Church, Beverley, and the shape of its bridge suggests that it may have been a droning instrument (plate 144). Those at March certainly are. It has already been observed that the word *kit* would have been applied to some of these varied rebecs (p. 31), as the narrow boat-shape which developed later in the century was yet to arrive.[16] Even in the seventeenth century, a manuscript written by Randle Holme gave a drawing of an ordinary rebec accompanied by the inscription 'A kit with foure bowed strings' (BL MS Harley 2027, fo. 272).

THE NUMBER OF STRINGS, AND THEIR TUNING

Since the time of Agricola, many writers have stated that the rebec had three strings and that they were tuned in fifths.[17] This is a generalization which needs to be modified to a considerable extent. While three is certainly the most frequent number to be seen in pictures and carvings, particularly those of the later period, there are many cases where the strings number from one to five, and occasionally to six. As far as the tuning is concerned, there seem to be no known English instructions extant from the Middle Ages, and the continental ones do not cover all the many types of rebec shown in the visual arts. Jerome of Moravia, in his *Tractatus de Musica* written in Paris some time between 1280 and *c*.1300 said that the 'rubeba' was tuned to *c* and *g*.[18] As he did not refer to other numbers of strings in this context, he was probably talking about the *rabāb* type, which has had two strings tuned in fifths for several hundred years. Agricola's *Musica Instrumentalis Deudsch* and Gerle's *Musica Teusch* also suggested tunings in fifths for their three-stringed instruments, which had bridges shaped in such a way that the strings could be sounded separately.[19] No one has left us tunings for all the countless instruments with four, five, or even six strings, which all sounded together above a flat bridge. Certain deductions can, however, be made about such instruments.

If there were three strings tuned in fifths, they would sound discordant unless the melody were kept to the top string and ended on a note which formed a consonance with the two lower strings. As the mediaeval rebec was normally played only in the first position, any melodies would therefore be restricted to five notes, e.g.

Ex. 1

and these do not contain the tonic. It is unlikely, therefore, that this tuning was often used on droning instruments.

Four strings tuned in fifths would be completely discordant from start to finish, and would give no suitable accompaniment to any mediaeval melody.

It is evident, therefore, that a different tuning must have been used from one that was only in fifths. The most obvious is a mixture of fifths and fourths, which of itself also produces the octave, and was recommended by both Jerome of Moravia and Tinctoris for the fiddle (pp. 65–6). On a four-stringed rebec tuned, for instance, to

Ex. 2

the drones would be consonant throughout.

There is, however, some evidence for strings being tuned in pairs, so that one could drone while its partner sounded a melody. It is particularly likely that this happened on rebecs with five or six strings, as the instrument was normally too small to take the variety of thickness that would be required, for instance, in strings sounding as follows:

Ex. 3

The following are suggestions for tunings compatible with mediaeval music, bearing in mind that they are only relative, as there was no standardization of pitch or of the sizes of instruments.

Ex. 4

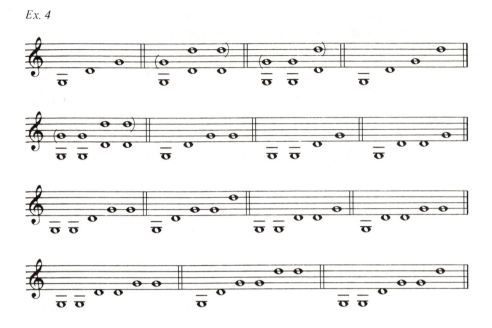

The cases of rebecs having a lateral *bordunus* would likewise vary according to what the minstrel wanted to play.

Much more freedom of tuning is possible for those instruments which have a curved bridge or its equivalent. Although each string can be sounded separately, paired strings can still be played together when required to give a melody with a single drone accompaniment. It is not until works of the sixteenth century that we have more positive information about the tuning of the rebec, and this comes from the German writers mentioned above, who said that it was tuned in fifths. It is only, however, with the 1545 edition of Agricola's work that specific notes are given for them, i.e.

Ex. 5   Discant   Alto &   Tenor   Bass

It will be noted that the bass rebec has four strings, but the others were of the three-stringed type which led to the textbook misconception that this was a standard number. It is not known to what extent, if at all, the bass rebec was used in England, as English pictures of instruments large enough to take its tuning are conspicuously lacking.

It has already been observed that a good many pictures are very inaccurate (pp. 3–4), and it is therefore not surprising that this often takes the form of an instrument having more pegs than strings. Sometimes the converse occurs, with instruments having more strings than pegs. This could also be due to some artistic aberration, but before dismissing the subject as nonsensical we should consider some of the examples. The one that stands out in particular is that from the Luttrell Psalter (plate 89), where there are two pegs and three strings, and it is quite obvious that the artist has deliberately attached two strings to one peg. At Oloron Cathedral the rebecs have four or five strings and three pegs,[21] while in the BL MS Sloane 3983, fo. 13 the upper of the two instruments labelled 'viola' has four strings and three pegs (plate 63). As pairs of strings were sometimes tuned at the unison, it might in theory be possible for two strings to be attached to one peg if they were to produce the same note. However, this cannot have been a very satisfactory arrangement, as the strings would be unlikely to stay in tune with each other for very long. It is another matter which calls for experimentation by instrument makers.

THE PLAYING POSITION

We have already seen how artistic licence affects not only the details of an instrument itself, but also the manner in which it is held; how, for instance, the playing position can be modified to suit the design of a painting, or to preserve intact a carving which might otherwise become damaged. Bearing this in mind, we can now consider the positions in which the rebec and its bow are most often represented in the visual arts.

Some of the earliest pictures of the rebec in England show it being played up at the shoulder in a manner similar to that of the modern violin.[22] However, a completely accurate portrayal of this attitude would be mainly a side view of the instrument, so for better artistic effect the painter depicted what could be seen from the front, namely the soundboard and its accessories. Typical examples are in the York Psalter (plate 21), the Canterbury Psalter (Oxford) (plate 30) and several other manuscript sources. In such cases as the BL MS Arundel 91, fo. 218^v (plate 6), the rebec is still held up at the shoulder but pointing downwards to a certain extent. By way of contrast, the example in the Winchcombe Bible points upwards (plate 16). During the fourteenth century two new positions became established, those of holding the instrument in the armpit and across the chest. The first is foreshadowed in the Bird Psalter (plate 51) and is clearly demonstrated at Lawford, after which it became an accepted manner throughout the remainder of the rebec's history. The second way, which is demonstrated at Worcester (plate 109), lasted certainly to the end of the Middle Ages, and almost always involved the use of a small bow. The practice of holding the rebec down on the lap (which is seen quite often in continental sources) does not appear in any English representation known to the present writer.

The technique of holding the bow is generally very similar to that of today, with the player's four fingers above the stick and his thumb below it. Typical examples are in the York and Luttrell Psalters (plates 21, 89). There are, however, cases such as that in Ely Cathedral, where the handle is gripped by the whole fist (plate 127), a posture often seen in connection with the larger fiddle (p. 68). The technique of gripping the bow from below might not be expected with English rebecs, as it is normally associated with instruments played down in the lap, but it does sometimes occur when they are held at the shoulder and point downwards. It can be seen in the BL MS Arundel 91, fo. 218ᵛ (plate 6), and the Vienna, Nationalbibliothek MS 1100, fo. 1, where the player is a blue animal with conveniently long 'fingers' (plate 5). The possibility of the player controlling the tension of the hairs is suggested at St. Mary's Hall, Coventry, but this example is a rarity (plate 110).

There seems to be no evidence of any pear-shaped plucked instruments in England before the rebec arrived, complete with its bow, perhaps soon after AD 1000; certainly they did not become fully established here until the fourteenth century. However, in the Lambeth Bible, fo. 309, dating from c.1140–50 there is an isolated musician sitting on the edge of an illuminated initial I(n anno) (plate 19). In his left hand he holds a rebec which rests on his right knee, and with his right fingers he plucks it. There is no plectrum. The extreme rarity of this picture suggests that the instrument is a plucked rebec rather than a member of the mandora (gittern) family, which did not become widespread in English art until after c.1300. There is, after all, nothing to stop anyone from plucking a rebec just for fun, even if it were not the orthodox way of playing the instrument. Perhaps the painter sometimes did it himself.[23] (The Apocalyptic Elders at Hardham are a different case, as described on p. 5.)

THE SOUND OF THE REBEC

From the great variety of instrumental shapes and patterns used during the Middle Ages it would seem that there must have been an almost equal diversity in the types of sound produced. Very few instruments of the rebec family would have sounded quite alike, and even those made to the same pattern by one maker may not have produced an identical effect. It is understandable, therefore, that widely differing descriptions were made of its tone, although certain characteristics predominate in continental and English writings. One is the frequent high pitch compatible with a small instrument, which was mentioned, together with its shrill quality, by Juan Ruiz, Archpriest of Hita, in his poem *Libro de Buen Amor* (c.1343): 'el rrabe gritador con la su alta nota'.[24] Other writers compare it to women's voices, notably Aimeric de Peyrac, Abbot of Moissac:

> Quidem rebecam arcuabant
> Muliebrem vocem confingentes[25]

while Chaucer's Friar in *The Canterbury Tales* actually uses the word itself to describe an old woman:

> Whan that they coomen somwhat out of towne,
> This somonour to his brother gan to rowne:
> 'Brother', quod he, '*heere woneth an old rebekke,*
> That hadde almoost as lief to lese hire nekke
> As for to yeve a peny of hir good.
> I wole han twelf pens, *though that she be wood,*

Or I wol sompne hire unto oure office;
And yet, God woot, of hire knowe I no vice.[26]

Over a century later John Skelton used the word 'rybybe' with the same meaning in 'The Tunnyng of Elynour Rummyng':

There came an old rybybe;
She halted of a kybe,
And had broken her shyn
At the threshold comyng in . . .[27]

The implication in these cases is not exactly complimentary. Tinctoris, however, must have known rebecs with different characteristics, judging from his own description in *De Inventione et Usu Musicae*:

And I am similarly pleased by the rebec, my predilection for which I will not conceal, provided that it is played by a skilful artist, since its strains are very much like those of the fiddle. Accordingly, the fiddle ['viola'] and the rebec ['rebec'] are my two instruments; I repeat, my chosen instruments, those that induce piety and stir my heart most ardently to the contemplation of heavenly joys. For these reasons I would rather reserve them solely for sacred music and the secret consolations of the soul, than have them sometimes used for profane occasions and public festivities.[28]

THE REBEC IN CONSORT

How can we be sure that when an artist depicts several instruments being played together, he is representing actual performance practice rather than just using his imagination? Apart from the obvious cases referred to on pp. 6–7 it is often very difficult to tell; we must use our discretion in each individual case, and, if possible, try out the combinations on similar reconstructed instruments to see if they work. There is, however, a general pattern which emerges when we have looked at a great many pictures, and this makes it apparent that certain instruments must have been played together a good deal, while others most probably were not.

It has been seen that instruments of the rebec family appeared in England from the early eleventh century onwards, in fact right through the period covered by this book, during which time its partners in art varied according to which instruments were then in fashion. This is particularly clear when it is a member of a duet. Among the plucked instruments its most usual partner to be found is the harp (which itself lasted throughout the Middle Ages and beyond), with occasional appearances of the psaltery. A duet with the gittern (citole) has yet to come to the author's notice, but from fourteenth-century sources onwards the rebec is to be seen with both the mandora (gittern) and lute. In conjunction with bowed instruments the chief partner is one of its own kind. Such a combination is well documented by references to the two German *gigatores* who worked at the Court of Edward I and presumably played together a good deal (p. 83). They were almost contemporary with the well-known miniatures of two *rabāb*-type rebec-players in the *Cantigas de Santa Maria* MS, fo. 118.[29] If there are any English pictures of a duet between a rebec and a mediaeval viol or fiddle they are extremely rare. This lack is not surprising, as the respective tone qualities of the instruments can be very different, and when played in the same register sometimes produce a jarring effect.[30] However, a possible case for them to play together would be if the rebec were playing a melody and the other instrument were droning at a lower pitch. More instruments which seem to be lacking in duet with the rebec in English art are those ancestors of the hurdy-gurdy, the two-man organistrum and its smaller successor known today as the symphony. Nevertheless, if the rebec is implied by the word *rebube* (p. 31), then such a combination is suggested in Lydgate's *Pilgrimage of the Life of Man*, where Miss Idleness talks of revels in a tavern:

> With al merthe & mellodye
> On rebube and on symphonye (p. 102)

Wind instruments are often difficult to classify when the artist has been careless about such essential details as the mouthpiece. It is safe to say that the rebec can be seen in duet with different types of pipe,[31] double pipes, double shawm, and panpipes. The single shawm certainly appears with it in continental sources, and this duet can be seen on one side of a quadrilateral capital in the crypt of Canterbury Cathedral (plate 13). However, as an adjacent side of the same capital shows animals playing a harp and a horn with fingerholes, it is possible that the sculptor had in mind not a duet, but a quartet in this case. In the Cambridge University MS Dd. viii. 18, fo. 110, two minstrels welcome David who returns with Goliath's head on a sword (plate 135). The rebec-player on the left is joined by a man with a pipe that is pointing sideways and is partly out of the picture. Its general angle suggests that it might be accompanied by a tabor which is hit by a stick in the performer's right hand, but unfortunately both are hidden. Cautiously, therefore, this group could be described as that of a rebec and a pipe-and-tabor. In the BL MS Harley 2838, fo. 45, music for a feast is being played on a partly hidden rebec and a long pipe which lacks a clear mouthpiece, is too narrow for a recorder, and is not sufficiently conical to be a shawm. Its shape suggests that it could be a three-holed tabor-pipe, but this is ruled out as it is being fingered by both hands. Hence it is best covered by the generic term *pipe* (plate 133).

Another type of duet is for the rebec and voice, well documented in Chaucer's *Miller's Tale* where Absalom, besides dancing 'after the scole of Oxenforde' is described thus:

> And pleyen songes on a smal rubible;
> Therto he song som tyme a loud quynyble.[32]

Somewhat later, in his 'Mumming at Hertford', John Lydgate (*c.*1370–1449/50) referred to an unfortunate man who 'with his rebecke may sing ful offt ellas!'[33]

The word *kit*, appearing as it does at the end of our period,[34] cannot be found in representative quotations with single instruments, but its use in consort with 'harpes, lutes ... basens and drommes' is vividly demonstrated in *The Christen State of Matrimony* of 1543 (p. 91).

Pictures of the rebec in consort can be seen in the following examples from Appendix D (pp. 151–61):

in duet, with
harp, *2.11.1*; psaltery, *2.14.1*; lute, *2.15.1*; rebec, *2.15.2*; pipe *2.15.3*; pipe-and-tabor, *2.15.4*; panpipes, *2.13.1*; shawm, *2.12.1*; double shawm, *2.14.2*;

in trio, with
harp and horn, *3.12.1*;[35] pipe and horn, *3.14.1*; harp, tabor-and-bells, *3.12.2*; two singers, *3.13.1*;

in quartet, with
mediaeval viol, psaltery and harp, *4.12.1*; harp and two horns, *4.12.2*; harp, wind instrument and horn, *4.11.1*.

Larger groups containing the rebec can also be found in Appendix D.

CHAPTER IV

The Crowd

❧

THE ORIGINS OF THE CROWD, AND ITS CONNECTION WITH THE LYRE

WHEREAS instruments of the rebec family apparently came to Europe complete with the bow, those of the crowd type represent the adaptation of the newly imported bow to the long established lyre. This new family of bowed instruments was not ancestral to the violin, as used to be supposed, but led directly to the later Welsh *crwth* which became an honoured instrument in Wales, and survived there until very recently.

The lyre was the chief plucked instrument of northern Europe in the early Middle Ages, but gave way to the superiority of the harp during the Romanesque period. Several examples have been excavated from the tombs of warriors, notably that from the seventh-century ship burial at Sutton Hoo in Suffolk.[1] Some of these instruments seem to have been of oblong shape with rounded corners, and it was this type which led to the crwth, although more exotic shapes can be seen in the slightly later visual arts, such as the carved instrument on a capital from the Abbey of Cluny, dating from *c*.1095.[2] The surviving fragments of the Sutton Hoo lyre show that it had six strings, and six and five strings respectively can be seen in the two eighth-century illustrations which served as models for the reconstruction of the Sutton Hoo instrument; these are the Vespasian Psalter, fo. 30[3] and the Durham Cathedral Library MS B. II. 30, fo. 81[4]. A development of this type of lyre, and one which could well have provided the link between it and the bowed ones, is that from the ninth-century Carolingian Bible of Charles the Bald, fo. 215[5] where the instrument has a neck against which the performer presses the three strings with his fingers, thereby having at his disposal far more notes than those produced by the strings on their own. These early lyres would undoubtedly have been plucked, as there is no known evidence of the bow in northern Europe until the early eleventh century.

TERMINOLOGY

The crowd is one of several instruments of which the terminology has long been, and still is, most confusing. Its ancestor the early mediaeval lyre seems to have been known to the Anglo-Saxons as a *hearpe*, according to such poems as the epic *Beowulf*, which dates from the period from which lyres, rather than harps as we know them, have been discovered in English excavations.[6] In the sixth century, however,

Venantius Fortunatus, Bishop of Poitiers, had referred in Latin to Britons singing with the 'chrotta',[7] and about two hundred years later the English Abbot Cuthbert used the word 'rotte' as a translation from the Latin 'cithara' in a letter to Archbishop Lullus of Mainz.[8] The related words *crot*, *cruit*, *rotta*, and *rote* have also been applied to the lyre, but in the last case especially, great caution is needed. *Rote* can also mean a triangular psaltery, particularly of the type used in the eleventh, twelfth, and thirteenth centuries,[9] quite apart from being a very vague poetical convenience because it happens to rhyme with *note*.

When the bow was first applied to the lyre, the instrument presumably continued for a time to use its existing names, but as it developed, and the plucked version went out of fashion, new ones appeared. These included *croude*, *crowde*, *crouthe*, etc., with positive evidence being provided by the early fourteenth-century Seal of Roger Wade the Crowder, where the musician's name followed by 'croudere' is accompanied by the likeness of his instrument and its bow (plate 62). The word *coriun* is also thought to have been used for the crowd, and can be found in Layamon's *Brut* (*c*.1200–25) in company with several other instruments played by King Blæðgabreat (see p. 80).

> ... ne cuðe na mon swa muchel of song
> of harpe & of salteriun. of fiðele & of coriun
> of timpe & of lire.[10]

When Chaucer said of the Friar in the *Canterbury Tales* 'Wel koude he synge and pleyen on a rote',[11] he may have meant the crowd, as the old mediaeval lyre was out of fashion in fourteenth-century England, as also was the triangular psaltery. However, the author of *Sir Tristrem* (*c*.1300) refers to a 'rote of yvere'.[12] A crowd would not have been made of such a substance, but a partly ivory harp has survived from fifteenth-century France, and is now kept in the Louvre.[13] Nevertheless, *rote* cannot always have meant a harp either during the later Middle Ages, judging from two lines in different parts of *Lybeaus Disconnus* (*c*.1325–50), 'Harpe, fydele and crouthe' and 'Harpe, fydele and rote'.[14] In such cases three different instruments are mentioned, so 'harpe' cannot be synonymous with 'crouthe' or 'rote' here. In the second of these two examples, 'rote' is used to rhyme with 'note', so in this case it may well be a poetical substitute for 'crouthe'. Chaucer's Friar did, however, sometimes play the harp.

Some of the fifteenth-century Latin and English descriptions of the crowd and its performers are as follows:

Nominale A	crowde	coralla
	crowdere	corallus
Catholicon	crowde	corus sine h litera (sine aspiracione A.) corista, qui vel que canit in eo.
Promptorium Parvulorum	crowde, instrument of musyke	chorus (See Appendix A.)

The Latin word *chorus* can, like *rote*, mean several completely different types of instrument, including a primitive form of bagpipe referred to in the spurious letter from 'Jerome' to 'Dardanus', and that type of string drum which has survived in the South of France under the names *tambourin basque* or *tambourin de Béarn* according to where it is found.[15] It is this instrument which is probably meant by Aimeric de Peyrac's much-quoted 'Quidam choros consonantes, Duplicem cordam perstridentes',[16] rather than the crowd, which in general had departed from France by the fourteenth century, when the poem was written. Higden's use of the word 'chorus' at Welsh feasts becomes 'crowde' in the translation of the BL MS Harley 2261, although Trevisa renders it as 'tabor' (p. 13).

Further ambiguities concerning the crowd appear in Palsgrave's use of the word 'rebec' to cover both it and the fiddle (p. 13), and in an example related by Galpin. He tells us that 'a certain John Hogan, in the year 1537, was reprimanded for "singing lewd ballads with a crowd or fyddyll" '.[17]

THE WELSH CRWTH

Before considering the crowd in detail, we should acknowledge the survival of certain bowed lyres in Scandinavia and Wales. Although there are considerable differences between them, those of Scandinavia can throw some light on the possible techniques of the mediaeval English crowd. The Welsh crwth, on the other hand, is the direct descendant of that instrument and of its counterpart in Wales, so it should be considered in some detail here.

Plate 154 shows a crwth made in 1742 by Richard Evans of the parish of Llanfihangel Bachellaeth, Caernarvonshire.[18] Of an almost rectangular shape, its outline is not far removed from that of the eighth-century lyre in the Vespasian Psalter, fo. 30ᵛ. The chief difference results from the presence of a neck and a fingerboard. Whereas on the plucked lyre the strings were generally stretched across a large part of the area between the two arms, here the arrangement is quite different. Four strings are stretched above the fingerboard, while two others are set to its left side (as seen with the yoke on top), branching off at a slight angle. At the bottom end the strings are attached to a tailpiece, while at the top they are fixed to pegs set in the yoke. However, before this takes place they pass through the yoke just above the nut at the end of the fingerboard, and then join the pegs behind. The soundboard is flat, and contains two round soundholes in its central area. The bridge is unusual, as while one of its legs rests in the normal way on the soundboard, the other passes right through a soundhole, thereby also becoming a soundpost. The back and sides of the instrument are carved from one piece of wood, and the arms are shallower in depth than the sides of the body. The performer's fingers and left thumb come through the gaps between the arms and the neck, and play in a similar manner to that of the violin, except that the thumb sometimes plucks the two lateral strings.

In the late eighteenth century the tuning of the crwth was given by Edward Jones and Daines Barrington as

Ex. 6

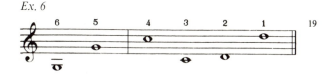

and this was followed soon afterwords by William Bingley's

Ex. 7

which Canon Galpin assumed should be an octave lower.[21] However, as J. Marshall Bevil has pointed out,[22] Jones also recommends that the top string should be tuned as high as possible without being broken, so his pitches were just relative to each other, and not necessarily Gs, Cs, and Ds. In that case, Bingley's tunings may also have been relative, and written down on the most convenient notes of the stave. Jones describes the strings as follows:

1. Y crâs-dant,	1. The acute string,	
2. a'i vyrdon,	2. and its burden.	
3. Byrdon y llorv-dant,	3. The accompaniment of the low string.	
4. Y llorv-dant,	4. The low string.	
5. Y Cywair-dant	5. The key note.	
6. a'i vyrdon.	6. and its base.[23]	

Bingley described

a bridge flat at the top, (and not, as in the violin, convex,) by which it follows that in drawing the bow across them the strings must all be struck at once, and thus produce, with proper fingering, not a succession of notes merely, but of concords.[24]

While a flat bridge would certainly be suitable for his tuning, some degree of curvature would be needed for those of Jones and Barrington, in order to avoid the continuing simultaneous droning of adjacent notes.

Jones tells us of 'eight orders of Musicians'. The 'four Graduated orders of Bards' are 'The Poet, or Invested Bard, of which there were 3 kinds: *viz.* The Harpist; the Crwthist; and the Singer.' The 'four Inferior orders, Non-Graduates, or Minstrels' consist of 'The Piper; The Juggler; The Crowder that plays on the three-stringed Crowd; and the Tabourer'.[25] From this we can infer that the crwth described above was that played by the superior musicians, while there was also a simpler three-stringed variety for the more ordinary minstrels. This was the type which can be seen in the BL Add. MS 15036, fo. 66, a Welsh manuscript of *c.*1797, containing tracings from the early seventeenth-century MS Havod 24 at Cardiff Central Library.[26] Some instructions for playing on the crwth can be found in the hand of Lewis Morris, dating from 1742, as addenda to the earlier Manuscript of Robert ap Huw, which itself dates from the early seventeenth century and contains tablature for the harp.[27]

							(1) West.	(2) West.	(1) War.	(2) War.	
	CUL	DCL	BL	Seal	OCL	CTL	Worc.	West.	West.	War.	War.	Shrews.
	11c.	12c.	13c.	14c.	14c.	14c.	14c.	c.1400		15c.		15c.
SHAPE												
Sides parallel, with one end rounded	▒											
Sides parallel, with both ends rounded		▒		▒				▒				
One end rounded, and widening sides			▒			▒						
Slight incurvation							▒					
Figure of eight												▒
NECK												
No neck apparent	▒	▒	▒									
Neck visible or implied				▒	▒	▒	▒	▒	▒	▒	▒	▒
SOUNDHOLES												
Two	▒		▒	▒	▒	▒	▒	▒	▒	▒	▒	▒
Three		▒										
BRIDGE AND TAILPIECE												
Frontal stringholder	▒	▒	▒					▒		▒		
Separate bridge				▒			?					?
Tailpiece					▒							
Possible combined bridge and tailpiece					▒		?					?
STRINGS												
Three	▒				▒					▒		
Four		▒	▒	▒				▒	▒		▒	▒
Five												
Six						▒						
Four plus two		▒										
PERFORMERS												
David's minstrels	▒											
Apocalyptic Elders			▒			▒						
Angels										▒	▒	
Man					▒		▒					
Man understood				▒								
No player		▒										

Abbreviations

CUL	Cambridge University Library, MS Ff.1.23, fo. 4ᵛ	11c.
DCL	Durham Cathedral Library, MS Hunter 100, fo. 62ᵛ	12c.
BL	British Library, Add. MS 35166, fo. 4ᵛ	13c.
Seal	British Library, Seal of Roger Wade the Crowder, Seal lxxxvii. 44	14c.
OCL	Oxford, Christ Church Library, MS 92, fo. 43	14c.
CTL	Cambridge , Trinity College Library, MS B.10.2, fo.4ᵛ	14c.
Worc.	Worcester Cathedral, misericord	14c.
West.	Westminster Abbey, Chapter House wall-painting (1=left, 2=right)	c.1400
War.	Warwick, St. Mary's Church, stained glass (1=left, 2=right)	15c.
Shrews.	Shrewsbury, St. Mary's Church, roof boss	15c.

Figure 1. *English Representations of the Crowd*

THE MEDIAEVAL CROWD AND ITS INGREDIENTS

Pictures of the English crowd are so rare that in thirty years of searching for mediaeval instruments in the visual arts, the present writer has come across only twelve, of which ten were already well known.[28] The periods from which these twelve examples date show that at least the instrument was known here throughout the Middle Ages (once the bow had arrived), being seen in the eleventh-century

Winchcombe Psalter, fo. 4^v (plate 1) and the late fifteenth-century roof carving from St. Mary's Church, Shrewsbury (plate 134), and being represented from each of the centuries between. The chart given in figure 1 gives the appropriate details of each instrument, and while it is risky to generalize from so few illustrations, it is worth while to observe the chief characteristics that do stand out.

Firstly, the basic outline of the instrument (regarding the soundboard as the front) show sides which are almost parallel, although sometimes with a slight bulging at one end as in the Cambridge manuscript mentioned above (plate 1). In this and in several other cases one end is rounded while the other ends with angular corners. The Seal of Roger Wade, which by reason of its presumed likeness to Wade's own instrument is a supposedly reliable witness, is one where both ends are rounded off with no right-angled corners (plate 62). The Oxford, Christ Church MS 92, fo. 43 represents a type where the sides widen slightly towards the yoke (plate 80), while the Worcester example shows the reverse to be true (plate 108). The only example with a completely different shape is the Shrewsbury roof carving, which takes the form of a figure of eight (plate 134).[29]

We have seen that the neck which became a feature of the Welsh crwth was already known on the Continent in the ninth century, as witnessed by the Bible of Charles the Bald, fo. 215^v,[30] and it appears on a bowed lyre of the eleventh century in the St. Martial Troper of French origin (Paris, Bibliothèque Nationale MS Lat. 1118, fo. 104).[31] It is not present, however, in the eleventh-century Cambridge manuscript (plate 1). Here there is the possibility that the soundboard may continue up to the yoke of the instrument because there is no line of demarcation for it, but the reliability of this picture has long been doubted. (If there *were* supposed to be a neck, the performer's fingers and thumb would be on each side of it, rather than coming over the upper end of the instrument.) It could equally be that the artist forgot that in most cases the soundbox ended where the arms began. Several examples of the early Germanic 'round lyre' can be found played with a bow in continental sources,[32] and in these the strings are quite free between the framework of the yoke, arms, and soundbox. The artist of the Durham instrument has been careful to indicate a somewhat fanciful design, but it does not include a neck (plate 7). Whether he forgot to put it in, or never intended one at all is a matter of particular interest, in so far as the string formation here is nearer to that of the later Welsh crwth than is any of the other known examples from mediaeval England.

All the other English examples have some form of neck, whether long or short. More problematical is the question of a fingerboard, which on so many mediaeval bowed instruments was not considered necessary. The Oxford, Christ Church MS 92, fo. 43 is one of several examples where the fingers press directly on to the neck itself (plate 80). In both the Seal of Roger Wade and the Worcester misericord the strings are carved in a raised block, which *might* suggest the presence of a fingerboard, but this is not definite (plates 62, 108). Unfortunately the Seal has become worn just at the point where the fingerboard would have been shown.

When soundholes are visible, which is not always the case, there are normally two, one placed on each side of the strings, as in the Seal of Roger Wade (plate 62). Only in the Durham picture are there three, if the rectangular designs are indeed soundholes at all (plate 7).

The bridge and tailpiece must be considered together. Sometimes they are not present as such, but there is instead a frontal stringholder as in the Durham manuscript (plate 7). In five cases, such as the Seal of Roger Wade (plate 62), there is a tailpiece of the normal type still used on most bowed instruments today, and in three instances, including the same example, there is clearly a separate bridge. Sometimes no bridge is indicated at all, thereby suggesting that it may be combined with the tailpiece, as in the Christ Church manuscript (plate 80). It is not known whether, during the Middle Ages, one side of the bridge was ever prolonged to create a soundpost, as in the later Welsh crwth (p. 29). In several cases, such as that of Christ Church, the soundholes are too far away from the bridge or its equivalent to make such a device possible, (plate 80), but in Roger Wade's instrument it might have happened (plate 62).

The number of strings varies from three to six, but the increase does not reflect a development through the Middle Ages, as the twelfth-century Durham manuscript is the only one which clearly shows the formation of four central strings and two lateral ones, as came to be the usual on the later Welsh crwth in its best form. As can be seen in figure 1, of the twelve examples two have three strings and two have five, but five have four, which does suggest a general tendency and is exemplified by the apparently reliable Seal of Roger Wade (plate 62). The five strings on one of the Warwick examples seem to be arranged in three courses of $2+2+1$, but they are all placed above the neck, as are the six strings at Worcester (plates 123, 108). (This last example, incidentally, has been reproduced over and over again in a very pretty drawing which has only five strings, and is quite inaccurate.)

As with the other instruments, the bow used with the crowd varied in its degree of length and curvature, and there is nothing to suggest that crowd bows were any different from those of the fiddle or rebec, although, like them, they were simpler than some of the bows used on mediaeval viols (p. 17).

The performers to be found playing the crowd in the sources quoted above are of the types that would be expected from mediaeval representations, except that there are no animals, devils, or grotesques. The earliest example is one of David's minstrels (plate 1); Apocalyptic Elders appear in sources of the thirteenth, fourteenth, and early fifteenth centuries (plates 43, 106, 111), and the only ordinary man is in the fourteenth-century Christ Church manuscript (plate 80). Angels are found at Worcester, Warwick, and Shrewsbury (plates 108, 123, 134). In the Durham source there is no player, as the instrument illustrates the section 'De Lira' in a description of the constellations.

THE TECHNIQUE OF THE CROWD, AND ITS TUNING

Judging from the different types of crowd represented in the arts, it would seem that their techniques and tunings must have varied a good deal. However, the instruments which are the most unusual are also the most unreliable, so extreme caution must be used in assessing their value.

Let us first consider the more reliable illustrations, those from the Christ Church manuscript, Worcester, Warwick, and Shrewsbury (plates 80, 108, 123, 134), which are all being played, besides those of Roger Wade's seal and Westminster, which are not (plates 62, 111). All these pictures show the instrument to have a neck. In the former examples the crowd is held at the shoulder and pointing downwards, and as with instruments of the fiddle family the player's thumb is to the left of the neck, with his fingers coming round to play from the right. As there are no lateral *borduni* the thumb is not immediately involved with the production of sound. It is possible that the Westminster instrument would be played down on the performer's lap, but as he is not playing at all, this cannot be certain (plate 111).

As the tuning of the mediaeval crowd is unknown to us, we can only guess at the possibilities, bearing in mind the known tunings of the eighteenth century, some possible parallels from Scandinavian folk instruments, and some known tunings of the mediaeval fiddle and rebec. The following suggestions are therefore entirely hypothetical.

Three strings. Possible tunings include (a) fifths or fourths or a mixture of both; (b) a re-entrant tuning such as *c' g' d'* which would enable the central string to be used for a melody, with the other two providing alternative drones.

Four strings. As these seem to be grouped in pairs, it is tempting to assume that they were tuned in the eighteenth-century manner but without the *borduni*, i.e.

Ex. 8

but they could also have been set to a pair of fifths.

Five strings. Here there are probably two double courses and a single one.

Six strings. Although they are evenly spaced at Worcester (plate 108), these strings are probably intended to be in three double courses, and it is possible that two of them really should be *borduni*, although they are not carved as such. There are two hypotheses which may be considered here. Firstly, the sculptor could have asked a friend how many strings the instrument should have, and the friend said six, without specifying that two of them should go off at a tangent at the side. Alternatively the sculptor could have known about *borduni* but thought they were too complicated to bother about in a small carving. However, these ideas may be quite unnecessary; perhaps the sculptor did, after all, intend the instrument to have three pairs of strings above the neck. Whatever the case, any instrument with double courses could have had the two strings of each pair tuned either to the same note, or else to an octave apart, as in the later Welsh crwth mentioned above.

In discussing the remaining pictures, it is best to move gradually backwards in time, and to take each illustration separately to see whether or not it is workable.

Cambridge, Trinity College MS B. 10. 2, fo. 4ᵛ (plate 106), c. 1380–95.

This seems to be an attempt by the artist to portray the instruments of the Psalms, although they are held by the Elders of the Apocalypse. The second part of Psalm 150 reads

> Laudate eum in sono tubae: laudate eum
>   in psalterio et cithara.
> Laudate eum in tympano et choro: laudate eum
>   in chordis et organo.
> Laudate eum in cymbalis benesonantibus: laudate eum
>   in cymbalis jubilationis:
> Omnis spiritus laudet Dominum. Alleluia.

The illustration shows the trumpet ('tuba'), psaltery ('psalterium'), harp ('cithara'), crowd ('chorus'), fiddles ('chordae'), portative organ ('organum'), and cymbals ('cymbala'). The 'tympanum' is left out. This may be because of the economical practice of having only two Elders with instruments in each panel, with the others sitting behind them so that only their heads can generally be seen (pp. 5–6). In fact the artist could have substituted a timbrel or tabor for one of the two fiddles, but perhaps he thought that 'in chordis' necessitated two instruments of the same type. However, he did make some attempt to depict a crowd, but a very strange one it is. Galpin points to its existence in his list of instruments in the visual arts,[33] but understandably ignores it in his text. As the strings seem to join together just where the fingers should be playing on them, the instrument can be dismissed as unworkable. Even if it were not within the context of the Psalms it might, nevertheless, still be recognized as an attempted crowd, as there is no other instrument in fourteenth-century English art to which it could bear any resemblance. The artist may have had in his mind something like the Christ Church example (plate 80), but he certainly had neither a reliable picture nor an instrument of that type in front of him while he worked.

BL Add. MS 35166, fo. 4ᵛ (plate 43). English, c. 1260–70

On first sight this example seems to be highly inaccurate because its four strings stop short before reaching the neck, and are spaced in such a way that they could not possibly all fit over it anyway. However, Otto Andersson has shown the great similarity of design between this instrument and the Finnish *jouhikantele*, which, like the Welsh crwth, was being played in an unbroken tradition until comparatively recently.[34] With a similar basic framework to that of BL Add. MS 35166, this instrument had a variable number of strings which passed from the lower end of the instrument to be tuned at the yoke. With the backs of his fingers, the performer touched the string nearest to the left arm of the instrument, and only that one provided the melody, with the others making an accompaniment. The actual neck at the centre of the instrument was not fingered at all. However, even if the British Library instrument is supposed to be played in that manner, it gives no indication as to what has happened to the strings after their disappearance from the picture.

Durham Cathedral Library, MS Hunter 100, fo. 62ᵛ (plate 7), c.1100–20

Having at last got back into the twelfth century, we surprisingly find a string formation which resembles that of the eighteenth, namely that of four central strings and two lateral *borduni*. However, in this case there are distinct problems. Firstly the *borduni* are on the right side of the instrument instead of the left, and secondly there is no neck. It is just possible that the artist meant the instrument to be for a left-handed player, resulting in the string arrangement being the opposite way round from usual, but if this was not the case, then he just made a mistake. The matter of the neck is very important, as on it depends the type of sound produced from the instrument. First of all, we must observe that there is no bow. This is not unusal, as if it is not being played the artist frequently does not bother to include the bow into the design, as has been seen in several pictures from the Apocalypse. It could be argued that this is a plucked instrument not intended to be bowed, but here we come up against the fact that plucked lyres do not have a tradition of the string formation 4 + 2, whereas bowed lyres do. The next step is to imagine the technique for playing such an instrument. If it were held up at the shoulder, there would be no means of supporting it with one hand while bowing with the other, unless the strings rested on the player's hand, thereby impeding performance on them. It might, however, be possible to play the instrument by holding it down on the lap and touching the strings with the fingers from the front. If this would not work, then it can be assumed that here, too, the artist made a mistake, and he should have included a neck. If this is the case, we can be justified in speculating as to whether or not the strings were tuned in the ways described by Jones, Bingley, and Barrington six hundred years later.

Cambridge, University Library MS Ff. 1. 23, fo. 4ᵛ. Winchcombe Psalter (plate 1), c.1030–50

This earliest known English example of a bowed lyre also causes problems. Here Asaph's fingers come over the yoke to touch the ends of the four strings. In the first place this would be difficult, as somewhere obstructing the fingers there would be pegs to hold the strings in position. Even if Asaph could overcome this problem he could only alter each string by about a tone, as the instrument is too wide for each of his fingers to come round and play on every string. If all the strings were on the same plane they would sound simultaneously, which would complicate the prospect of tuning with this system of fingering. However, if the frontal stringholder were curved, then it would be possible to play on each string separately, and by tuning the strings a third apart, an octave of notes could be obtained from each open string and one finger on it. Due to lack of similar evidence from elsewhere, it is unlikely that this actually happened.

Having considered the crowd as it appears in English sources, we can now see which of their characteristics are recognizable in *Dyvaliad Crŵth* (a Delineation of the *Crŵth*) by Gryffydd ab Davydd ab Howel, who lived in the late fifteenth and early sixteenth centuries:

A fair coffer with a bow, a girdle,
a fingerboard, and a bridge; its value is a pound;
it has a frontlet formed like a wheel,
with the short-nosed bow across;
and from its centre it winds in a ring,
and the bulging of its back is somewhat like an old man;
and on its breast harmony reigns,
from the sycamore music will be obtained.
Six pegs, if we screw them,
will tighten all its chords;
six strings advantageously are found,
which in the hand produce a hundred sounds;
a string for every finger is distinctly seen,
and also two strings for the thumb.[35]

This is not completely illuminated by the surviving evidence, so it is to be hoped that further illustrations will come to light. The last eight lines are clear, and include the information that sycamore wood was used for part of the instrument. The first part of the poem, however, is still of uncertain interpretation. Otto Andersson has suggested that the 'girdle' 'might possibly refer to something akin to the band of birch bark in the Carelian bowed-harps. This cannot originally have had any other function than to keep the soundboard on the resonator'.[36] The crwth in the Victoria and Albert Museum has a strip of ivory across the upper end of the soundboard,[37] and this could certainly be regarded as a 'girdle', although there is no such thing on the instrument by Richard Evans (plate 154). There is one, however, in the BL Add. MS 35166, fo. 4^v (plate 43), which has already been compared by Andersson to the Finnish 'bowed-harp'. The value of a pound is useful information which can be added to that taken from expense accounts and other literary sources, concerning the prices of instruments. 'It has a frontlet formed like a wheel' may mean that the rounded part was the yoke, as suggested by Andersson,[38] or that it was the lower end, as put forward by Bevil.[39] Certainly either view can be corroborated by the eight-shaped carving from Shrewsbury (plate 134), which is very near to Wales. 'And from its centre it winds in a ring' could perhaps refer to the type of round disc found in the Durham example (plate 7), but apparently nowhere else, so it remains uncertain. 'The bulging of its back is somewhat like an old man' can be explained by the actual meaning of the Welsh word *crwth*, which is given in William Owen's *A Dictionary of the Welsh Language* (1803) as 'any body swelling out, a bulging . . . a kind of box scooped out of a piece of wood and rounded . . . a musical instrument with six strings . . .', and William Richards's *Welsh Dictionary* (1828) as 'anything swelling out; a bulge . . . a crowd, a violin'.[40] Although the few remaining pictures do not provide clear evidence of this bulge (by reason of their being shown mainly from the front view), Bevil has made the reasonable suggestion 'One might surmise that the crwth was at one time characterized by a vaulted back'.[41] 'On its breast harmony reigns' may well indicate the playing together of two or more notes through the use of drones.

While not all of this poem can be satisfactorily explained within the context of our present knowledge, we must remember that it may have applied to one particular instrument that the poet knew, or even owned, and that with the lack of standardization still present at that time, there may have been few other crwths around which fitted all the details of the poem.

THE SOUND OF THE CROWD

Many passages from literature seem to indicate that the crowd generally sounded at least two notes at once, as did the later crwth. Gryffydd's passage 'On its breast harmony reigns' comes close to some commentaries on the Psalms, where the word 'chorus' is often translated by 'croude' (p. 50). Such examples come from the fourteenth-century Psalter of Richard Rolle of Hampole:

Ps. 149.3.   *Laudent nomen eius in choro; in tympano & psalterio psallant ei.*

Loue thai his name in croude: in taburn and in psautere synge thai til him. In heuen thai sall loue in croud. that is, in perfite charite, when na strife sall be, bot derest anhede . . .

Ps. 150.4.   *Laudate eum in tympano & choro: laudate eum in chordis & organo.*

Louys him in taburn and croude; louys him in strengis and orgyns. Louys him in taburn. that is, in fleyss chawngid til inmortalite and in passibilite. for taburn is made of a dryid scyn. and in croude, that is, in pesful felagheship and concord of voicys . . .

Ps. 150.5

. . . In there instrumentis that he neuens is perfeccioun of all musyke, for blast is in the trumpe, pouste in the harpe and in chymys voice the croude, in the whilke instrumentis of musyke gastly melody is bitakynd.[42]

THE CROWD IN CONSORT

In *Musical and Poetical Relicks of the Welsh Bards* (1794), Edward Jones says 'The sound of the Crwth is very melodious, and was frequently used as a tenor accompaniment to the Harp'.[43] There seems no reason to believe that this was not already an ancient tradition, and indeed, the two instruments are carved together in performance on a late sixteenth-century Welsh bed now kept at Cotehele House, Cornwall.[44]

Two references from John Wycliffe's translation of the Bible may or may not throw light on mediaeval performance. The brother of the Prodigal Son heard 'a symphonye and a croude' on drawing near to the family house.[45] Jephte, on the other hand, was received by his daughter with the sound of the crowd and timbrel:

> Forsothe to Jeptee turnynge aȝens into Maspha, his hous,
> aȝencam to hym his oonli goten douȝter with tymbrys and chorys.

Different versions say that she came to him with 'tympanys and croudis' and with 'croudis daunsynge'.[46]

Singing with the crowd is suggested in the *Canterbury Tales*, if the Friar's 'rote' was indeed that instrument; although 'well koude he synge and pleyen on a rote' does not expressly say that he did both things at once, equally it does not deny the possibility.

These quotations can be joined by records of actual historical events to show that the crowd was an accepted instrument on festive occasions. One such event was an Eistedfodd in 1176, at which crowders competed with other minstrels as part of the general entertainment, and the musicians did not all have to be Welsh:

At Christmas in that year the Lord Rhys ap Gruffudd held court in splendour at Cardigan, in the castle. And he set two kinds of contests there: one between bards and poets, another between harpists and crowders and pipers and various classes of music-craft. And he had two chairs set for the victors. And he honoured these with ample gifts. . . . And that feast, before it was held, was announced for a year through all Wales and Scotland and Ireland and the other islands.[47]

At the Feast of Westminster in 1306 the payments to minstrels included eight to crowders, of whom about half were either Welsh or connected with Wales. Further evidence of crowders performing at feasts comes from poems such as *Sir Orfeo*, which is quoted on p. 96.

In a more allegorical context the crowd again appears with many instruments in *The Passetyme of Pleasure* by Stephen Hawes:

> There sate dame musyke/with all her mynstralsy
> As taboures/trumpettes/with pypes melodyous
> Sakbuttes/organs/and the recorder swetely
> Harpes/lutes/and crouddes ryght delycyous
> Cȳphans/doussemers/wᵗ clarycymbales gloryous
> Rebeckes/clarycordes/eche in theyr degre
> Dyde sytte aboute theyr ladyes mageste.[48]
>
>   (1517 version)

In spite of these and many other descriptions of crowders playing with several other musicians, pictures of the instrument being used in ordinary human situations during our period are very elusive. It can be seen in the hands of David's minstrels, or of Apocalyptic Elders, or of angels, although it should be remembered that the feathered angels who play it at Warwick may be based on humans dressed up (p. 7) (plate 123). The Christ Church manuscript shows it in the hands of a man who is one of ten minstrels each in his or her own separate panel in the border of a page, where one of the central pictures also contains a positive organ and a harp (plate 78 and Appendix D). While the relevant 'orchestra' might have been played together in real life, it is unfortunately not represented in a life-like setting.

Certainly the crowd was a rare instrument in mediaeval England, but English music was enriched by the presence of crowders from Wales and the surrounding districts. Edward I, for instance, asked the Abbot of Shrewsbury to lend him his crowder so that this minstrel could teach the instrument to one from the household of the Prince of Wales.[49] That there were, however, crowders normally resident in London can be deduced from the following announcement of 1323:

On the first Sunday in Lent ... a minstrel, Roger Wade by name, a crowder, solemnly celebrated his own interment, as though he had been dead, and had masses sung for his soul, both he himself and others in his company making offering, so that many persons marvelled thereat. And this he did, because he put no trust in executors; but by reason of this act, some persons of the religious orders would have withdrawn from him his livery, which he had bought from them for the term of his life; he himself however died soon after Easter.[50]

(*Chronicles of Old London, etc.*, 1863, p. 258)

CHAPTER V

The Mediaeval Viol

FROM the previous two chapters we have seen that the bowed instruments which are known to have been used in England before the Norman Conquest belonged to the families of the rebec and the crowd. Several examples show that by the 1120s they had been joined by a different type (plates 9, 10), for which no individual name survives. The author prefers to call it the *mediaeval viol*, on account of the fact that in England it was normally played down in the lap with the bow gripped from below, as was the much later viol of the Renaissance period. Some authorities, such as Bachmann, include this instrument with good reason among the basic family of the mediaeval fiddle, and it is true to say that on the Continent there was often less distinction between the two instruments than in England. It can be said, for instance, that according to southern European sources either instrument could be played up at the shoulder or down on the lap, whereas in England the normal practice was for the viol to be played in the downward position and the fiddle at the shoulder or across the chest. By this very distinction itself, it would seem that the English did regard the two basic types as belonging to somewhat different species, and they will therefore be considered as such in this book.

TERMINOLOGY

As the mediaeval viol had no particular name by which it could be distinguished from the other bowed instruments, it must have been covered by the Latin *viella* and *viola*, the French *vielle* and *vièle*, the German *fiedel*, and the English forms of *fithele*, while its player would have been a *viellator*, *violator*, *vidulator*, *vilour*, *fiedeler*, or *fitheler*. These names, however, also cover the instruments and performers mentioned in the next chapter (p. 62), so for the period in which these two basic types overlapped (late twelfth century to early fourteenth) it is almost impossible to know which instrument is being referred to in literature. For this reason, pictorial sources will be used almost exclusively in this chapter.

THE SHAPE AND INGREDIENTS

Normally the sides of the mediaeval viol were incurved, to a greater or lesser extent. A very smooth incurvation can be seen in the St. Alban's Psalter, p. 56 (plate 10), where the instrument is narrower than most of its type. On p. 417 of the same manuscript, however, the indentation is much more pronounced, resulting in the instrument known in German today as the *Achtformfidel* because of its shape resembling that of a figure of eight (plate 11). Sometimes there is a parallel section in the centre of the body between the two bouts, as demonstrated in the Cambridge, Trinity College MS O. 4. 7, fo. 112 (plate 8). On other occasions there is a double indentation, resulting either in a point on each side, as in the Brailes Psalter (plate 37), or in a domed shape, as in the Great Canterbury Psalter, fo. 54^v (plate 23). In the British Library MS Arundel 157, fo. 71^v, this central part becomes just large enough to form a new bout of itself (plate 29). The carving in the doorway at Barfrestone is too worn to show much detail, but it does seem to have had some kind of central indentation (plate 27).

All these basic types can be found in pictures of the twelfth and thirteenth centuries, although during the latter period there was a tendency towards more instruments of the smoother shape, as can be seen in the New York, Pierpont Morgan Library MS G. 25, fo. 5^v. In the Amesbury Psalter, fo. 55^v there is a slight hint of corners such as can be seen on certain members of the gittern (citole) family, which had recently arrived in England (plate 40).

As the mediaeval viol existed at a time when manuscript illustrators normally showed the 'full face' view of an instrument, there are comparatively few cases where any indication is given as to the shape of its back. Of the surviving carvings, that at Barfrestone is too dilapidated to give any clear indication (plate 27). The statue at Oakham, on the other hand, has been sculpted in such a way that not only the front is seen clearly, but also the sides. These seem to be of a similar depth all round, and their edges suggest that the back may be intended to be flat (plate 24). The carving at Westminster Abbey cannot be seen so clearly as that at Oakham, due to being in the north aisle arcading and extremely difficult to observe from below (plate 38). An important continental source, one of the viols in the *Portail Royal* at Chartres Cathedral, leaves no room for doubt as it is flat against the wall from rib to rib.[1]

In most cases the neck is distinct from the body, even though probably carved from the same piece of wood. This is demonstrated by the Winchester Psalter, fo. 46 (plate 20), in contrast to the York Psalter, fo. 21^v, where it is formed by gradual tapering (plate 22). Most pegholders are flat, except in a few cases where the artist has gone out of his way to produce an exotic design. In the St. Alban's Psalter, p. 417, for instance, it is impossible to see how the pegs would have fitted, or how the strings would have been joined to them (plate 11). Fingerboards can be seen at Oakham (plate 24) and in the Cambridge, St. John's College MS K. 30, fo. 86 (plate 26), but even in continental sources they are comparatively rare, with examples including a broken carving on a capital in Geneva Cathedral, and an illustration in the Paris, Bibliothèque Nationale MS Lat. Nouv. Acq. 1392, fo. 113^v. These latter date from the twelfth and thirteenth centuries respectively. In no representation of a mediaeval viol of any nationality has the author found any frets.

At the lower end of the instrument the strings were generally fixed to a tailpiece which itself was attached to an end projection. These projections sometimes became very large, as in the Cambridge, Trinity College MS B. 11. 4, fo. 85 (plate 34), and the

St. Alban's Psalter, p. 417, where the exotic crown-like shape matches that of the pegbox (plate 11). Here the tailpiece itself is also of a design unusual for England, but more akin to those on French carvings, notably at Oloron Cathedral.[2] In the BL MS Arundel 157, fo. 71^v, the end projection is very wide, possibly to give some means of support to the instrument, and also to sustain the wide raised section which seems to be an early form of frontal stringholder (plate 29). At Oakham there is a form of hookbar (plate 24), which can be found in various continental examples, such as the Worms Bible, fo. 3^v.[3] Also at Oakham there is one of the rare English cases of a visible separate bridge (another is in the Winchester Psalter, fo. 46, plate 20), one which is not only flat but also very low, so all the three strings would almost certainly have been sounded together. As with the other bowed instruments the number of strings was varied, although the most usual seems to have been three. The Cambridge, Trinity College MS B. 11. 4, fo. 128 shows an instrument which may be intended to have a *bordunus* at the side (plate 35), but this picture is not very carefully depicted, and the author has never yet seen one where a mediaeval viol does have a clear lateral drone string.

The shape of the mediaeval viol, particularly when it resembled a figure of eight to a greater or lesser degree, gave the artist more scope for imagination than did, for instance, the rebec. This is particularly noticeable with regard to the soundholes. In many cases, such as both illustrations from the St. Albans Psalter (plates 10, 11), there are two holes in each of the two bouts, one on either side of the strings. Even within this manuscript itself there is contrast between the small circular holes on p. 56 and the larger half-moon shapes on p. 417. William de Brailes, in the Cambridge, Fitzwilliam Museum MS 330, leaf 5, also has four soundholes, but those of the upper bout are of a different shape from the lower ones (plate 37). In the Winchester Psalter, fo. 46 and the Cambridge, Trinity College MS O. 4. 7, fo. 112, where there is a parallel central section, the soundholes are narrow rectangular slits which run parallel to the sides (plates 20, 8). The York Psalter, fo. 21^v also has central slits, as well as two small round holes on either side of each bout (plate 22). In the Evesham Psalter, fo. 7^v there is one soundhole on one side of the upper bout, and one on the other side of the lower bout. The viol in the BL MS Arundel 157, fo. 71^v has a large round hole in each of the upper and lower bouts, and a small hole (or holes?) in the central section (plate 29). In the thirteenth century, however, there was more of a tendency to have one hole on each side of the strings at the central part of the body, such as the surprisingly modern pair in the Cambridge, Trinity College MS B. 11. 4, fo. 128 (plate 35).

It has been noted above that the bow of the mediaeval viol was often elaborate and furnished with a handle (p. 17). In most cases it is seen to be long, and the degree of curvature varied as with the other instruments of its period.

THE SIZE, SOUND, AND TUNING OF THE MEDIAEVAL VIOL

Among the normal bowed instruments of the twelfth century the viol must have been capable of producing the deepest sounds, judging by the size of those in the St. Albans Psalter (plates 10, 11), and the Cambridge, St. John's College, MS K.30, fo. 86 (plate 26), and, to take a continental example, that of the Worms Bible, fo. 3ᵛ.[4] There were, however, much smaller sizes, such as that of the Winchester Psalter, fo. 46 (plate 20), which would have been about the same size as certain rebecs. These different sizes do not, however, indicate any kind of standardization any more than they do with the rebec or the fiddle, and there is absolutely no suggestion of regular 'consorts' of mediaeval viols.

Nothing is known of the tuning, but judging from the low flat bridge on the Oakham instrument (plate 24), there must have been some such viols where the strings all sounded together, and were therefore presumably tuned to a mixture of fifths and fourths, such as some of those suggested on p. 36.

The dissertation upon which this book is based included the remark 'Of the actual sound of the instrument we shall know little or nothing until it is being made again for performance'.[5] That was written c.1970, and between that year and 1986 there has been a great advance in the making of old instruments. The mediaeval viol, however, is one of the last to be resurrected, and although there are a few examples now being made (some of them quite spurious), it will still be some time before an adequate assessment can be made of their average types of sound.

THE MEDIAEVAL VIOL IN CONSORT

Of all the mediaeval bowed instruments, perhaps with the exception of the crowd, the viol is the most difficult to place in music and society, partly because of the ambiguity in the names by which it was known, and partly because, during the two centuries when it flourished, there were fewer pictures of ordinary human situations than there were in later years.[6] (The instrument is normally seen in the hands of David, of the Elders of the Apocalypse, or of angels, and these last are mainly from after 1200.) Only the carving at Barfrestone seems to represent normal life (plate 27), in the form of village revels, if the musical animals involved can be considered as minstrels dressed up (pp. 8, 101). Here the seated man playing a viol does show that the instrument was sometimes included among joyful rustic occasions. At Oakham the viol is played by a very dignified man whose head has been partly broken off (plate 24), but he is one of several performers who each adorn a separate pillar and there is no evidence to suppose that they are necessarily playing together. In the Cambridge, Trinity College MSS O. 4. 7, fo. 112 and B. 11. 4, fo. 128 (plates 8, 35) and in the Amesbury Psalter, fo. 55ᵛ (plate 40), the player is a single man sitting in an initial. In none of these cases is there firm evidence to suggest that the player is David (although he might be), contrary to the Winchester Psalter, fo. 46, where he wears a type of crown and is seated in the initial B(eatus vir) with the hand of God raised to him (plate 20).

Pictures of the mediaeval viol in duet are rare, the two examples in Appendix D showing it with a harp and fiddle respectively. In trio it can be found with a harp and psaltery, and in quartet that combination is joined by a rebec. On the whole, however, it seems to appear in larger groups, as can be seen in Appendix D. As suitable pictures of it in consort are so rare, three thirteenth-century French examples are included here to supplement the listed English ones.

The following numbers from the Appendix show sources for the instrument in small groups:

in duet, with
harp, *2.13.2*; fiddle, *2.13.3*;

in trio, with
harp and psaltery, *3.13.2*;

in quartet, with
rebec, harp and psaltery, *4.12.1*; rebec, harp and double pipe, *4.13.4*;

and also, from French sources,

in trio, with
horn and chimebells, Paris, Bibliothèque Nationale, MS Lat. Nouv. Acq, 1392, fo. 113ᵛ;

in quartet, with
fiddle, harp and horn, Paris, Bibliothèque Nationale, MS Lat. 238, fo. 114ᵛ; symphony, harp and psaltery, Copenhagen, Royal Library, MS G.K.S. 1606, fo. 22ᵛ, Christina Psalter.

One of the latest English pictures of a mediaeval viol occurs in the cope now in the Museo Civico at Bologna (plate 77).[7] This was embroidered between 1315 and 1335, and, like many other copes of the time, consists to a great extent of arcading with a biblical scene, or a sacred person or event, within each arch. In one row of arcading, the spandrels contain a row of thirteen minstrel angels which, because of their very stylized presentation, are unlikely to represent actual performance practice. They do, however, contain some of the chief instruments used in the early fourteenth century, and among these are to be seen, in adjacent spandrels, a mediaeval viol and a fiddle. This was the period during which the latter instrument completely superseded the former in popularity, and was to hold a unique position in England for the next two hundred years. The viol disappeared completely in this country, according to the lack of visual evidence of it, and its Renaissance successor which was brought by musicians from Flanders, Italy, and Germany to the Court of Henry VIII was a very different instrument. This will be discussed in Chapter VII.

CHAPTER VI

The Fiddle

THROUGHOUT its history the word *fiddle* has often been used in a generic sense, and among its members can be found such widely diverse instruments as the dancing master's kit and the modern double bass. We have seen how, during the Middle Ages, it was applied to the families of the rebec, crowd, and mediaeval viol, and it is a safe word to use for the many hybrids which cannot safely be attributed to any of the more definite categories.

There was, however, one family to which it was applied in the more particular sense, and which has become known today as that of the *mediaeval fiddle*. (Henceforth the word *fiddle* in this book will apply to that instrument unless otherwise stated.) This had unending variations within itself, but among the most usual types two main characteristics stand out. One is a clear distinction between the body and the neck of the instrument, even if they are carved from one piece of wood (as in the Yugoslav *gusle*) (plate 155), and the other is a flat or nearly flat back. While neither of these two characteristics were absolutely essential to the fiddle or to each other, they do appear together in the most popular examples.

Such instruments can be traced back to the eleventh century in Byzantine sources such as the Theodore Psalter (BL Add. MS 19352, fo. 191),[1] dating from 1066, and by about 1150 they were well developed in Spain and France. In England, however, such fiddles that did exist at that time were more primitive instruments. If more advanced ones were ever brought here by visiting Troubadours during the reigns of Henry II and his son Richard I (d. 1199), they certainly did not appear frequently in the English visual arts until well after 1200.

TERMINOLOGY

These simple forms of fiddle appear in English art from the time when most educated people in this country spoke French or Anglo-Norman. French literature, such as would have crossed the Channel in the twelfth-century Norman and Plantagenet entourage, includes the word *viele*, which at that time could have covered both the mediaeval viol and the fiddle. The same provision applies to the Latin words *vidula*, *viella*, and *viola*, which also appear in contemporary sources.

The English language was written down by few scribes and poets during this period, and surviving forms of the word *fiddle* are rare. However, as Aelfric's 'fidicen' of *c*.1000 is rendered 'fiþela' in a twelfth-century version of his vocabulary (p. 12), we can assume that the same word was used throughout the Romanesque era, as it emerges with frequency in English literature soon after 1200. We can also assume that during the thirteenth century it became applied more and more to the instrument to be considered in this chapter, which we call, in the particular sense, the *mediaeval fiddle*.

Its early spellings were generally *fiðele*, *fiþele* or *fithele*, and in the fourteenth century they had been joined by *fethill*, *fydele*, *fythele*, *fyþele*, *viþele*, etc. By 1500 the names also included *fiddill*, *fidle*, *fidylle*, *ffythele*, *fydel*, *fydell*, *fydle*, *fydyll*, *fylh*, *fythil*, *fyyele*, *phidil*, and *vythule*. The word *vyell* was used in 1483 and *viallis* c.1500 (p. 72), and these are almost certain to have meant the fiddle as there is no evidence of the Renaissance viol having arrived in England so early (p. 72). Further reference to the fiddle and its players, in English and in Latin, can be found in Appendix A and in Henry Holland Carter's *Dictionary of Middle English Musical Terms*.

THE FIDDLE IN ENGLAND

The earliest English pictures of fiddles are very similar to those of rebecs, and perhaps can best be included among the hybrid types. They have an oval body which gradually tapers towards the neck, but there is a point at which the two parts become distinct from each other. Such an example can be seen in the Florence, Biblioteca Medicea Laurenziana MS Pluteus xii. 17, fo. 2ᵛ dating from *c.*1120 (plate 9). This illustration is notable for two reasons, firstly as being one of the earliest pictures of a fiddle in an English source, and secondly because the performer is an angel. At this period musical angels were normally restricted to blowing horns in the Apocalypse and scenes of the Last Judgement, and it was not until the thirteenth century that they frequently appeared in heavenly 'orchestras'. Here, however, there are six performing angels, three with bowed instruments, and the others playing a harp, horn, and psaltery in *De Civitate Dei* by St. Augustine.

A rather similar fiddle can be seen on an exterior corbel at Romsey Abbey (plate 12). This instrument has a wider body than the previous example, and the sculpture indicates a curved back. There are four strings, probably four pegs in the somewhat damaged pegbox, and a bridge and tailpiece which, if not actually combined, are set very close to each other. In the Lambeth Bible, fo. 67 a man wearing an animal head holds a small oval-bodied instrument on his lap, without playing it. Here the neck is clearly distinct from the body, and as only the front view can be seen, it is impossible to ascertain the shape of the back (plate 18).

Of these three instruments the first has a very long bow, only slightly curved, the second has a very short one (probably restricted by the nature of the carving), and the third has a bow of medium length.

From the thirteenth century onwards the fiddle became one of the most popular instruments in England, as it was on the Continent. Its main shapes were oval, as in the BL Add. 28681, fo. 100 (plate 50), elliptical as in the Trinity College Apocalypse, fo. 22 (plate 41), and with incurved sides as shown in the BL MS Royal Roll 14. B. v (plate 49). It is generally accepted that at this period the back and sides were carved from one piece of wood, and possibly also the neck. In the soundboard the soundholes were most often c-shaped, although the Evesham Psalter, fo. 7^v is one of the few cases where they show a resemblance to the f-shaped holes of the violin. The strings were normally attached to a tailpiece at the lower end and to a flat pegbox at the upper end. The number of strings was very varied, and many fiddles had a lateral *bordunus*, such as that in the Angel Choir at Lincoln Cathedral (plate 46).

The fourteenth century saw a greater variety of fiddle shapes. While the elliptical body became the most usual, oval ones decreased in number and those with incurved sides increased. The influence of the gittern (citole) can be seen in the pointed corners of fiddles in the Cambridge, Trinity College MS B. 10. 2, fo. 4^v and in the Litlyngton Missal, fo. 221^v (plates 106, 105), while in the latter manuscript the rounded sides of the fiddle on fo. 121 show the influence of the lute (plate 104). An important development of this period is the appearance of fiddles where the back was carved separately from the sides, and then stuck on to them, sometimes with the edges overlapping, as on the violins of today. This new characteristic, which may perhaps seem suggested in the Spanish Romanesque doorways at Santiago de Compostela and Orense Cathedrals,[2] can be seen in carvings at Hanwell (plate 92), Beverley Minster (nave), Lincoln Cathedral (cloister), and on a misericord at Hereford Cathedral (plate 64). While these examples show that the new technique was now known in England, such instruments as were made from it were presumably in a minority for a long period while the older method continued, that of carving the back and sides in one piece. The shape of the back is evident from a good many pictures at this period. Among fiddles with a flat back are examples at Norwich Cathedral (plate 65) and Cley Church, while a corbel from St. Mary's Abbey at York shows a deeply vaulted back. Pegboxes were still flat or cup-shaped in most cases, although the Peterborough Psalter, fo. 57 suggests a right-angled turn (plate 57), which was rare in English sources so soon after 1300. The conventional tailpiece acquired rival methods of attachment at the lower end of the instrument, notably the direct connection of the strings to an end projection, as in the Litlyngton Missal, fo. 221^v (plate 105), or to separate pins as in the Gorleston Psalter, fo. 35 (plate 70). The Litlyngton Missal, fo. 121 and the Cambridge, Trinity College MS B. 10. 2, fo. 30 also show fiddles with frontal stringholders, reflecting the influence of the lute (plates 104, 107). Frets appear on a good many fiddle pictures from *c*.1300 onwards, with notable examples in the Ormesby Psalter, fo. 9^v and the Bohun Psalter (London), fo. 29^v (plates 72, 102).

There are fewer surviving English representations of fiddles from the fifteenth and early sixteenth centuries, for the reasons given on p. 3; hence we have to be particularly careful about making generalizations about this period. However, certain points can be noted. The elliptical shape continued to be the the most popular, varying in size from such large instruments as that of Hillesden (plate 138), to the very small example in the Hours of Elizabeth the Queen, fo. 7 (plate 115). A somewhat exotic shape can be seen in the roof of Loughborough Church, dating from *c*.1450, and the rectangular type seen so often in French manuscripts of the period is found on a benchend at Altarnun, carved after 1523 (plate 146). The two fiddles discovered on the *Mary Rose* also had straight sides, and one of them shows that its back and sides were carved in the old manner from one piece of wood. A fiddle erected in the roof of Knapton Church in 1503 shows its sides to be tapering, a characteristic of the old gittern (citole) (plate 140). The influence of the lute, however, can again be seen in a round-bodied stained glass fiddle of 1501 in Great Malvern Priory (plate 139). Its soundholes are still in the old-style pair, with one on each side of the strings, as are those at Hillesden (plate 138), or from the *Mary Rose* (plates 150, 151), but the example from the Hours of Elizabeth the Queen is one of several which have a rose instead (plate 115). This fiddle also has a pegbox which turns back at a right-angle from the neck, and ends with a carved animal head, while the BL MS Harley 2838, fo. 44^v, on the other hand, shows a sickle-shaped pegbox (plate 132). A plain right-angled one can be seen on one of the fiddles on the late fifteenth-century screen in York Minster. In the church at Broad Chalke, a roof angel plays a fiddle with two soundboards at different levels, one containing two c-shaped soundholes and the other a rose (plate 117); in general shape it is remarkably like the fiddle of St. Caterina de' Vigri (p. 2)[3], although proportionally of a larger size.

We have already seen that in England the lateral *bordunus* went out of fashion on the rebec after *c*.1300 (p. 33). It survived longer on the fiddle, but at the time of writing the author knows no English representations of it from the late fourteenth century onwards. In Italy, however, it was frequently represented in the arts until the time when the fiddle turned into the Renaissance *lira da braccio*.

One of the latest 'English' fiddle pictures from this period is to be found in a sketch, possibly by the German artist Hans Holbein the Younger, of a triumphal arch designed for the Coronation celebrations of Anne Boleyn in 1533 (plate 149). Here one of the Muses plays a fiddle across her chest. Its details are not clear, but the main points to emerge are incurved sides, c-shaped soundholes, a sickle or scroll-shaped pegbox, and a curved bow. The musical setting of this picture will be considered on pp. 95–6.

THE STRINGS AND THEIR TUNING

Apart from the apparent disappearance of the *bordunus*, there seems to be no distinct pattern as to the number of strings used at different periods during the Middle Ages. Any number from three to six was quite usual, and occasionally there were two or seven or eight.[4] Sometimes the pictures show them grouped in pairs, when each of the two strings presumably sounded at the same pitch, or else an octave apart. This applies particularly when there are six or more strings. However, certain representations show six strings to be spaced quite evenly, and these may or may not have been tuned in pairs. The following list shows examples of the most usual string formations:

Single strings
3 Peterborough Psalter, fo. 57 (plate 57)   14c.
4 Howard Psalter, fo. 55ᵛ (plate 69)   14c.
5 York Minster, south aisle glass (plate 113)   15c.
6 Hillesden Church (plate 138)   15c.

Paired strings
2 + 2 York Minster, tower sculpture (plate 129)   15c.
2 + 2 + 2 Saxlingham Nethergate Church (plate 116)   15c.

Single strings with bordunus (+ 1)
2 + 1 Navenby Church (plate 83)   14c.
3 + 1 Oxford, Bodleian Library, MS Douce 131, f. 20 (plate 91)   14c.
4 + 1 Lincoln Cathedral, Angel Choir (plate 46)   13c.
5 + 1 Exeter Cathedral, Minstrels' Gallery (plate 86)   14c.

Paired strings with bordunus
2 + 2 + 1 BL Add. MS 28681, fo. 100 (plate 50)   13c.

How were these instruments tuned? In the lack of English instructions we have to turn again to continental sources, chiefly those of Jerome of Moravia and Johannes Tinctoris. Jerome of Moravia, writing between 1280 and 1300, described three different tunings for a five-stringed 'viella':[5]

Ex. 9

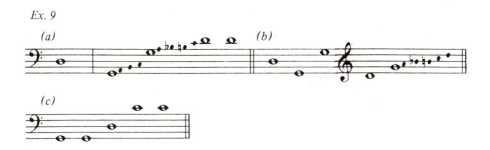

He names the notes that can be stopped by the fingers for the first two tunings, and says that for the third one they are produced in the same way (all the stopped notes mentioned by him are shown here in black).

In the first tuning the *d* is specified as a lateral *bordunus*, from which no other notes can be produced, so it is impossible to play a complete scale on the fingerboard (or neck) from the bottom *G* to the top *a'*. However, Jerome points out that the bottom *e* and *f* can be played an octave higher.

The second tuning has all the strings placed over the fingerboard, as 'it is necessary for secular songs and for all others—especially irregular ones—which frequently wish to run through the whole hand'. However, this tuning is re-entrant, starting with *d* and followed by *G g d' g'*. Christopher Page has suggested that the second and third strings should be an octave course of *G*s, to be sounded together, and that 'the instrument's sound picture would have been rich in octave ambiguities'.[6]

With the third tuning of *G G d c' c'*, the fingers could produce an octave from *G* to *g*, and an extra *a* could be added by the fourth finger, but there would be no *b♭* or *b♮* before the appearance of the two *c* strings. It would seem that with this tuning the bridge should be shaped in such a way that the three bottom strings could be played together, when drones were needed based on *G*, and that similarly the top two strings could be played with each other, one of them giving a drone to the other's melody. Alternatively, if they were sufficiently close together, they could be a double course touched simultaneously by the fingers.

As Jerome's *G* would need a longer pitch than most pictorial fiddles could take, its actual pitch has long been a matter for doubt. Christopher Page has now shown that in order to indicate all the notes that the fiddle could produce, Jerome had to set the bottom string at the bottom of the Guidonian Hand.[7] This, however, was only a theoretical convenience, and the actual pitch could be set wherever was most suitable for each individual instrument, according to its size.

Tinctoris, in his *De Inventione et Usu Musicae* (*c*.1487), said that the 'viola' had 'either three simple strings tuned to a pair of fifths,[8] which is the most usual, or five strings tuned unevenly in fifths and unisons' ('sive tres ei sint chorde simplices ut in pluribus: per geminam diapentem: sive quinque (ut in aliquibus) sic et per unisonos temperate: inequaliter').[9] By 'unisons' he may have meant octaves; these would produce the interval of a fourth which was 'unequal' to the fifth below it, resulting in an ascending 15151 formation. Alternatively, he may have intended a tuning in fifths where the upper two pitches were repeated at the actual unison, i.e. 15522. This would still have involved 'unequal' tuning to the extent that there was not the same distance between every string. He gave no specific pitches, but these two suggestions could be interpreted, for instance, as

Ex. 10

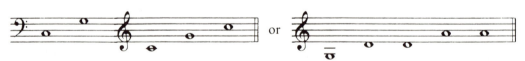

or notes relative to those.

Christopher Page has drawn attention to two other useful sources. One is the *Summa Musicae*, which dates from between 1274 and 1307, and possibly originated in Paris. The author of this work, while not actually specifying the 'viella', refers to stringed instruments 'which are tuned in the consonances of octave, fourth and fifth; by variously stopping with the fingers the players of these make tones and semitones for themselves'.[10]

The second source is a fourteenth-century treatise probably written by the Parisian composer Jean Vaillant (Berkeley University MS 744). It includes diagrams of certain instruments with the pitch letters marked on their strings, and one of the instruments looks very much like a fiddle. Its body is almost rectangular in shape, and it has a frontal stringholder to which are attached four strings marked *c d g c*, the latter one presumably being *c'*. Below the diagram is the statement 'Thebeus the Arab loosened the lower string, adjusting a fourth between it and its neighbour', resulting in *A d g c'*.[11]

From the first three treatises we can see that a tuning in fourths, fifths, and octaves was predominant, but that there was a good deal of variation in their arrangement. Jean Vaillant has given us a tuning largely in fourths, but including one interval of a second. There is, however, one further point to be considered here: did he really mean that instrument to be played with a bow? No bow is depicted, and the frontal stringholder gives the impression of being flat and low, with the result that all the strings would have been sounded together. Such a tuning would have been cacophanous if one melody were accompanied by three drone strings, but it could have been adequate if the performer were adept at double stopping; however, we have no idea as to what extent this practice existed during the Middle Ages, beyond a melody being accompanied by drones. It cannot be ruled out that this may have been intended to be a plucked instrument of the gittern (citole) family. Such instruments flourished during the lifetime of Jean Vaillant (d. 1361), and their shapes varied considerably, with the main characteristic that their sides were approximately parallel and the back either flat or only slightly curved.[12] There were, therefore, distinct similarities between certain fiddles and gitterns (citoles), and confusion between the two could easily arise, particularly if the instrument were unplayed and with no bow or plectrum in sight. Apart from the general appearance of Vaillant's instrument, there is the point that all the other instruments he describes are plucked, namely the harp, psaltery, and mandora (gittern). It would seem strange, therefore, to leave out the ubiquitous gittern (citole) in favour of one out of several bowed instruments, and this uncertainty has arisen because he did not label this diagram. *If* he did intend the instrument in question to be plucked, then there is no problem about its tuning as the strings would not be sustained all together; the source would then be omitted from those giving tunings for the fiddle.

THE PLAYING POSITION

The chief methods of holding the fiddle in performance are very similar to those of the rebec (p. 37), and again we must bear in mind the conditions imposed by artistic licence. A good many pictures show the instrument to be held up at the shoulder and parallel to the ground, as in the Peterborough Psalter, fo. 57 (plate 57). By far the greater number, however, have it held at or near the shoulder, but pointing downwards to a slight extent, as in the Ormesby Psalter, fo. 9ᵛ, or to a greater extent as in the Huth Psalter, fo. 89 (plates 72, 47). Another way was to hold it across the chest. This was very popular in Germanic countries,[13] but less so in England. It occurs mainly in sources from the fourteenth century onwards, and is represented here by a stained glass example in the church (now a museum) of St. Peter Hungate, Norwich (plate 125). Another late mediaeval development is when the fiddle is held in the armpit, as in the BL MS Harl. 2838, fo. 44ᵛ (plate 132). Pictures of fiddles held down on the lap are very rare indeed in English sources. Apart from some ambiguous sources of the thirteenth century where the instruments may in any case be mediaeval viols, and one picture in the Bohun Psalter (Oxford), fo. 58, the author knows at present of only two examples, both dating from after 1400. One is a fiddle played downwards by an angel in the roof of Buckden Church (plate 130),[14] and the other is in stained glass of the south aisle at York Minster (plate 113). Here a musician is holding a fiddle which rests against his knees, at the scene when St. John the Baptist's head is brought in on a charger; it is not certain, however, whether in this case the instrument is actually being played at all.

Some of these pictures pose the question as to how the fiddle could easily be played. As there is no chinrest, a really good hold can only be obtained by the player gripping the instrument between his jaw and his shoulder, as appears in the BL Add. MS 28681, fo. 100 (plate 50). In this way he can play the most complicated types of mediaeval music without the instrument slipping. When the fiddle leans against the shoulder, and points downwards to a greater or lesser degree, the activities of the fingers are limited, as they are partly involved in supporting the instrument. In some cases the player's cheek is against the lower rib of the instrument, as in the Steeple Aston Cope (plate 76), but this is unreliable in performance and must be due to artistic licence. The instruments which point almost straight downwards could not be used for very complicated music, but in such a position they could play simple drones, or melodies on the top string with drone accompaniment. If a fiddle is held across the chest, it cannot be played really successfully without a strap to keep it in position. This is sometimes shown in continental sources, such as the Velislav Bible, fo. 72, a Bohemian manuscript dating from c.1340.[15] If the fiddler ever changed the positions for fingering, which is considered on pp. 28–9, he would have needed to hold the instrument firmly.

The majority of mediaeval pictures show the bow to be held with its hairs facing away from the player—the opposite way to that of the modern violin bow—with exceptions including the Litlyngton Missal, fo. 221ᵛ and the Oxford, Bodl. MS Bodley 691, fo. 1 (plates 105, 93). The actual grip on the stick is often like that of today, with the thumb below it and four fingers above, as shown in the Peterborough Psalter, fo. 57 (plate 57). There are, however, cases such as that of the window at Ringland, where the little finger is not touching the stick at all (plate 74). This technique is sometimes used on the violin today, but the author's own experience has shown that, while giving more freedom in one respect, it is also conducive to dropping the bow. Another manner is to have two fingers above the stick and two below it, as seen in the choir roof boss at Exeter Cathedral and the stained glass at St. Peter Hungate, Norwich (plates 53, 125). A further grip, involving the whole fist, can be found in a good many representations including that of Gloucester Cathedral (plate 96). While on first sight it might seem to be due to ignorance on the part of the artist, experimentation shows that in certain types of lively music this grip works well, given a suitable bow.

THE SOUND OF THE FIDDLE

Bearing in mind the obvious truth that with their very varying shapes mediaeval fiddles must have produced very different sounds, we are left with the impression that on the whole the fiddle was highly regarded. Certainly it was by Jerome of Moravia, who, immediately after describing it in his treatise, came to his dedication 'ad honorem domini nostri ihesu christi . . .'.[16] Its versatility was acknowledged by Johannes de Grocheo in his *De Musica* of *c*.1300, when he said that it could play 'every musical form'. Tinctoris in the fifteenth century declared that, with the rebec, it stirred his heart 'most ardently to the contemplation of heavenly joys'.

English literary sources frequently mention the fiddle's part in celebrations and merriment, one example being from the *Laud Troy Book* (*c*.1400):

> He sette hit there with mochel song,
> With ffythel, harpe, and mynstrasie,
> With mychel merthe and melodye.[17]

and the metrical *Life of St. Brandan* (*c*.1300) gives a good imitative description of its sound:

> And he with flykerynge of his wynges made
> a full mery noyse lyke a fydle, that hym
> seemed he herde never so joyfull a melodye.[18]

A noteworthy remark, which will strike a chord of sympathy from players of all types of fiddle today, is Konrad von Megenberg's assertion that 'when the air is damp the organ and fiddle sound less sweetly than when the weather is fine'.[19]

THE FIDDLE IN CONSORT

Among the instruments classified as loud and soft ('haut' and 'bas') during the later Middle Ages, the fiddle on its own counts as soft, and is frequently depicted being played with other soft instruments. However, although one string on its own would not make a very loud sound, four or five strings sounded together could, so it is not surprising to find pictures of small groups in which a fiddle plays with, for instance, a shawm, bagpipes, or a trumpet. It is reasonable to suppose that in such combinations the fiddle involved would generally have had a flat bridge.

When a fiddle is seen as half of a duet, its most usual partner is a plucked instrument. Of these, the harp was popular throughout the Middle Ages, the gittern (citole) in the thirteenth and fourteenth centuries, and the lute in the fifteenth. The psaltery and mandora (gittern) also appear in duet with it, but not so often.

In partnership with another bowed instrument, it appears most often with another fiddle, and the discovery of two fiddles together on the *Mary Rose* lends weight to the evidence of the pictorial records. As the fiddle ousted the mediaeval viol these two are seldom seen in duet, with the BL Add. MS 28681, fo. 100 being a rare example (plate 50). Nor is the rebec a frequent partner, because its tone often jars against that of the fiddle. If a mediaeval picture does exist of the fiddle playing in duet with a crowd, it has yet to be revealed.

The portative organ and fiddle appear together frequently in continental pictures, and to a somewhat lesser extent in English ones, from *c*.1300 onwards. Experience of playing the two instruments together shows that they can blend extremely well.

Listing the fiddle's duets with other wind instruments can be a problem, as many of them can only be classified as a 'pipe' for the reason mentioned on p. 40. However, certain points have emerged. Firstly, the author has found no instance of a fiddle playing alone with a recorder. It does appear often with the pipe-and-tabor and also with the shawm, although in some cases these are not clearly defined, and might be intended to be short trumpets. Bagpipes also occur occasionally. What might be unexpected is the frequent appearance together of the fiddle and the trumpet, and of this there are several representations and references; a possible explanation has been given on p. 69.

Among percussion instruments to be found with the fiddle are the chimebells and the tabor, besides the related clapping of hands. While a timbrel would be suitable and indeed can be seen in continental sources, it has yet to appear in an English one known to the author.[20]

From expense accounts there are many payments to a fiddler with one or two other musicians. Sometimes it is not clear whether they actually performed together, but on other occasions it can be assumed that they did, as when several fiddlers played while the Princess Eleanor, sister of Edward III, was in St. Paul's Cathedral before going to Holland in 1332:

> Diuersis vidulatoribus, facientibus menestralcias
> suas coram cruce ad hostium boriale in ecclesia
> Sancti Pauli, London, de dono domine Alianore,
> ibidem, per manus thesaurarii, ultimo die Aprilis
> xij d.[21]

It can also be assumed that Bestrudus and Beruche, the 'vidulatores' from Geneva, must have played together in duet when they toured England in 1302 and 1303.[22] When a similar combination of instruments appears more than once in accounts, this does suggest that the musicians concerned were used to playing together. Two such examples come from the Royal Household accounts of James IV of Scotland. On 23 September 1497, a gift of 18*s*. 0*d*. was made to Pais, taborer, and Bennet, fiddler,[23] and on 9 May 1504, 14*s*. 0*d*. was paid to a taborer and a fiddler in Leith.[24]

Pictures of the fiddle in ensembles of three or four instruments normally show it to be accompanied by those with which it appears in duets, and these can be supplemented by further references in literature and accounts. In larger groups, of about eight or more, the instruments are of course more varied, and sometimes include almost all the main types in use at the given period, although such groups must be treated with particular caution (p. 6).

An interesting entry appears in the Household Book of the Prince of Wales for the thirty-first year of the reign of Edward I:

Gift of 12.0d each to Thomasinus the fiddler, John Garsie and John de Cataloyne, trumpeters, and John the nakerer, minstrels of the prince, making their minstrelsy before the prince at Neubotel on the day of the Holy Trinity, of the Lord's gift for four black cloaks of his livery bought for them.[25]

Two trumpets and a pair of nakers can often be seen played together, and it is possible that in this case they formed part of the proceedings, such as fanfares, while the fiddle played at different times. However, as there is much pictorial evidence for the fiddle playing in small groups with the trumpet (p. 69), so this quartet may actually have taken place.

There are numerous references to the fiddle playing with the voice, one of the most famous being 'To a woman that singeth with a fidell 2s' from the Privy Purse expenses of Henry VII in 1495.[26]

Representations of the fiddle in small consorts can be found in Appendix D as indicated:

in duet, with
harp, *2.13.4*; psaltery, *2.14.3*; gittern (citole), *2.13.5*; mandora (gittern) (or plucked rebec?), *2.14.4*; lute, *2.15.5*; mediaeval viol, *2.13.3*; fiddle, *2.15.6*; portative organ, *2.14.5*; double pipe, *2.14.6*; pipe-and-tabor, *2.14.7*; shawm, *2.14.8*; double shawm, *2.14.9*; bagpipes, *2.15.7*; trumpet, *2.14.10*; chimebells, *2.13.7*;

in trio, with
harp and psaltery, *3.14.2*; harp and gittern (citole), *3.14.3*; psaltery and mandora (gittern), *3.14.4*; harp and trumpet, *3.13.4*; shawm and handbells, *3.13.5*; bagpipes and gong, *3.13.6*; chimebells and bagpipes, *3.14.5*;

in quartet, with
harp, gittern (citole) and double pipe, *4.14.1*; harp, gittern (citole) and trumpet, *4.14.2*; three singers, *4.14.3*.

THE BELLOWS-AND-TONGS, AND OTHER SKITS

The subject of the fiddle is incomplete without reference to the numerous skits on it which occur in mediaeval art. Prominent among them is that of the bellows-and-tongs, in which the bellows are held up at the shoulder and the tongs are placed above them as a bow. This occurs in the Ormesby Psalter, fo. 24 (plate 73), while on a fourteenth-century misericord at Lavenham Church, Suffolk, the 'bow' may be a crutch. The bellows in fact look more like a rebec than a fiddle, but their back would be flat. They are sometimes replaced by an actual fiddle, while the 'bow' becomes a garden rake, or a similar object. This can be seen in the BL MS Royal Roll 14. B. v (plate 49). Flemish manuscripts of the early fourteenth century abounded in such curiosities, notable examples being found in the Oxford, Bodl. MSS Douce 5 and Douce 6, where the instruments are caricatured by a jawbone, a ram's head, a gridiron, and many other such objects. A rather different skit of the fifteenth century occurs on the screen at York Minster, where two adjacent angels 'blow down' a bow and arrow respectively ...

CHAPTER VII

The Renaissance Viol

❧ ❧

UNTIL very recently the early history of the Renaissance viol was one of the many important musical subjects waiting to be thoroughly investigated. Although firm evidence of it could only be found from the late fifteenth century onwards, numerous modern performers played this instrument, even in its Baroque form, in music going back as far as the twelfth century. Now the matter has at last been tackled by Ian Woodfield, who finds that the earliest known pictorial evidence for the Renaissance viol comes from the area around Valencia in the second half of the fifteenth century, and that it had travelled to Italy, possibly by means of the Aragonese Court at Naples and the Borgia connection in Rome, by about 1490. While most of the Spanish pictures show flat-bridged instruments which could broadly be described as bowed guitars, mainly suitable for accompaniment, the Italian sources show that in that country the viol was developed into a deeper-sided instrument with a curved bridge. There it was made in several different sizes, and became an ideal instrument for consort music.[1]

TERMINOLOGY

In his *Dictionary of Middle English Musical Terms*, Henry Holland Carter gives two references to words which might on first sight be interpreted as Renaissance viols.[2] The first is from Caxton's *Knight of the Tower*, printed in 1483: 'Syre Geffroy called hym before hym and demaunded hym where his vyell or clauycordes were',[3] and the second example is from the *Coventry Pageant of the Shearman and Taylors* (*c*.1500) where Herod says that he shall wake to the sounds of 'trompettis, viallis and othur armone' (p. 92). As, however, there is no definite evidence of such viols in England at that time, and as they had only recently become established in southern Europe, it could be that these English names applied to no more than the old-established mediaeval fiddle which was going through certain alterations of spelling. Later on the words *vialles*, *vyalles*, *vyolls*, and *veoldes* referred to instruments played at the Court of Henry VIII by foreign musicians, and these are more likely to have meant the actual Renaissance viol.

In a similar way the Latin word *viola* was used for both instruments. Thomas Stapleton refers to the young Thomas More playing it as a recreation from his studies (*Tres Thomae: Vita Thomae Mori*, Douai, 1588, p. 25), but as More was born *c*. 1478 this instrument would almost certainly have been the fiddle. When the viol did arrive he welcomed it into his family circle, where it can be seen in the pictures by Holbein which are described later in this chapter; by that time, together with its predecessor, it, too, bore the name *viola*.

THE RENAISSANCE VIOL IN ENGLAND

As yet, no English viols are known to survive from the period covered by this book, but it is certain that by the end of that time viols were being used in England. From the second decade of the sixteenth century onwards they were mentioned with increasing frequency, generally as being played at the royal Court by musicians from Flanders, Germany, and Italy, and before 1530 they had begun to appear, though very rarely, in the English visual arts.

In 1515 the Flemish viol players Matthew, Philip, and Peter van Wilder came to England, and in the same year viols were mentioned for the first time in the Revels Accounts, where Richard Gibson described them as 'strange' instruments (p. 94). The royal expenses for the year 1517 show the entry

To pay Matthew de Weldre, the king's minstrel and player upon the lutes and veoldes, his wages monthly, at the rate of 20 marks a year.

Greenwich, 7 Jan, 8 Hen.VIII.[4]

It is, however, just possible that this musician may have played the viol at the English Court as early as 1506, if his instrument had survived a shipwreck in the entourage of Philip of Castile (p. 84).

In 1526 the royal musicians included two other foreigners, Hanse Hossenet and Hanse Highorne (Peter Holman suggests that they were Germans), who were each paid 33s. 4d. per month,[5] and by 1531 they had been joined, albeit for a short time, by the apparent Englishman Peter Savage.[6] By 1540 there were eight 'Vialles': the two Germans mentioned above, besides 'Alberto da Venetia, Vincenzo da Venetia, Alexandro da Mylano, Zuan Maria da Cremona, Ambrose de Milano, and Romano da Milano'. (Although their names suggest that they may have been Italian, Holman has now shown that they were in fact Sephardic Jews of families which had originally gone to Italy from Spain.)[7]

Some of these musicians were involved in the funeral solemnities of Henry VIII in 1547,[8] and in the same year an inventory of the King's instruments, drawn up at the request of his son Edward VI, included

xix Vialles greate and small with iii cases of woodde
couered with blacke leather to the same

and

A chest collored redde with vi Vialles hauinge the Kinges Armes.

The inventory also mentions

Foure Gitterons with iiii cases to them: they are caulled Spanishe Vialles,[9] and Woodfield has suggested that these might have been early Spanish viols which came to England as the result of Prince Arthur's marriage to Catherine of Aragon in 1501.[10] If this is so, Herod's 'viallis' at Coventry (p. 72) could be more debatable, although the present writer still tends to feel that they were mediaeval fiddles. However, it is not certain that these 'Gitterons' were bowed instruments at all, as that very name suggests plucking, and 'vialle' in this context may be an anglicization of 'vihuela', which is associated even more often with plucking than with bowing.

There is evidence of other noble households collecting viols from the 1520s onwards, and the first known pictures of them come from the household of Sir Thomas More, the Lord Chancellor from 1529 to 1532. In about 1527 his family group was sketched by Hans Holbein the Younger, in preparation for a larger painted portrait. The drawing, which was taken to Erasmus at Basel in 1528, shows a large viol hanging up on the wall behind the family (plate 148). Due to being a brief preliminary sketch it does not give much detail, but the outline shows the bouts to be delineated clearly by corners. There is a central rose, and two smaller soundholes in the upper bouts; a tailpiece is sketched, but the bridge is not clear, and there are frets. Near the instrument is a memorandum, thought to have been written by Holbein after consultation with More, to say that in the painting it must be replaced by instruments lying on the sideboard to the left of the picture.[11]

Until very recently it was believed that the subsequent painting had not survived, but that an exact copy of it, made by Rowland Lockey in the 1590s, was to be seen at Nostell Priory near Wakefield.[12] (Lockey also did similar but not identical portraits, including in them younger members of the family who could not have been in the earlier design; these versions can be found in the National Portrait Gallery, the Victoria and Albert Museum, and the British Museum.) However, damage by water and smoke during a fire at Nostell Priory in 1979 caused the picture to be cleaned, and analysis of a fragment by a team from Arizona University declared that the painting could after all date from the 1520s and therefore be a genuine work by Holbein. This has been disputed by the Oxford Research Laboratory for Archaeology and the History of Art, which says there could be a margin of error of 150 years either way in such an analysis. Meanwhile Mr Jack Leslau, a retired jeweller who has studied the painting for many years, believes that Holbein himself did the painting c.1540, five years after More's death in 1535.[13] Whatever the outcome of this art-historical wrangle, the viol still belongs to the sixteenth century, and is either by Holbein or is a direct copy of his work.

The instruments lying on the sideboard in this painting (plate 147) are in fact quite different from those in the sketch at Basel. The lute is larger, and clearly shows six courses, while the viol bow lies across it. The bow was omitted in the later paintings by Lockey, perhaps because he thought it made the lute look untidy, but its appearance in the Nostell Priory version verifies the fact that the other instrument is a viol rather than some kind of guitar, which otherwise might have been possible. (*If* the painting is after all by Lockey, the inclusion of the bow against his natural inclinations does suggest that he was really trying to copy the original.) This instrument's body is tantalizingly obscured by the head of Margaret Gigs, More's adopted daughter, but even so, it can be seen that the instrument is by no means the same as that in the original sketch. Its outline is much smoother, and is more of the type represented by the viol by Giovanni Maria da Brescia in the Ashmolean Museum. In the painting there are two small c-shaped soundholes in the upper bouts, but they face outwards, whereas those on the sketch face inwards. The tailpiece and end button are clear, and part of a bridge can be seen; there is a long neck and a fingerboard, but no frets, which is unusual but not unknown in a viol (compare the large fretless viol in Matthias Grunewald's Isenheimer Altar in the Musée Unter-linden at Colmar). The bow is fairly short and somewhat curved, with black hairs and a carefully-shaped nut, possibly of ivory, into which they are fitted at the lower end.

We may wonder why the design of the viol is so different from that in the original sketch, and in the lack of any further knowledge on the matter, any answer can only be hypothetical. It could be, for instance, that Sir Thomas More had viols of different shapes and sizes, and decided to substitute a smooth one for that with more distinct corners. On the other hand, Holbein may have had a smoother viol more easily accessible when he was working on the painting, and decided to use that instead. Whatever the case, both pictures are of great importance for the history of the viol in Tudor England.

Further evidence is not pictorial, but comes from expense accounts. Those of the Earls of Rutland show the date on which a set of viols was paid for, the cost of their strings (some apparently from Brussels, besides the lute 'menekyns' which came from Venice), and the fact that they were of sufficient bulk that a man had to be employed to help in their transport:

1537:
Item paid the 27th day of July for four viols bought at London, 53s 4d.

1540:
To a man to help to bring the viols between Croxton and Belwer, 2d.
11 July 1541:
To Richard Pyke for strings for the virginals and viols that he bought at London, 10s.[14]

11 March 1542:
To Pycke for two dozen of lute strings called 'menekyns' at 20d. the dozen, and ten dozen of 'bressell' [Brussels] strings for the viols at 3d. the dozen, 5s. 10d.[15]

In 1538 a 'sett of violles' was owned by the Earl of Hertford, [16] and in the same year the Marquis of Exeter had among his servants a certain Thomas Harrys who played the viols and several other instruments. Two years later Sir John Wallop wrote from 'Veronne' to Thomas Barnaby, saying that he wished his own servant to be taught how to play the viols.[17]

Were all these viols in England of foreign importation, or had the future great school of English viol-makers already begun? It seems that it had, according to the following piece of evidence cited by Gerald Hayes:

We may just mention the one remaining link with our early school of craftsmen that laid the foundations upon which the Elizabethan makers, Bolles, Pemberton, Strong, Ross, and others, built their splendid work. This is Richard Hume, by some set down for a Scotsman for his name and the provenance of the evidence. That he was English is shown by this Edinburgh document of 1535:

> Item to the Kingis Grace to Richard Hume, Inglismanne, quhilk suld mak violis to the Kingis Grace, to by stuffe for the samin, xx lib.[18]

Whether or not Hume was one of the first English viol-makers of the Renaissance, the craft of making these instruments must have been learned from somewhere, and if the makers did not actually go abroad to study, they must surely have observed the viols brought to this country by the visiting foreigners. These instruments would not have been standardized, any more than those in the two very different pictures by Holbein (plates 147–8), and they would presumably not have acquired such later characteristics as the soundpost, which is absent from the earliest surviving viols.[19]

The tunings, too, were varied, among the sources which survive from the Continent. Agricola, for instance, gives the following tunings in the 1528 edition of his *Musica Instrumentalis Deudsch*:

Discant:	*f*	*a*	*d'*	*g'*	*c''*	
Alto and Tenor:	*c*	*f*	*a*	*d'*	*g'*	
Bass:	*G*	*c*	*f*	*a*	*d'*	*g'*[20]

It will be noted that only on the bass viol are there the six strings which became the traditional number. However, the Nostell Priory painting, of which the original lost version is contemporary with the Agricola document, indicates that six strings were already known in England. They may or may not have been tuned according to the method indicated by Ganassi in his *Regola Rubertina* of 1542–3, i.e.

Discant:	*d*	*g*	*c'*	*e'*	*a'*	*d''*
Alto and Tenor:	*G*	*c*	*f*	*a*	*d'*	*g'*
Bass:	*D*	*G*	*c*	*e*	*a*	*d'*[21]

This is the tuning which became traditional, showing at last some standardization in contrast to the ever-changing ideas of the mediaeval musicians. Ganassi does, however, recommend the occasional use of viols with only three or four strings.[22] His title-page shows three viol-players holding their instruments between their knees, with the bows gripped from below, as was usual in pictorial sources from the Continent. The book is itself a manual for players of much experience, thereby giving an outline of the capabilities of the instrument, and being of great value to performers of today.[23] It is also possible that the ways recommended by Ganassi were those in which Vincenzo da Venetia, Alberto da Venetia, and their compatriots played at the Court of Henry VIII.

CHAPTER VIII

The Trumpet Marine?

❦

B Y the middle of the fifteenth century a new bowed instrument had appeared on the European scene. It was an adaptation of the old rectangular monochord, which had a movable bridge to determine the notes of its one plucked string, and was used mainly for purposes of instruction. Already in the twelfth century it was being altered, as witnessed by a capital in the Abbey of Vézelay, where the instrument is shaped very much like an elongated triangle, with the narrowest part serving as a neck where the performer could stop the string with his fingers.[1]

It was to such an instrument that the bow was added, apparently after 1400, and the number of strings was no longer restricted to one.[2] A Flemish painting of the School of Jan van Eyck, *The Fount of Grace* or *The Triumph of the Church over the Synagogue* (now at the Prado, Madrid) shows it with four strings grouped in pairs, thus presumably representing two unisons or octaves.[3]

The earliest names for this instrument are uncertain, although it has been suggested that it may have been covered by the existing word *monochord*. In 1511 Virdung described it in his *Musica Getutscht* as 'Trumscheit', a name which it has kept since then in Germanic countries. The later Italian, French, and English names *tromba marina*, *trompette marine*, and *trumpet marine* have yet to be completely explained, although various theories have been offered. What does seem certain is that the 'trumpet' part is due to its similarity to that instrument, as both were then normally restricted to the notes of the harmonic series. In the trumpet marine these were produced by the strings being touched lightly by the thumb, or occasionally by the fingers, between the bow and the bridge. The bridge was not set firmly, as it is on instruments of the violin family, but one foot was free to vibrate against the soundboard, causing a 'buzzing and snarling' to quote Praetorius.[4] In some of the later instruments the bridge was combined with the soundpost, as in the Welsh crwth (p. 44).

Continental sources show the trumpet marine to be held in different ways. In Memling's triptych of *Musical Angels* in the Museum of Fine Arts at Antwerp, it is held up and pointing outwards,[5] a posture confirmed in the *Dodecachordon* (1547) of Glareanus (Heinrich Glarean), who said that 'players go about through the streets with the instrument's point fixed at the breast'.[6] On the other hand, a fifteenth-century French manuscript, BL Add. MS 27697, fo. 105ᵛ, shows an early example of the manner which later became normal, that of resting the instrument on the ground with the pegbox at the highest point.[7]

Was this instrument ever played by English minstrels? According to Glareanus it was used in Germany and France, and it can be found in the Netherlandish and Italian art of the period.[8] English art of the fifteenth and early sixteenth centuries seems to be lacking (at present) in any portrayals of the trumpet marine in its most usual continental types, but there are two illustrations which seem to resemble it more than anything else. One is in the stained glass of the Beauchamp Chapel at Warwick (plate 124), dating from c.1447, and the other is on the screen at York Minster, dating from 1475–1500 (plate 136). The Warwick instrument is by shape long and narrow, and tapering to its pegbox as in the continental types. It seems to have seven strings, arranged in groups of two, three, and two, which fit into the respective three archs of the frontal stringholder or bridge. Instead of the angel performer pointing it outwards, with the pegbox touching his chest or shoulder, or else holding it so that the lower end rests on the ground, he is playing it just as if it were a fiddle. His left hand fingers the strings near to the pegbox, almost on a level with his waist, while the wider part of the instrument passes over his shoulder and out at the back some way beyond and above his head. He is bowing on the strings between his left hand and the bridge, as on the fiddle, instead of between the fingers and the pegbox, as on the more normal type of trumpet marine. In this way he cannot be producing the necessary harmonics of the latter instrument, so is presumably pressing the strings down firmly, as on the former. The bow is long, and has twisted hairs, and they are facing away from the performer.

The York instrument is of a somewhat smaller size, although the basic shape is similar to that at Warwick; here, however, there are only two strings. The important point is that it is being held and played in the same manner, which gives rise to the question that such a technique might have been usual on instruments of the trumpet marine family in England, although they were rare. On the other hand there is a posssible reason for both, although it is entirely hypothetical.

It is known that John Prudde went abroad to study foreign glasswork before making the windows for Warwick in 1447, and that he used actual glass from Flanders.[9] It could be that while there he saw a trumpet marine of the type shown by Memling, and decided to use it in his own design for Warwick. He may not have sketched it *in situ*, or perhaps he sketched it without a player, and if he had not seen the instrument before it would be quite understandable for him to make a mistake in the manner of performance while trying to reproduce it from memory. Over a quarter of a century later the designer of the York screen may in turn have seen the Warwick glass, and then borrowed from it the idea of the trumpet marine for his own work. However, it should be admitted that he did not borrow several others of the Warwick collection, and this theory can therefore only rest in the realm of remote hypothesis. If more examples of this strange form of the trumpet marine should turn up in the English art of the period, then we can become convinced that something like it did exist, and more information may be forthcoming.

CHAPTER IX

Fiddlers

❧❀❧❀

BEFORE considering the occasions on which bowed instruments were used, we should first look at the musicians who played them, and who could all, in the generic sense, be described as 'fiddlers'.

In the lower strata of society the people themselves were illiterate, and it is uncertain to what extent they played bowed instruments at all during the early period. Dr Bachmann has searched in literature and come to the conclusion that 'Nowhere in any of the pre-fourteenth-century sources do we find reference to the use of the fiddle among the "lower" social strata—the world of serfs and villeins, artisans and day-labourers'.[1] We must, however, give a thought to the somewhat crude rebec-players who adorn the corbel-tables of so many Romanesque churches, such as that of Kilpeck (plate 17), and allow for the possibility that at least some of them may have been from among those categories. As for the later period there is no doubt, and Bachmann quotes from the French poem 'Bellefoiere' which mentions 'the sound of the bagpipe and the hoarse rebec of the cowherds' ('du son de la musette, du rebec enroué des vachers').[2]

Slightly above these amateur musicians in the social scale, there came the minstrels who earned their living through playing, but were nevertheless also illiterate. Without written music, they learnt their repertoire by the aural tradition of hearing others playing it, and they improvised a good deal. They were not only musicians, but also jugglers, acrobats, and general entertainers; a group of such minstrels can be seen with David in the Anglo-Saxon source BL MS Cott. Tiberius C. vi, fo. 30^v (plate 2), and in many sources of the Romanesque period. A good idea of the variety of instruments they could play is given in the poem 'Fadet Joglar' by the Troubadour Guiraut de Calanson (*fl. c.*1200) who was himself a *jongleur* of Gascony.[3] He mentions several instruments of the string, wind, and percussion families, including 'la guiga', and their number indicates a general all-roundness which was possible in an age when technique was not so advanced as it is today. The very fact that the changing of positions on bowed instruments was apparently unknown for a large part of the Middle Ages meant that once the basic techniques of bowing and fingering had been mastered, together with a good sense of intonation and awareness of sound, there should have been no great difficulties.

The type of minstrel who wandered around without a regular job was often a trouble-maker and denounced by clergy and laity alike. Thomas of Chobham, Subdean of Salisbury, writing *c.*1216, regarded such men as 'damnabiles',[4] and would certainly have included in that category the rebec-player sitting in the stocks on a fifteenth-century capital in the church of South Molton, Devonshire.

Higher up the social ladder were to be found fiddlers who definitely could read, among them those of the University of Paris to whom Jerome of Moravia was speaking in the last part of his treatise *De Musica*.[5] Urban T. Holmes has suggested that many of those who were employed by the nobility had 'served their apprenticeship in Church music' before branching off to become professional instrumentalists.[6] This would certainly have taught them to read music, but for the completion of their studies as performers most fiddlers would also have received training from musicians of repute.

Just as *jongleur*-type minstrels were versatile, so were those of higher standing. Robert Manning of Brunne gives us a description of such versatility in the person of Glegabret in *The Story of England*:

> A syngere of þe beste get;
> Of song & of mynstrecye
> Alle men gaf hym þe maystrie;
> þe note he couþe of alle layes,
> Of mynstrecye al þer assayes;
> He couþe so mykel musyk & thume
> þat þe people [saide] in his tyme
> He was þe best of ffythelers,
> Of iogelours & of sangesters,
> ffor he was euere glad & gamen,
> ffele in seruise held he samen.
> Of ioye & song was his spel;
> Was he neyþer irous ne fel,
> Bot led his lyf in melodye
> Ynto þe tyme þat he schold deye.[7]   (see p. 43)

In *Lybeaus Desconus* (*c*.1350–*c*.1400) the dwarf Teandelayn is reputed to play several instruments in addition to his other talents:

> Myche he couþe of game,
> With sytole, sautrye yn same,
> Harpe, fydele and croupe.

(Another version of the poem refers to 'harpe, fethill and crowthe'.)[8]

Court minstrels are sometimes listed in the expense accounts as playing more than one instrument. An example is Adam Boyd, who served at the Court of James IV of Scotland. At Easter 1497 the accounts mentioned him as a fiddler,[9] but on 18 December of the same year he was paid for his services as a taborer.[10] At the Court of Henry VIII of England, John Severnake played the rebec for many years, and later the flute, which had recently become fashionable in England.[11]

Although court minstrels were not normally employed to play as many instruments as those mentioned by Guiraut de Calanson, they did have other duties besides their musical ones. Some were soldiers, such as three of the crowders who played at the Feast of Westminster in 1306. These were 'Johannes le Crouther de Salopia',[12] 'Sagard Crouther'[13] (William Sagard), and 'Tegwaret Croudere',[14] while a soldier fiddler was 'Johannes le vilour domini J. Renaud'.[15] 'Thomas le Croudere' was a yeoman archer.[16] One of the most important fiddlers was 'Le Roy Druet', who owed his title to being King of the Heralds.[17] During the reign of Edward III (d. 1377) William Crowder was an archer,[18] while a 'Tagwaret le Crouder' was a footman.[19] Robert Fytheler seems to have captured otters for the Prior of Durham, although it is uncertain how far this was a regular job. At any rate, he was paid for doing it. Walter le Vyelur is known to have been a painter (p. 31).[20] John Stevens has pointed out that by the time of the Reformation there were servants in noble families who, among other things, could play instruments as well, although this may not have been the original reason for their employment. Such a servant was Thomas Harrys, who worked for the Marquis of Exeter. In 1538, when he was thirty years old, it was recorded that he 'luteth and singeth well and playeth cunningly upon the viols and divers other instruments'.[21]

The established minstrels wore distinctive clothing, either the livery of the household to which they were attached, or of the town to which they belonged. The two Minstrels' Pillars at Beverley show the importance with which the minstrels of that town were regarded. In the Minster, a fourteenth-century bracket (against which there used to rest the banner of St. John of Beverley) shows three minstrels wearing similar clothes. One is a fiddler, playing the elaborately carved instrument shown in plate 95. Unfortunately this is badly damaged, but the two instruments with which it was played are now non-existent. In St. Mary's Church, the better known sculpture of minstrels on a nave capital dating from c.1520 show performers of a pipe-and-tabor, rebec, lute (?), and shawm (plate 145).[22] They are elegantly clad, and wear special chains to denote their position.

Certain types of clothing, even if not registered as the livery of a household or town, were regarded as normal apparel for a minstrel. An incident in the fifteenth-century *Knight of La Tour Landry* tells how a young squire appeared at a feast wearing a German-style coat which was mistaken for that of a minstrel. As a result, a knight who was present 'axed hym, where was his fedyll or his ribible, or suche an instrument as longithe vnto a mynstrall',[23] indicating also that such bowed instruments were among those most often associated with this craft.[24]

Some pictures show women playing instruments. How far they had to earn their living by it is uncertain, but it was done in the poem *Sir Beues of Hamtoun* by Iosian, a princess who was living incognito in Greece:

> While Iosian was in Ermonie,
> ȝhe hadde lerned of minstralcie,
> Vpon a fiþele for to play
> Staumpes, notes, garibles gay;
> þo ȝhe kouþe no beter red,
> Boute in to þe bourȝ anon ȝhe ȝed

And bouȝte a fiþele, so saiþ þe tale,
For fourti panes, of one menstrale;
And alle þe while, þat Saber lay,
Iosian eueriche a day
ȝede aboute the cite wiþ inne,
Here sostenaunse for to winne.[25]

Certainly the 'woman that singeth with a fidell' earned her 2*s*. from Henry VII in 1495.

Many English minstrels travelled abroad especially for the purpose of furthering their musical studies, particularly during Lent, when occasions for performance at home were limited. One of these musicians was Merlin, a 'vidulator' who was given leave of absence to go to the minstrel schools on the Continent, together with the bagpipers Barberus and Morlanus, in February 1334.[26] Merlin had already been allowed to go to France three years earlier, although on that occasion the reason was apparently not recorded.[27] Each time, however, he received a grant towards his expenses.

The fact that Merlin, a royal minstrel, went abroad for a refresher course in Lent, implies that he came back with new repertoire, and that most, if not all of it was continental. Other instances of the dispersal of music, and presumably also of instruments, can be assumed from the frequent occasions when members of the nobility travelled abroad, taking their minstrels with them. Such an event was in 1332, when the Princess Eleanor, sister of Edward III, travelled to Holland for her marriage to the Count of Guelders. Among her large retinue were several minstrels, and the household accounts refer to the fiddler Richard playing at Rosyndale in Holland:

Ricardo vidulatori, facienti menestralcias suas coram domina Alianora, de dono eiusdem domine et per preceptum eiusdem, apud Rosyndale, xxiij die Maii, per manus proprias
                                                                                                    xij   d.[28]

Even in warfare, minstrels accompanied their lords abroad, and these minstrels were not always only trumpeters and drummers. When Henry V was preparing the journey which culminated in victory at Agincourt in 1415, the list of his minstrels for the expedition included one Snyth Fydeler.[29] Earlier, when the future Henry IV joined the Germans in a type of crusade against the Lithuanians in 1390,[30] he made several payments to musicians, although it is not clear whether the fiddlers mentioned were his own or local ones:

Item iij fithleres existentibus cum domino apud Dansk in quadragesima per manus senescalli ex precepto domini   xiij s.   iiij d.[31]

In these, and in many other instances, the fiddlers were able to become acquainted with the continental music and instruments, and to enrich their repertoire for audiences at home in England.

The reign of Edward I shows a great advance in the number of instruments used in England, according to the evidence of the visual arts and of expense accounts. These new instruments include the lute, portative organ, timbrel, clappers (ancestors of the castanets and sometimes known as 'bones'), and nakers, besides the appearance of frets on fiddles. A brief survey of this King's life will show to what extent his own travels may have influenced the colouring of the English musical scene.

The son of Henry III and Eleanor of Provence, he was born in 1239, during the period which produced the famous canon 'Sumer is icumen in'. At the age of fifteen he went to Spain, and was knighted there by King Alfonso X 'The Wise' of Castile, that poet king who may have composed some of the *Cantigas de Santa Maria*. (Certainly the chief manuscript containing them was compiled for him, and besides including over 400 sacred but unliturgical songs, it is one of the best pictorial sources of thirteenth-century instruments in Spain.) Edward then married Alfonso's half-sister Eleanor at the nearby Abbey of Las Huelgas, which had strong connections with England, and an international repertoire of music.[32] During the next few years he spent a good deal of time in France, administering Gascony for his father, and being entertained there by the music of the Troubadours. The year 1270 saw him on the Seventh Crusade with Louis IX (St. Louis) of France, thereby coming into contact with the sounds and instruments of the Saracens. He ascended to the English throne in 1272, while still away, and returned home in 1274, passing through Italy with rousing receptions, and presumably hearing some of the *laude spirituali*, of which many have survived. From then onwards he spent more time in England, but made a notable contact with the East in 1289. The Ilkhan Argun of Persia sent a mission to Europe, and as a result of its visit to London, Edward sent a return ambassador in the person of Sir Geoffrey Langley. Gifts were exchanged on each occasion. John Harvey has attributed to these incidents the strong oriental influence which appeared in English art at about this time.[33] Eleanor of Castile died in 1290, and in 1299 Edward married Margaret of France, daughter of the French King Philip III. It was during her time that the Feast of Westminster was held in 1306, and Phelippe de Coumbray, 'vidulator' of the King of France, came to this country especially for the occasion, being given ten marks by Edward I on returning to his own country.[34]

Other foreign minstrels at the Feast of Westminster were three German 'gigatores'. Two of them, Heinrich and Conrad, appeared regularly in the royal household accounts from 1301 to 1306, with the rank of groom,[35] and Constance Bullock-Davies has pointed out that they were almost certainly the 'Gygors' mentioned in an account of 1299.[36] They were joined in March 1306 by a third 'gigator', Conrad le Peper, who had been sent to England on the orders of the King of Germany.[37] He was due to go home in April, but finally stayed on for the feast on 22 May, and returned with his two compatriots soon afterwards.[38]

During the time that Heinrich and Conrad were playing in England, visits were made by two 'vidulatores' from Geneva, called Bestrudus and Beruche (and other variants on those names). They played before the Prince of Wales during two days at Newcastle-on-Tyne and Durham during 1303, before 'returning to their own district'.[39] 'Bestruche' was then paid 76s. 0d. for his expenses for 'remaining in London, in the prince's instructions, for 102 days in the months of July, August, September, and October after the Prince's departure for Scotland'.[40] During the following year they were again recorded as being in England.[41]

Two other German 'gigatores' were at the English Court in 1331, during the reign of Edward III. They were Hanekin de Bavaria and Hanekin de Cologne, who came by order of the Queen, Philippa of Hainault, and she is recorded as having given a saddle to Hanekin de Cologne at Melton.[42]

Visiting musicians such as those mentioned above would normally have brought their own instruments with them, even if they happened to buy English ones while in this country. During the fourteenth century the basic characteristics of bowed instruments were broadly similar in England, Germany, and Switzerland, even though there were some local differences in details. In 1506, however, there took place an event which may possibly have influenced the history of instruments in England.

Philip the Fair, son of the Emperor Maximilian I and Mary of Burgundy, was sailing to Spain, having become King of Castile on the death of his mother-in-law Isabella. With him went the members of his Flemish chapel (part of the Burgundian inheritance) and a good number of instrumentalists, one ship being allotted to the musicians. Off the English coast there was a violent storm, causing them to be shipwrecked, so the whole company had to take refuge in England. Henry VII received the King of Castile with great hospitality at Windsor, and from the words of an anonymous chronicler, it has been interpreted that both Flemish and English minstrels entertained the guests at the feasting:

Et il ne fault point demander . . . sy la compagnye fut bien receue et bien festoyée, et s'il y eust force bon vin et bonnes viandes, et se tous instrumens n'y estoient oys . . .[43]

We could wish that the chronicler had been more specific about the instruments, as this was a crucial time in their development. Judging from pictorial sources, England was still using the old mediaeval ones to a great extent, while on the Continent certain Renaissance instruments were becoming established, notably the viol and the crumhorn, which were to play such an important part later on in the music at the court of Henry VIII. The vital question here is whether or not the Flemish minstrels managed to save their own instruments from the shipwreck. If they did (a real musician would instinctively want to rescue his instrument before the rest of his baggage), and if these instruments included even one Renaissance viol, that banquet at Windsor might have been the first occasion on which such an instrument was played in England. Although this is a hypothesis, it should be noted that on arrival at Orense in Galicia later in the same journey in 1506, the King of Castile's 'Joueulx d'Instrumens' included one 'Mathis de Wildre',[44] and that among the King of England's minstrels in 1517 was 'Matthew de Weldre . . . player upon lutes and veoldes' (p. 73). If this was the same man, that he was already playing on 'veoldes' in 1506, that 'veoldes' were in fact Renaissance viols, and that he saved his instrument(s) from the shipwreck, then it is not far-fetched to suppose that the court at Windsor heard the viol at that early date. Yet even if it did, there is no definite evidence of such viols in England until the second decade of the century; from that time onwards it was played regularly first by the Flemish musicians and then those from Germany and Italy who were established members of the Court of Henry VIII.

ANIMAL MUSICIANS

We have already seen that minstrels sometimes dressed up as animals, a prominent illustration coming from the Shaftesbury Psalter where a drummer appears in the costume of a bear (plate 15). Sometimes the reverse happens, and animals are dressed up to parody human scenes. There are, however, cases where the performers are just ordinary animals, the result of an artist's whim. How can we decide which of these can be taken at face value, and which have a hidden meaning? This is a vast subject, and one which is far beyond the scope of the present work. A pig, for instance, can be a symbol of St. Anthony the Hermit, or of the Devil,[45] or of other subjects, but it can also be just a pig. To decide which it represents needs a careful study of the context into which it is set.

The animals seen most often with bowed instruments vary according to their period. During the twelfth and thirteenth centuries the rebec and fiddle were most often played by a ram, as in Bristol Cathedral (plate 32), or a goat, as in the BL MS Lansdowne 420, fo. 12^v (plate 36). The winged ram with a long tail in Canterbury Cathedral is widely believed to represent a devil (plate 13). These minstrels were joined by the sheep, and c.1300 the predominant animal fiddler became the cat, which can be seen in the BL MS Harley 6563, fo. 40, and in carvings at Hereford (plate 64), Wells (plate 88), Northleach, Fawsley (plate 141), and Beverley Minster (plate 143), among other sources. The last three date from the sixteenth century, and by 1587 there was an inn called the 'Catte and Fidle' at Old Chaunge.[46] It was at about this time that there appeared the famous nursery rhyme:

> Hey diddle diddle, the cat and the fiddle,
> The cow jumped over the moon,
> The little dog laughed to see such sport
> And the dish ran away with the spoon.[47]

John Skelton may have been referring to it in his 'Garlande of Laurell' of 1523

> And what blunderar is yonder
> that playth didil diddil?
> He fyndith fals mesuris out of
> his fonde fiddill.[48]

On the other hand, a more likely reference to it may be found in Thomas Preston's *A lamentable tragedy mixed ful of pleasant mirth, conteyning the life of Cambises, King of Percia*, printed in 1569:

> They be at hand sir with stick and fidle
> They can play a new daunce called Hey didle didle.[49]

A final suggestion that the poem was probably new at this period is the unfortunate fact that in none of the known mediaeval representations of a cat and a fiddle is there also to be found a cow jumping over the moon, a laughing dog, or a dish running away with a spoon.[50]

CHAPTER X

Bowed Instruments in English Society

❧

BOWED INSTRUMENTS IN CHURCH, IN SACRED PROCESSIONS AND IN PREACHING

THE use of instruments in mediaeval churches has been the subject of much controversy, and doubtless will continue to be so for many years to come. Before considering it in detail, we should be aware of two basic and obvious facts. These are that in the normal course of events, conditions vary from country to country, and from one period to another. The history of church music has included many swings of the pendulum, from simplicity to complexity and back again, and the use of instruments has followed the same pattern.[1] It is therefore most unlikely that the customs regarding them should have remained exactly the same in England from the time of the Norman Conquest to that of the Reformation.

What is certain is that within the liturgy the only instrument to be used regularly throughout the Middle Ages was the organ, and it seems that on special occasions chimebells were also played.[2] The possibility of other instruments being used in church is, however, suggested by the Englishman Magister Lambertus (otherwise known as 'Pseudo-Aristotle'), who worked in Paris around the year 1270. After mentioning 'organa, vielle, cythara, cytole, psalterium et similia', he refers to the part played by music itself in church:

Utilitas autem ejus magna est et mirabilis et virtuosa, valdeque fores ecclesiae ausa est subintrare. Nulla enim scientia ausa est subintrare fores ecclesie, nisi ipsa tantummodo musica.[3]

Unfortunately Magister Lambertus did not make it clear whether the 'vielle', etc., were played during the actual liturgy or for non-liturgical occasions. With the latter, however, we are on firmer ground, as there are several references to fiddles and other instruments being played in church apart from the liturgy itself, particularly when the King or another member of the Royal Family was there on a visit. Richard Rastall has listed several such occasions, with different instruments involved, and a few of them are given here.

In May 1297 Edward I went to Chichester Cathedral and found Walter Lund, a local harper, playing his harp by the tomb of St. Richard of Chichester.[4] In the following month the King gave £4. 8*s*. 4*d*. to fourteen minstrels who, in his presence, played before the image of Our Lady in the crypt of Christ Church, Canterbury.[5] On 15 April 1331, a fiddler named John was among several minstrels who played in the same place in the presence of Queen Philippa, and John was given 2*s*. 0*d*. to share between them.[6] Thirty-eight years later, Hanekin Fythelar played there while the King was making his offering and was given 6*s*. 8*d*., and on the same day John Harpour received 3*s*. 4*d*. for harping in St. Augustine's Church, Canterbury.[7] On 1 April 1371(?), 13*s*. 4*d*. was paid to

minstrels making their minstrelsy before the image of the Blessed Mary in the crypt of Christ Church, Canterbury, and before the shrine of St. Augustine in St. Augustine's Church, Canterbury.[8]

Rastall also mentions various payments to musicians, including fiddlers, for making their minstrelsy 'before the Cross in the north chapel of St. Paul's, London'. One such occasion was when the Princess Eleanor was on her way to Holland in 1332 to become the Countess of Guelders. She stopped at St. Paul's Cathedral and made her offering at the Cross, and while she was there music was played by several fiddlers (the payments were to 'diuersis vidulatoribus').[9] This Cross has been described by G. H. Cook as the

Crux Borealis, the miraculous Rood near the north door of the Cathedral. It stood on a beam that spanned the north transept at the triforium level, and according to tradition was carved by Joseph of Arimathea and was discovered by King Lucius in A.D.140 . . . Liberal offerings were made at the Northern Rood, near which was an iron chest for the purpose.[10]

Certain illustrations may or may not throw light on the performance practice of mediaeval church music as far as bowed instruments are concerned, and for what they are worth they should be described here.

It has already been seen that David and his musicians often appear in the initials *B(eatus vir)*, *E(xultate Deo)*, and *C(antate Domino)* which start the Psalms 1, 81, and 149 of the Vulgate. Sometimes the initial C is occupied by a group of singers, and in a few cases they are accompanied by a player of a bowed instrument.

The first example can be seen in the Venice Psalter, fo. 115, an English manuscript of the thirteenth century (plate 45). Two men sing by a lectern showing the words 'Cantate dño canticū', and immediately behind them stands a man playing a rebec. The ground that they stand on is green and undulating (grass?), and the background contains nothing.

The other two examples date from the fourteenth century. In each case the initial C contains three singers in ecclesiastical vestments, standing in front of a lectern, while a fiddler plays just *outside* the initial. The Vaux Psalter, fo. 145[v] shows on the lectern a scroll (its writing is stylized and incomprehensible) which is being unrolled by the right hand of the foremost singer, his left hand being raised as if conducting. The singers are standing on a flat surface, and behind them are three pointed arches, between which the background is painted gold. Just outside the initial, but immediately behind the singers, can be seen a fiddler. He is small in proportion to the singers, and stands on a ledge projecting from the centre of the initial, in a position from which he can see the scroll on the lectern (plate 66).

The third example is from the Bodl. MS Liturg. 198, fo. 91ᵛ (plate 100). Here again there are three singers wearing vestments, and one of them is opening a large book which rests on the elaborate lectern. They are in the centre of the initial C, and in the doorway of a somewhat stylized building. Just outside the initial there is again a performing fiddler, but this time he faces outwards and not in the same direction as the singers. A man leans out from the building towards the fiddler, supporting himself on the battlements and the foliage of the border, and his hands almost touch the pegbox of the instrument.

Clearly there are similarities among these three cases. It could be said that they provide an indication of bowed instruments being played with singers in church music, yet in no case is the entire group to be seen inside a church in a liturgical context. While the first two examples suggest that the instrumentalist is involved in the same performance as the singers, this is not so obvious in the third case. What part is played by the man leaning out over the battlements? Is he trying to hear the music of the fiddler, or is he perhaps trying to persuade an ungodly minstrel to come into church, with or without his instrument, and to mend his ways?

These pictures are stylized in other respects than that of their settings. Only in the first instance are the words 'Cantate Domino' seen to be written on the manuscript in front of the singers. On the other book, and on the scroll, the artist has made no attempt to show the text, so it can be assumed that the illustrations do not represent an accepted way of performing the 149th Psalm. It could be that, as the singers and instrumentalists are always performing at the same time, the pictures just represent the symbolic answer, from different types of musicians, to the call to glorify God. On the other hand, two factors do suggest that these could be groups such as sometimes played together in church. The first is that the clerically-dressed singers are in small groups, such as would have performed sacred polyphony. The second is that each instrumentalist is using a long bow, such as would have been necessary for playing slowly-moving tenor parts. At this time very little written music descended lower than c, so such parts would have been within the range of certain fiddles. The rebec in the Venice Psalter, however, is unlikely to have descended so far, given the short sounding length of its strings, but it could have played one of the upper parts, provided its tone blended well with the voices (plate 45).

In this context a mention should be made of the statement by Bachmann that

It is interesting to note the comment by the Abbé Aimery de Peyrac, from Moissac (*c*.1300), that the Choral or cantus firmus lost none of its beauty if played from time to time on a bowed instrument.[11]

For this source Bachmann refers to the remark by Edmund Bowles that

In 1316, Abbot Aimery du Peyrac of Moissac observed that the charm of plainchant lost almost none of its sweetness when played on a vielle.[12]

This, however, is based on a misunderstanding of two adjacent sentences by André Pirro:

Transmise par certains instruments, d'ailleurs, la caresse du chant ne perdait presque rien de sa douceur.

> *Quidam rebecam arcuabant*
> *Quasi muliebrem vocem confingentes*

remarque Aimery du Peyrac qui fut abbé de Moissac de 1371 à 1407.[13]

The Abbot of Moissac did not actually say that the rebec was joining the voices in plainsong, or that a bowed instrument played the cantus firmus in polyphony, which is suggested in this misunderstanding. The date 1316 appears in Pirro's sentence *after* those mentioned above, and has a quite different connection.[14]

Processions often gave the minstrels an opportunity to play their various instruments, and this is borne out by many continental pictures; it has been suggested, however, that they would probably have stopped playing when they entered the church.[15] Nevertheless it should be remembered, albeit hypothetically, that such an occasion as the feast of Corpus Christi (instituted by Pope Urban IV in 1264) was so important that it was one of those times when instruments might have been played in church.[16] Bowles has cited several cases of stringed instruments being used in Corpus Christi processions,[17] and of these certain continental examples include bowed instruments; his English examples do not, however, although he does refer to the harp and lute being played together in this context.[18]

The procession of the Ark of the Covenant in mediaeval art may be considered a parallel to that of Corpus Christi, as far as mediaeval instruments are concerned. Hence it is worth while to notice the Tickhill Psalter's illustration on fo. 64ᵛ, where the Ark is borne in procession to the accompaniment of a fiddle played by David, as well as a trumpet (plate 60).

One practical point should be mentioned here concerning the Corpus Christi procession today. It normally starts from the altar, passes out of the church (if this is possible), and eventually returns to the altar. However, if there is heavy rain it stays inside all the time. When this happened during the Middle Ages, any string minstrels would have had to play within the church, unless they were actually forbidden to do so.

Among the celebrations of the mediaeval gilds were processions which led to and away from a church. The Gild of St. Elene at Beverley (founded in 1378) had its own ceremonial which may well have included instrumentalists among the musicians:

An alderman and two stewards are chosen every year. At the year's end, the alderman and stewards, and the bretheren and sisteren of the gild, meet together, on the feast of St. Elene. And then a fair youth, the fairest they can find, is picked out, and is clad as a queen, like to St. Elene. And an old man goes before this youth, carrying a cross, and another old man carrying a shovel, in token of the finding of the Holy Cross. The sisteren of the gild follows after, two and two; and then the brethren, two and two; and then the two stewards, and after all follows the alderman. And so, all fairly clad, they go in procession, with much music, to the church of the Friars Minor of Beverley; and there, at the altar of St. Elene, solemn Mass is celebrated, and every one of the gild makes offering of one penny. The Mass ended, and all prayers said, they go home; and, after dinner, all the gild meet in a room within the hall of the gild; and there they eat bread and cheese, and drink as much ale as is good for them. Afterwards, they choose, by unanimous assent, out of the best men of the gild, an alderman and two stewards, for the next year; and to these must be handed over all the goods of the gild.[19]

It is an unpleasant but undeniable fact that during the Middle Ages, and later, there were abuses which detracted from the dignity of the Church. They can be represented here by an example from *The Cristen State of Matrimony* (1543) which makes an early reference to the kit:

Early in the mornyng the weddyng people begynne to excead in superfluous eatyng and dringkyng, whereof they spytte untyll the halfe sermon be done, and when they come to the preachynge they are halfe droncke, some all together. Therefore regard they neyther the prechyng nor prayer, but stond there only because of the custome. Such folkes also do come to the churche with all manner of pompe and pride, and gorgiousnes of rayment and jewels. They come *with a great noise of harpes, lutes, kyttes, basens, and drommes*, wherwyth they trouble the whole church, and hyndre them in matters pertayninge to God. And even as they come to the churche, *so go they from the churche agayne*, lyght, nice, in shameful pompe, and vaine wantonesse.[20]

Music as an aid to preaching had already been established by the seventh century, when St. Aldhelm stood on a bridge and sang to attract a crowd. Then he gave them a sermon.[21] At the end of the Middle Ages, certain performing preachers provoked a virulent poem, *The Image of Ipocrysy*, which was attributed to John Skelton, but has now been proved to date from after his death in 1529. The third part of the poem starts with the words

> Of prechers nowe adayes
> Be many Fariseyes ...

and later continues with

> Thus these sysmatickes
> And lowsy lunatickes,
> With spurres and prickes
> Call true men heretickes.
> They finger ther fidles
> And cry in quinibles
> Away these bibles,
> For they be but ridles![22]

RELIGIOUS DRAMA

Religious drama of the Middle Ages can be broadly divided into two basic types. On the one hand there was liturgical drama, which was an extended trope within the context of the liturgy; it was sung, in Latin, and was performed inside the church. On the other hand there were the miracle plays and mystery plays, which were mainly spoken and mainly in the vernacular, and while some took place inside, most of them were performed out of doors.

There is very little evidence for the use of instruments in liturgical drama. *The Play of Daniel* suggests it by the words

> Simul omnes gratulemur resonent et tympana;
> Cytharistae tangant cordas; musicorum organa
> resonent ad ejus praeconia

which have been translated as

> 'Joy!' we cry in all accordance; let the drums resound for him;
> Let the strings of harps be smitten; all the instruments in hand
> loudly proclaiming Darius king.[23]

In the *Presentatio Beatae Virginis Mariae in Templo* two 'pulsatores' were called for, without actual specification as to the nature of their instruments.[24] Neither of these dramas originated in England, the first being from Beauvais and the second from Avignon. Although it is not impossible that bowed instruments were occasionally used in such works in England, there seems to be no actual evidence that they ever were.

More information is available about miracle and mystery plays. Bowles has pointed out that in continental dramas Christ was accompanied by players of 'soft' instruments, and that in the Innsbruck *Himmelfahrt* play these were specifically bowed ones: 'Primo exiit Ihesus cum suis angelis, procedit cum vialatoribus'.[25] Many English sources are tantalizing. They give such directions as 'Tunc cantant angeli' without saying what the angels are to sing, or to whether they are to be accompanied. Many plays had a 'mansion' representing Heaven, which contained musical angels, some of them singing and others playing instruments when they were needed.[26] A foretaste of sounds, even if not an actual rubric for them, appears in *The Coventry Pageant of the Shearmen and Taylors* (c.1500), where Herod says 'Trompettis, viallis and othur armone Schall bles the wakyng of my maieste'.[27]

We have already seen that the early sixteenth-century roof bosses in the north transept of Norwich Cathedral represent scenes from the lost Norwich Mystery Plays, and that some of these bosses contain musicians (p. 7). They include a lutenist playing and singing during the Resurrection of the Innocents, and a bagpiping shepherd approaching Bethlehem.[28] Other biblical incidents appearing in mediaeval art may not represent a particular play at a particular time, but they sometimes show signs of dramatic presentation. A fifteenth-century example can be seen in the stained glass of the south choir aisle in York Minster, where a minstrel holds, and possibly plays, a fiddle (plate 113). M. D. Anderson has described the way in which this picture may have been based on actual drama:

In a window of the south choir aisle of York Minster, Herod, Herodias and their company, with a musician in attendance, are visible from the knees up above a horizontal beam with a curtain hanging below it. In the lower foreground the execution of St. John the Baptist has been carried out and the head is being placed in the charger by a servant. As there are no plates or goblets on this horizontal bar to suggest Herod's table, it is tempting to conjecture that the glazier was remembering a play in which the feast took place on the upper stage and the decollation of the saint on the ground immediately in front of the curtains of the lower room through a gap in which the substitution of a dummy for the living actor could have been achieved with some verisimilitude.[29]

Bearing this in mind, it is easy to imagine a dramatic setting as the basis for a series of pictures from the Queen Mary Psalter, showing scenes from the life of St. Catherine, which is known to have been dramatized during the Middle Ages.[30] On fo. 282 she is seen in prison being visited by the Empress, and behind her are two angels, one playing a fiddle and the other a gittern (citole) (plate 68). The prison wall is so low as to be, in a practical sense, quite useless, as the saint could easily climb over it. In a dramatic presentation, however, this adaptation of reality would be necessary in order to show the audience the double situation of St. Catherine in prison and the Empress approaching the building from outside.

SECULAR DRAMA

Although mystery and miracle plays were not performed within a liturgical frame-work, they were still basically on religious subjects. The completely secular entertainments, which increased in number towards the end of the Middle Ages, included mummings, disguisings, interludes, fixed plays, and court spectacles, and music was a common ingredient to them all. Several of the surviving plays contain references to bowed instruments, either within the text or as a definite instruction for musicians. In John Rastell's interlude *The Four Elements* (*c*.1517), Humanity says

> This dance would do mich better yet
> If we had a kit or taberet.[31]

In the somewhat later *Gammer Gurton's Nedle* (possibly written during the reign of Edward VI and therefore strictly speaking beyond the period covered by this book), Diccon, speaking alone at the end of Act II, says to the musicians

> In the meane time felowes, pype upp your fiddles,
> I saie take them
> And let your freyndes here such mirth as ye
> can make them.[32]

John Redford's *Wyt and Science* (*c*.1539) includes the use of viols, which may or may not have played for the 'galyard' danced by Wyt and Honest Recreacion. Later on the direction says 'Here the[y] cum in with vyols', and soon afterwards Woorshyppe says

> Then let us not stay here muet and mum,
> But tast we thes instrumentes tyll she cum.

Fame, Favor, Ryches, and Woorshyppe then sing the song 'Excedynge Mesure', at the same time playing upon their instruments.[33] They return again at the end of the play: 'Heere cumth in fowre wyth violes and syng "Remembre me", and at the last quere all make cur[t]sye, and so goe forth syngyng'.[34]

Such fixed plays could be performed in many different places, given good actors and the right circumstances. In Court, however, dramatic performances were often designed for special occasions, and the actors were members of the nobility accompanied by court musicians. Some of the entertainments which took place during the reign of Henry VIII were described by Richard Gibson in the *Revels Accounts*, and they give a good idea of the instruments which were used on such occasions.

On 6 January 1513, Gibson himself had to produce a pageant called the 'Ryche Mount'. This was an elaborate mountain, decorated with symbolic plants such as broom for Plantagenet, which was drawn into the hall by two 'myghty woordwossys or wyld men'. Six lords stood at the foot, and when a door opened in the side of the Mount, six ladies came out and a dance ensued. Six minstrels stood on this pageant, and four others played for the dance. The instruments mentioned are 'rebecks' and 'tambourines', but at this period the latter word, like the French *tambourin* and the English *tabouret*, often meant the pipe-and-tabor combination, which was much associated with dancing. On Christmas Day, 1514, 'rebecks', 'taborets', and 'drumbyllslads' (drummers) played for a mumming in which the King himself took part.[35]

A year later, viols were mentioned for the first time in the *Revels Accounts*. On 6 January 1515, the Court at Greenwich was 'full of strangers, French, Spanish, German', and by Sir Harry Gyllforth's instructions Gibson prepared a pageant

kawlld the wryttyng there over, the Pavyllyon un the Plas Parlos. there was a pavilion on a 'pas' or stage, of crimson and blue damask, with a gold crown and a bush of roses on the top, and hung with blue tartron. At the 4 corners, 4 brickwork towers, a lord in each dressed in purple satin broidered with gold wreaths and letters H and K. On the pageant, 6 minstrels with strange sounds, as sag[ebutts], shawms, viols, &c., dressed in blue and white damask. At the foot, 2 armed knights with swords in their hands, 'maintaining the place', dressed in crimson satin. Also gentlemen of the Chapel, viz., Mr Kornyshe, Mr Krane, Mr Harry of the Chapel, with the children. These gentlemen first declared the intent of the pageant by process of speech; then entered 3 armed knights in yellow satin, 'with noise of drombyllslads, in fierce manner, making a goodly tourney; then 6 woodwos entered suddenly and parted the tourney; after which departure the 3 knights un rescuing the four knights and their ladies', who were dressed in crimson and plunket satin. They descended and danced before the presence of the King's grace and the Queen's grace, and after returned to the said pageant, the which with press was spoiled.[36]

MUSIC OF PUBLIC CELEBRATIONS AND
EVERYDAY LIFE

Up to this point we have considered the use of bowed instruments in the liturgy, in religious works apart from the liturgy, in set plays whether sacred or secular, and in specially prepared dramas of the Court. The other occasions on which these instruments took part are so numerous and varied, yet most of them so interconnected, that they cannot easily be separated for the purpose of study. Many of them are basically dramatic in character, but only happened once, being living drama as opposed to historical or fictional representations.

Such, for instance, are the celebrations which took place for a royal wedding, or when a royal personage entered a town, or returned to the country after a long absence abroad. Scenes would be acted on pageant stages, while market crosses and water conduits would also be used as focal points. Often the action would contain a symbolism pertinent to the event (this happened particularly when a joust was the centre-piece of a *pas d'armes*),[37] and besides the main drama, there might be groups of angels in appropriate places. The reconciliation of Richard II to the City of London in 1392 was such an event. One of the musical attractions was described by Richard Maydiston:

The conduit distils red wine instead of the usual water and there is ample for a thousand people to drink. A heavenly host is stationed on the top of it who sing songs with pleasing skill. Gold coins are scattered on all sides by maidens which flutter down like leaves or flowers.

One of the pageant stages carried a representation of the Trinity, surrounded by angelic singers and instrumentalists.[38]

The chronicler Froissart has given a regrettably short summary of the events which took place to celebrate the wedding of Edward III to Phillipa of Hainault in 1329:

And Sir John of Hainault, Lord Beaumont, her uncle, did conduct her to the city of London, where there was made a great feast, and many nobles of England, and the queen was crowned. And there was also great jousts, tourneys, dancing, caroling, and great feasts every day; the which endured the space of iii weeks.[39]

Such occasions might involve civic processions, when trumpets and shawms provided music which could be heard afar off. If many gilds were taking part in a procession, each one might have its own minstrels, in all giving a good variety of sound to the spectators as they went past, as can still be found today in such traditional events as the Munich Beer Festival, or in military parades containing many different regimental bands.

During Anne Boleyn's Coronation procession in 1533 she passed a 'mervelous connyng pagyaunt' of Mount Parnassus. 'On the mountayne satt apolo, att his ffeete satt Calliope, and on every syde of the mountayne sate iiij muses playng on seuerall swete Instruments' (BL MS Harley 41, fo, 5ᵛ). Fortunately a design has survived for this very subject, believed to be by Holbein, although it does not coincide with the description in every detail. It shows a triumphal arch with mountains on the summit, and amidst them Apollo sits enthroned beneath an eagle. In his left hand he holds a harp, while with his right he conducts the Muses; four of them are singing, and the others play a fiddle, lute, pipe-and-tabor, triangle, and crumhorn, this last being, like Apollo himself, a sign that the Renaissance had finally arrived in England (plate 149).

Mediaeval pictures of David being greeted after his victory over Goliath give some idea also of the use of bowed instruments in processions. In the Cambridge University Library MS Dd. viii. fo. 110, David is shown holding up the giant's head on a sword, while minstrels welcome him with a rebec and a pipe (plate 135).[40] In the Tickhill Psalter, fo. 17, a more varied combination is presented. David is preceded by two trumpeters, a fiddler, and a gittern (citole)-player, while behind him there are two more trumpeters and two rebec-players (plate 61).

The fifteenth-century poem *Sir Gawain and the Carl of Carlisle* also describes a procession which includes both loud and soft instruments:

> Trompettis mette hem at þe gate,
> Clarions of siluer redy þerate,
>   Sertayne wythoutyn lette;
> Harpe, fedylle, and sawtry,
> Lute, geteron and menstracy
>   Into þe halle hem fett.[41]

At a subsequent feast

> ... minstrells sate in windowes faire
> And playd on their instruments cleere.[42]

Other literary descriptions, however, are more explicit about instruments being played during the actual feasts:

> In þe castel þe steward sat atte mete,
> & mani lording was bi him sete.
> Þer were trompours and tabourers,
> Harpours fele, & crouders:
> Miche melody þai maked all,
> & Orfeo sat stille in þe halle
> & herkneth; when þai ben al stille
> He toke his harp & tempred schille.
>
> *Sir Orfeo* (c.1330)[43]

> Syr Kadore lette make a feste,
> That was fayr and honeste,
>   Wyth hys lorde þe kinge,
> Ther was myche menstralse,
> Trommpus, tabours, and sawtre,
>   Both harpe and fydylleyng.
>
> *Emaré* (c.1400)[44]

Turning to visual sources, we find fewer minstrels in pictures of feasts. Among sources in England the greatest number known to the author is five, which appears on the Braunche brass in St. Margaret's Church, King's Lynn (plate 101). This brass was made in Flanders to commemorate Robert Braunche (d. 1364) who was the Mayor of King's Lynn, and his two successive wives Letice and Margaret. Among the many engravings on it can be seen a peacock feast, an event which took place on special occasions during the Middle Ages.[45] Twelve people, including a king and queen, are sitting at a long table covered with food. On the right side a woman carries in a dish and presents it to a man at the end of the table; she is followed by a shawm-player and two trumpeters. On the left more food is carried in, preceded to the table by musicians playing a fiddle and a mandora (gittern). It could be that these two groups would have approached the table in turn, with one set of musicians playing first, and then the other, thus giving a contrast between 'loud' and 'soft' music. The artist, however, would have had to show them all playing together. On the other hand it could also be that both groups did enter at once, with all the musicians playing simultaneously for most if not all of the time. Judging from many poetic accounts, it does seem that very varied groups played together at feasts.

Another case of food being carried in to the accompaniment of music occurs in the Queen Mary Psalter, ff. 184ᵛ–185, where a fiddler walks in front of the dish-bearers (plate 67). On fo. 203 of the same manuscript, two men in the lower border play a fiddle and gittern (citole), apparently connected to a feast on fo. 202ᵛ.

The Trinity College Apocalypse, fo. 22, shows a feast where a harper sits in front of a table and a fiddler at the end of it (plate 41). We have already seen that these two instruments appear together a great deal in mediaeval art (p. 69), and experience shows that their sounds blend together very well. Both are known to have been used regularly in the performance of epic poems and songs, and Tinctoris said that 'over the greater part of the world the viola with a bow is used . . . in the recitation of epics'.[46]

The minstrels of the Trinity College Apocalypse (plate 41), from their context of a sacred banquet, can certainly be classified among Thomas of Chobham's good minstrels who 'cantant in instrumentis suis gesta principum et alia talia utilia ut faciant solatia hominibus'.[47] In a fifteenth-century copy of the *Speculum Humanae Salvationis* the instruments played at a feast are a rebec (only partly visible) and an unidentifiable pipe (plate 133).

In view of the paucity of English pictures where more than three minstrels are performing together at a feast, a mention should be made of one in a French *Bible Moralisée*, BL MS Harl. 1527, fo. 36ᵛ. This dates from the mid-thirteenth century when connections between England and France were strong. In the illustration four minstrels sit in front of a table, playing a fiddle, symphony, harp, and psaltery, and the psaltery-player plucks his strings with a plectrum in his left hand, while conducting with his right hand. This is a good instrumental combination, and one which could make quite a penetrating sound, although not so forceful as that of trumpets and shawms. (It is illustrated in Remnant, *Musical Instruments*, plate 180.)

We have seen that literature describes many minstrels at feasts, but pictures indicate fewer. Let us now consider the Feast of Westminster, held on Whit Sunday 1306. It took place in Westminster Hall (which had been newly decorated with wall-paintings for the coronation of Edward I in 1274), and was the occasion on which Edward I knighted his son, who was soon to become Edward II. Accounts survive of payments to the minstrels who were present, and a great number they were,[48] being not only those attached to the Royal Household, but also minstrels of other noblemen who had made the journey to London for the occasion. They received varying amounts of money, some having a specific fee while others were included in a lump sum to be allocated as thought fit. The players of bowed instruments are listed as variants of the following.

Vilour (French), Vidulator (Latin)

These could have been players of either the fiddle or the mediaeval viol, but the former instrument is more likely as the latter was already going out of fashion. It is possible, however, that both types of instrument were used.

Crouder, Crouther

There can be no doubt that these were players of the crowd. The instrument was then used little or not at all in France and southern Europe, so the scribes at Westminster, not knowing what to call it in French, referred to it by the names current in England.

Gigour

The musicians described thus were almost certainly rebec-players, as the word *gigue* seems to have applied to the rebec family at that time (pp. 30–1), and there are no other words in the accounts which could refer separately to this instrument.

The list which follows gives the names of the minstrels as recorded in the accounts; those in Latin are therefore in the dative case.

Vilours and Vidulatores
[Guillot] de Roos vilour   (identical with Guillot le Vilour)
Robert le Vilour
Vidulatori Domine de Wake
Gilloto Vidulatori Comitis Arundellie
Ricardo vidulatori Comitis Lancastrie
Johanni le vilour domini J. Renaud
Andree vidulatori de Hor'
Phelippe de Coumbray
Le Roy Druet
Ernolet
Richard Rounlo
Thomasin vilour Mons. Le Prince
Thomelin de Thounleie
Martinet le Vilour qui est oue Le Conte de Warewike

Crouders
Johann Le Croudere
Tegwaret Croudere
Nagary le Crouder Principis
Sagard Crouther
Dauid le Crouther
Johanni le Crouther de Salopia
Thome le Croudere
Audoeno le Crouther

Gigours
Henri le Gigour
Corraud son compaignon
Le tierz Gigour[49]

Le Roy Druet was a 'King of the Minstrels' and is referred to elsewhere as a 'vidulator' in the service of the Earl of Gloucester.[50] Phelippe de Coumbray was a 'vidulator' to the King of France, brother of Edward I's Queen Margaret, and he came to England especially for the feast (p. 83). Payment was also made to a certain Merlin, who may or may not have been the same Merlin who appears in later accounts as a fiddler. (There were various other Merlins in royal service around this time.)[51]

The question arises as to how and when these minstrels performed. Unfortunately there is very little description of what took place during the feast, and no reference to minstrels actually playing. However, Nicholas Trevet in his *Annales* said that

On the same day, after the King, surrounded by the new knights, had taken his seat at table, a great concourse of minstrels ('menestrellorum multitudo') entered, carrying a drapery with manifold ornamentation, in order that they might invite and induce the new knights especially to vow some deed of arms before the device. The King himself vowed first . . .[52]

According to the *Flores Historiarum*

. . . two cygnets or swans, ornamented with golden nets or gilded pipings, were brought in in showy splendour before the king; an agreeable spectacle to those looking on. After he had surveyed it, the king vowed a vow to God in heaven and the cygnets (or swans) that he purposed to set out for Scotland, to avenge the injury done to Holy Church, the death of John Comyn and the broken faith of the Scots.[53]

It can be assumed that music was played while the banner was carried on and also for the appearance of the swans, but it is unlikely that all the minstrels played at once. Groups who had had time to practise together would probably have taken it in turns to play at different points in the proceedings. As to the music during the feasting, some idea can be gained from the very large size of Westminster Hall. Not only the King's table would have been laid out, but also many others. The great number of guests would have made some considerable noise, so it is possible that small groups of minstrels entertained different tables, perhaps even moving around from one table to another. Only when trumpets played fanfares might there have been something approaching silence, and fanfares were reserved for special moments. Pictures of feasts at this period generally show only the King's table, so that what went on in the rest of a crowded hall is open to conjecture. Singing and dancing would doubtless have played their part afterwards, if not actually during the feast itself.

Minstrels attached to noble households had other musical duties to perform than playing for dancing, singing, and entertainments at feasts. The Earl of Northumberland's Household Book begun in 1512 describes some of the activities of a group consisting of a rebec, lute, and tabret (probably a pipe-and-tabor):

ITEM My Lorde usith and accustomyth to gyf yerly when his Lordschipp is at home to his Mynstraills that be daly in his Houshold as his Tabret Lute ande Rebek upon New-Yeres-Day in the mornynge when they doo play at my Lordis Chambre doure for his Lordschipe and my Lady xxs. Viz. xiijs. iiijd. for my Lorde and vjs. viiijd. for my Lady if sche be at my Lords fyndynge and not at hir owen And for playing at my Lordis sone and heir Chaumbre doure the Lord Percy ijs. And for playinge at the Chaumbre doures of my Lords Yonger Sonnes my Yonge Maisters after viijd. the pece for every of them—   [xxiijs. iiijd.][54]

Dancing and singing were ingredients of society at all levels. The author of *Sir Beues of Hamtoun* (*c*.1300) tells us that Josian could play 'staumpes' on a 'fiþele'. These would have been *estampies*, which were danced by only two or three people, and may be represented by the BL MS Egerton 1151, fo. 47, where the instruments concerned are a fiddle and a gittern (citole) (plate 44). The same combination of instruments occurs in the Queen Mary Psalter, fo. 174 for a different type of dance performed by two men and two women in the border of fo. 173^v. In the BL MS Cott. Domitian A. ii, fo. 8, a single woman dances while two grotesque men play a fiddle and a pipe and tabor (plate 82).

In the metrical life of *St. Thomas* (1285–95), dancing and singing are included among the chief celebrations after a wedding:

> At þis bruydale was plei i-nouȝh: song and gret hoppingue,
> Tabours and fiþele and symphanye: stiues and harpingue . . .[55]

while in *Launfal* (*c*.1400) more attention is given to the actual dancing itself:

> The quene yede to the formeste ende,
> Betwene Launfal and Gauweyn the hende,
>   Ande after her ladyes bryght,
> To daunce they wente alle yn same,
> To se hem play hyt was fayr game,
>   A lady and a knyght.
> They hadde menstrales of moch honours,
> Fydelers, sytolyrs, and trompours,
>   And elles hyt were unryght;
> Ther they playde, for sothe to say,
> After mete the somerys day,
>   All what hyt was neygh nyght.[56]

In the fifteenth-century *Squyr of Lowe Degre* the chief reference to music comes with the return of the squire who was thought to be dead. Although the word 'songe' is mentioned, there is no specific allusion to dancing, but it can reasonably be assumed that this took place, as the revels went on all night:

> There was myrth and melody,
> With harpe, getron and sautry,
> With rote, ribible, and clokarde,
> With pypes, organs, and bumbarde,
> With other mynstrelles them amonge,
> With sytolphe and with sautry songe,
> With fydle, recorde, and dowcemere,
> With trompette, and with claryon clere,
> With dulcet pipes of many cordes;
> In chambre revelyng all the lordes
> Unto morne that it was daye.[57]

It has already been seen that mediaeval fun and games often involved dressing up, whether as angels, animals, grotesques, or other beings, and that this could happen equally on a village green or in a palace. The descriptions which follow here are of pictures which are or may be based on such real life entertainments.

The B(eatus vir) initial of the twelfth-century Shaftesbury Psalter shows a familiar instrumental duet, but here it is accompanied by percussion (plate 15). On the left of the picture a bearded man plays a one-stringed rebec, while the man in the centre tunes a harp. To the right is a great bear with a tabor suspended round his neck; this he plays with his fingers, from which small bells are jingling, and there may also be bells round his ankles, similar to those which have survived in Morris dancing to this day. Without doubt this character is a man dressed up; not only does the costume look man-made, but the player's knees bend forward. If he were a real bear, the hind legs should bend backwards at the main joints.

Also dating from the Romanesque era is the south doorway at Barfrestone Church, where musicians occupy adjacent roundels (plate 27). In one of them a bear plays a harp, while an acrobat bends over backwards. The central figure of the lower roundel is a man seated and playing a mediaeval viol (p. 57), with a dog playing a pipe on the right and a hare with panpipes on the left. The contents of these roundels would appear to be connected, and the position of these animals' legs suggest that they too are humans dressed up. The rebec-player to the left of these roundels does seem to be an ordinary minstrel in everyday clothes.

Animal musicians are again involved in the fourteenth-century Bodl. MS Douce 131, fo. 20 (plate 91). Here two men are having their own joust on foot with swords, in the manner known as 'barriers'.[58] Behind the left-hand figure a sheep plays a fiddle, while on the right a dog plays a shawm. Although this could possibly be based on a game that the painter had seen, the musicians are not obviously human beings in animal clothing, and the presence of a cat chasing a mouse between the jousters seems to indicate that here the artist was just having a bit of fun.

Of a somewhat different nature is a picture from the Alfonso Psalter, fo. 17^v, dating from the thirteenth century (plate 48). A man in tattered clothes plays a fiddle, and beside him are two apes, one holding bagpipes (but not actually blowing them), while the other is either hitting a gong or juggling. Apes can certainly be taught to do a great deal, and what these two are doing is not beyond the bounds of possibility. It could be that the ape with the gong provides a rhythmic accompaniment to the fiddle, while the other one dances around with the bagpipes. This would provide a good sight, whether or not the bagpiper did try to blow its instrument, and if it did, any result would be good entertainment for the spectator.

There is a good carving of village revels round a window in the church at Lawford in Essex. Canon Galpin has described it as follows:

Lawford has something to offer us of the greatest interest and in absolute perfection: nothing less than an English merry-making of the middle of the fourteenth century. It is sculptured in the arch mould of the easternmost window on the north side of the chancel and owing to its elevation has escaped uninjured. It reveals the dancers and tumblers interwoven hand with foot and forming a grotesque rollicking chain over the arch: well up on the right is the piper with his tabor, which, as his hand is otherwise engaged, is tucked lightly under his right arm— a quite unusual position for this small drum. On the other side is the rebec-player with his little bow hard at work, whilst just above him stands the Lord of Misrule with a demure Maid Marian on the opposite splay of the arch. As there appear to be no bells on the dancers' legs we can hardly call it a Morris dance: in fact the subject is a little too early for that popular pastime in England. The subject is, we believe, unique among the extant examples of English ecclesiastical art.[59]

However, the object which Galpin identified as the tabor is in fact the foot of the man above the piper in the window carving, where arms and legs are intertwined in a curious manner.

The mediaeval tavern provided not only drink and company, but also plenty of music. According to literature, this music was often played on the rebec, if that really was the instrument meant by the word *ribible* and its variants. It certainly fits into this context more suitably than the fiddle. In *Piers Plowman*, Gluttony, with good resolutions, is on his way to church, but is hailed by Betene the Brewestere and persuaded to enter the tavern where he finds, among others, 'a rybibour and a ratoner, a rakeare and hus knaue' (C text).[60] Chaucer tells us that Perkyn Revelour, an apprentice in the 'craft of vitailliers', 'loved bet the taverne than the shoppe ... Al konne he pleye on gyterne or ribible' (*The Cook's Tale*).[61] In Lydgate's *Pilgrimage of the Life of Man* Miss Idleness says

> I teche hem ek, (lyk ther ententys)
> To pleye on sondry Instrumentys,
> On Harpe, lut, & on gyterne,
> And to revelle at taverne,
> Wyth al merthe & mellodye,
> On rebube and on symphonye ...[62]

However, in the same author's *Reson and Sensuallyte*, a description of instruments in the Garden of Deduit includes

> Harpys, fythels, and eke rotys,
> Wel accordyng with her notys,
> Lutys, Rubibis, and geterns,
> More for estatys than taverns.[63]

This seems to imply that, while 'lutys, rubibis and geterns' were often used in taverns, these particular ones were too good for such treatment.

CHAPTER XI

The Use of Bowed Instruments in Music

❧❧❧

FROM the visual arts, from literary sources and from expense accounts, a picture has emerged of the different types of bowed instruments used in mediaeval and early Renaissance England, and of their use in society at that time. Now we must consider the actual *raison d'être* of these instruments, namely their part in the making of music. This investigation has a dual purpose. Not only does it attempt to show what could have been done on such instruments and in certain types of music, but it also hopes to contribute to the performance of mediaeval music today. It does not, however, attempt to fathom the nature of the improvisation which would have been a normal part of the minstrel's trade, apart from noting a few basic principles.

Just as mediaeval instruments were not standardized, neither was it customary before the sixteenth century to compose for certain instruments to the exclusion of others, except in such cases as keyboard instruments, lutes, and trumpets.[1] A rare example for a bowed instrument seems to occur in the thirteenth-century motet 'In seculum viellatoris', where the tenor part is set to the music for the words 'In seculum' from the plainsong Easter Gradual 'Haec dies'.[2] There are several hypotheses as to the meaning of the title. It could have been that the actual 'In seculum' part in the tenor was to be performed by a player of a mediaeval viol or fiddle, or even that the piece itself was composed by a musically literate *viellator*. As it has no words, there is good reason to suppose that the whole motet was written for instruments. However, it is not of English, but of French origin, and no parallel compositions survive from England at that period. The general lack of 'orchestration' at this time does emphasize the need for very careful experimentation with regard to the capabilities of each instrument, and to the combinations of sound which led eventually to the Tudor 'broken consort'.

Before considering the music itself, we should be aware of three main points which govern any decision concerning the choice of bowed instruments. These points would have been obvious to minstrels in the Middle Ages, but, having lain dormant for several hundred years, they still need to be fully absorbed by the 'early music' specialists of today.

1. The instrument chosen must be of a basic type which existed during the period when the selected music was being performed, and not one which was invented many

years after that music was forgotten. Thus the rebec and crowd (of appropriate types) can be used in suitable music of the whole period covered by this book, the mediaeval viol from the early twelfth century to the early fourteenth, the large fiddle from the early thirteenth to the mid-sixteenth, the Renaissance viol from the second decade of the sixteenth century, and the violin from the fourth decade. The trumpet marine can perhaps be used in music of the fifteenth and sixteenth centuries, but not as a representative of the more usual bowed instruments of that time. Admittedly the instruments did alter within these periods, and the average musician of today cannot afford to have, for instance, a choice of four or five rebecs according to the age of the music to be performed. In this respect a certain amount of compromise may be accepted. What cannot be tolerated, however, is the use of modern covered strings on newly constructed 'mediaeval' instruments, if these make any pretence to authenticity. Such strings were used on fiddles in the 1960s, when that type of instrument was reappearing, but there is absolutely no excuse for them to be fitted to those made in the 1980s, when so much research has been, and is still being done, into mediaeval music and its performance.

2. The shape of the bridge is of paramount importance. A piece of music which remains consistently in one mode can be played to advantage with one or more drones, and therefore needs an instrument with a flat bridge or its equivalent, so that all the strings can sound together. In this way the drones will normally be of the tonic and dominant notes, but if only one drone is needed, an instrument with a curved bridge and lateral *bordunus* can be used. When a piece of monophonic music changes its mode, or when a polyphonic piece in several parts is to be played by several instruments, then an instrument without built-in drones is essential. Ideally any professional fiddler of today should be equipped with two fiddles, one for music with permanent drones, and one on which each note can be played separately.

3. The choice of a bow is also a matter to be considered very carefully. It has already been seen that bows were interchangeable during the Middle Ages (p. 17), and any player of mediaeval instruments who has experimented with them will know that different bows are suitable for different pieces of music, even when played on the same instrument. Some pieces sound better with a taut bow, and others with a more relaxed one and even so the choice can still be affected by the acoustics in the place of performance. As a general rule, short and taut bows are suitable for fast and lively music where little slurring is needed, while longer bows are better for the sustained notes of tenor parts, and for music where a good many notes need to be slurred together. The many variations between these extremes will become known to the player through experimentation and experience.

THE USE OF BOWED INSTRUMENTS IN MONOPHONIC VOCAL MUSIC

Plainsong

The use of stringed instruments in plainsong is even more problematical than their use within a church building. Although it has been shown that they did sometimes play in churches (pp. 87–91), we do not know to what extent, if at all, they were actually used in plainsong. However, there is no reason why this should not have happened in certain circumstances, with appropriate music and suitable instruments. The following considerations, therefore, are entirely hypothetical, but they should be made.

Perhaps the most likely instance is during the singing of hymns in processions, whether inside or outside a church. We have seen that bowed and plucked instruments were sometimes used on such occasions, when the minstrels involved were playing melodies they knew well. Simple tunes like that of the hymn 'Pange lingua,'[3] which is not restricted to any particular season of the Church's year, are eminently suitable for instrumental doubling of the vocal line, by nature of their almost syllabic settings.

Within the Proper of the Mass, the most syllabic movement is the sequence, and as this only appears on the more important feasts of the Church, it is a probable candidate for instrumental doubling. Certain sequences could also take a drone, among them the 'Victimae Paschali laudes' of Easter.[4] The other parts of the Proper are in general so melismatic that instrumental doubling would be detrimental to the flow of the chant. The same can be said for many settings of the Ordinary of the Mass, such as that of No. IX, *Cum Jubilo*, which is sung on feasts of Our Lady.[5] Theoretically this could take a drone, but such accompaniment is perhaps more likely to have taken place on an organ. Paradoxically, the Mass settings which are more syllabic are less likely to have had instrumental support, because they were sung on less important occasions, when string minstrels would not normally, if ever, have been called for. Typical of these is Mass XVIII *Deus Genitor alme*, which is sung on ferial days in Advent and Lent.[6]

So far these hypotheses have been applied to churches and cathedrals where there was a competent choir and also an organ. There were, however, many small village churches which for a long time could not afford an organ, and which cannot have had such expert singing. Whether they more often used the organistrum or other instruments to help out the liturgy is a matter of great food for thought.

As the liturgical Office is part of the daily life of a monastery or a collegiate church, it is unlikely to have been decorated by the use of 'extra' instruments, except perhaps when the trope of a liturgical drama was interpolated. However, certain parts of it, such as the antiphon 'Salve Regina'[7] and the hymn 'Te Deum laudamus'[8] were often taken from their usual contexts and sung on special occasions. Such events would include the times when a king was making an offering at a cross or a statue, besides at appropriate points in mystery and miracle plays, and in those civic celebrations when minstrels dressed up as angels and played 'heavenly music' (p. 95).

Monophonic Song other than that of the Liturgy

The plainsong of the liturgy was not, of course, the only corpus of sacred monophonic song to survive from the Middle Ages. There were also many songs which were entirely sacred in character but quite unconnected to the liturgy. This was because the

Church played a far greater part in the lives of ordinary people than it does today, so it was quite natural for those people to sing songs of a religious nature as well as secular ones, whether they were ploughing a field or having a break from study in Oxford or Cambridge.

It is unfortunate that the English repertoire of mediaeval solo song is so small compared to that of the Continent, and particularly to that of France. From the period of the Troubadours very little has survived to show what it was like. We know that certain Troubadours visited the Courts in England of the French-born Henry II and his wife Eleanor of Aquitaine,[9] but their art did not take root here on any noticeable scale; nor did the desire for posterity which is apparent from their names being so often included in their songs. The English songs of St. Godric (c.1069–1170) have survived, not so much on account of their musical value, but because of their place in the life of a very holy man whose deeds were carefully recorded by his contemporaries.[10] They certainly cannot be regarded as typical of English 'secular' songs, most of which were probably not written down at all, but were either handed down orally from one musician to another, or else improvised on the spur of the moment and then forgotten. It could be that some of the songs which appear in English thirteenth-century manuscripts are in fact rare survivals from an earlier age. It is certain that the following remarks on instrumental participation apply just as well in practice to the Troubadour songs as to the English ones of a century later, so they can be presumed to apply equally well to the unknown songs of Romanesque England.

We have already seen Johannes de Grocheo's remark (c.1300) that the 'viella' could play 'every cantus and cantilena and every musical form'. Just which instrument he meant (although it is presumed to be the fiddle) is hardly relevant to the present point at issue—that of performing songs on bowed instruments—as the basic methods would have been similar on the rebec, mediaeval viol, and fiddle, bearing in mind the above-mentioned needs concerning the bridge and the bow. The following, therefore, are some of the most usual ways in which a bowed instrument could take part in a song.

1. The Instrument alone

First of all, the song could be played as a straight instrumental solo, with no accompaniment. A work such as 'Ja nuns hons pris' by Richard Coeur-de-Lion (hardly an 'English' song, but included here as its composer was King of England) could have been played on a rebec, mediaeval viol, or primitive fiddle in England during the twelfth century, or on a more advanced fiddle if played in certain parts of the Continent at that time.[11] As the piece cannot take a regular drone, the instrument would have had to be of a type where the strings could be sounded separately.

Any ornamentation would have been at the discretion of the performer. An example of different settings of one piece can be seen in two of the several surviving versions of 'Angelus ad Virginem'. Figure 2a shows a very simple setting, taken from a manuscript of tropes and proses,[12] while figure 2b gives a much more elaborate

(a)

An - ge - lus ad vir - gi - nem sub - in - trans in con - cla - ve,

Cambridge University Library, Add. MS 710, fo. 127
(transcription from Dobson and Harrison, *Medieval English Songs*, p. 261)

and a thirteenth-century English translation

(b)

Ga - bri-el, fram he-ven - king sent to the mai-de swee - te,

London, BL MS Arundel 248, fo. 154
(transcription from Dobson and Harrison, op. cit., p. 263)

Figure 2. *Contrasted settings of 'Angelus ad Virginem'*

version.[13] The differences between the two versions are seen in the addition, in figure 2b, of repeated notes, passing notes, and auxiliary notes. These are typical ornaments of the thirteenth and fourteenth centuries, and could be used to decorate any song if the performer thought fit. Such a song as 'Bryd one brere' contains such devices already,[14] but can be ornamented further to good effect.

Many pieces can take drones as we have already seen, a prominent example being the thirteenth-century 'Worldes blis'.[15] This is suitable for an instrument where the strings are on the same plane, or for one with a very slightly curved bridge and a very slack bow. Here, however, there is room for another hypothesis. Because it moves almost note by note, and, by reason of its gloomy nature, is slow, this *could* be played on one string alone if the performer changed positions, thereby gaining a drone from an adjacent string even if the bridge were curved and the other strings could not be touched by the bow. If, for instance, two strings were tuned to G and D, the whole melody could be played on the D, allowing the G to drone.

2. The Instrument as Accompaniment to the Voice

As accompaniment to a voice, the actual role of a bowed instrument depends on its pitch in relation to that of the singer, and this could vary from one case to another. The chief methods of accompanying songs are summarized here (they are more varied than those possible for plainsong), and any of them could have been used by the woman who sang with a fiddle and was rewarded with 2s. by Henry VII in 1495.

The most simple way is to double the voice at the unison, or at an octave above or below, depending on what is appropriate. Adding an extra part above is witnessed by Chaucer in *The Miller's Tale*, where Absalom sang a 'loud quynyble' to his 'smal rubible'. Parallel thirds and sixths, which often occur in mediaeval English compositions, are listed by Guilelmus Monachus in his *De Preceptis Artis Musicae* (*c*.1450) as being among the characteristics of English style,[16] so it would be natural for an English fiddler to include them also among his methods of accompaniment, where appropriate.

More complex is the use of heterophony, where the minstrel plays around the basic song melody with elaborate ornamentation. Such techniques as applied to mediaeval instruments have not survived in an unbroken tradition in England up to the present day, so we do not know how it was done here during the Middle Ages. We can certainly get some idea from the performance of folk singers in other parts of Europe, such as those of Yugoslavia who sing and accompany themselves heterophonically on the *gusle*. There is, however, no evidence that their actual style of doing it is similar to that of mediaeval England, and indeed, it may have been very different.

The use of the drone has already been seen in connection with instrumental solos, and its value is just as great when accompanying the voice. It can consist of one or more strings, either open or stopped by fingers, if these are not already occupied in doubling the voice or creating heterophony on other strings. The drone is often consistent, sounding throughout a piece and sometimes creating an almost hypnotic effect. It can, however, be very tiring to the performer, particularly if the drone is being fingered to suit the pitch of the singer's voice, in such long works as 'Samson dux fortissime'.[17] This survives in the same manuscript from Reading Abbey as 'Sumer is icumen in' (BL MS Harley 978), and is the type of piece which could have been performed at monastic feasts. It is known that monasteries sometimes employed minstrels, particularly harpists and fiddlers, whose co-operation would have been welcome in such a long work. If a harpist and a fiddler were both involved in 'Samson dux fortissime', they could alternate droning and playing with or around the voice, thereby lightening the task for each other. So far the fiddle has been mentioned in this context because there are so many pictures of it being played at feasts. However, as 'Samson dux fortissime' dates from the thirteenth century, other suitable bowed instruments for it at that time would have been the rebec, crowd, or mediaeval viol. Because of its position of being held down in the lap, this latter instrument would make the task of droning much less onerous than a fiddle, which in England was held up at the shoulder, or leaning against it and pointing down, or later held across the chest, none of which could be called restful postures. Bachmann has suggested that when an instrument points downwards it may be droning, as the activity of the left hand is limited by such a position.[18]

Although a great many pieces can take one drone throughout, there are others where it needs to be varied, for instance going from C to D and back again. Here a parallel can be drawn with the long notes in the tenor parts of much church music, but in such cases the compositional procedure is reversed, with the upper parts being composed to fit the pre-existing tenor, instead of a drone being inserted beneath the given melody.

The third chief function of a bowed instrument in the performance of monophonic song is to provide an introductory prologue, besides occasional interludes, and perhaps an epilogue. Bachmann has cited many Continental examples of these,[19] and it can be assumed that to some extent the same practices would have prevailed in England, although with possible differences in style, and also sometimes in instruments. There are, however, some English descriptions which support the use in this country of at least one of these methods. The prologue, for instance, is described with some form of the verb *to go*. In Dan Michel's *Ayenbite of Inwyt*, the first phrase of the 'Pater noster' is described as follows:

þet is ase ane inguoinge of þe viþele.[20]

John Lydgate, in *The Pilgrimage of the Life of Man* (dating from 1426, but based on the French version of 1335 by Guillaume de Deguileville) wrote

And thys menstral than a-noon
Maade hys ffythele for to gon,
And song wyth-al fful lustyly.[21]

The implication here is that once the minstrel had started to play, he then began to sing.

On the other hand, there is some evidence in continental sources that when the voice entered, the fiddle stopped. Alternatively the instrument could, after its 'inguoinge', continue with the voice in one of the ways mentioned above—doubling the melody at the unison or at a fixed interval apart, elaborating it by heterophony, or playing a simple drone. Songs surviving from before the fourteenth century have no specifically instrumental introduction, as their words start with the first note of the music, so any 'inguoinge' would have been improvised, perhaps based on the music that was to follow. Since that time, however, songs have survived which do have a textless section before the voice enters and between phrases, and presumably these would have been played on an instrument.[22] Bachmann has pointed out that in the great majority of such songs written before the fifteenth century these textless sections could in fact support a drone themselves,[23] so they may have been sung to the accompaniment of a drone fiddle. These observations, however, apply mainly to Germanic music, where most of such songs are to be found. Unfortunately there are very few surviving English monophonic songs of the fourteenth century, and in all of them the text starts at the beginning of the music. Nevertheless the textless introduction in the lower part of the polyphonic 'Thys Yool, thys Yool' of *c*.1400 indicates that as the practice was known in polyphony in the British Isles, so it may also have existed in the performance of English solo songs, whether or not a drone was suitable in each individual case.

THE USE OF BOWED INSTRUMENTS IN POLYPHONY

As with monophonic music, mediaeval polyphony can be grouped into sacred and secular compositions, and within the sacred category there are liturgical and unliturgical works. Again we do not know to what extent instruments were used in them, and this can only be open to conjecture.

Magister Lambertus, who has already been mentioned within the context of church music, lived during the period from which English ecclesiastical polyphony is best represented by the so-called *Worcester Fragments*, and many of these are suitable for instrumental participation in appropriate circumstances. Either each of their parts could be doubled by an instrument, or any selected part, or the tenor could be played on an instrument alone, below the other voices. If this doubling was not done by an organ (and not all churches had organs at that time), the most suitable instrument would have been a fiddle with separately-sounding strings, provided that its lower ones were sufficiently strong to sustain the important tenor line. An appropriate piece is the troped 'Kyrie' from Worcester '... Anges anima—Lux et gloria—Kyrie eleyson'.[24] Here the decorated 'Kyrie' of Mass I (now known as *Lux et origo*)[25] is given in a rhythmic pattern (not consistent throughout) in the tenor part, while the two upper parts have different texts. The very fact that the plainsong of the tenor is taken from a Mass sung at Easter suggests that, being composed for a very special occasion, it might have been allowed to use 'extra' instruments.

The *Worcester Fragments* contain music from the thirteenth century and the first part of the fourteenth. A later stage in compositional procedures is reached in the *Old Hall Manuscript*, which for many years was kept at St. Edmund's College, Ware, and is now in the British Library as Add. MS 57950. This contains music of the later fourteenth century and *c*.1400. Here there are settings of the Mass which include textless parts, not only for the tenor voice, but also in the upper parts. Such an example is the Gloria by Queldryck, a composer about whom very little is known.[26] In this piece there are two tenor parts without words, often moving note against note, and above them are two parts for counter-tenors. Normally one of these lines moves in fast notes with the text, while the other accompanies it with a slower-moving line, and they frequently change roles. Only rarely do they both sing the text together. Although the textless parts may have been intended for vocalizing, it is also possible that they may have been played on an organ, or perhaps occasionally on other instruments. It could be that sometimes the organ played the lower parts, with fiddles taking the alternating textless parts above, and perhaps even doubling the voices where the words are written out.

Consideration must also be given to the possibility of sacred music being played on instruments alone. This is unlikely to have happened as part of the liturgy itself (with the exception of the organ playing alternately with the choir, or during its absence), but it could have taken place before or after services on special occasions, and particularly in sacred drama. Among the suitable types of music are settings of antiphons, such as Leonel Power's 'Ave Regina coelorum' which sounds very well when played on a portative organ and fiddle together, the organist playing the two upper parts in the right hand while the fiddler plays the bottom one.[27]

Carols held an important place in the ceremonial sacred music of the fifteenth and early sixteenth centuries. Written in English, Latin, or a macaronic mixture of both, and sometimes of French, they included celebrations for Christmas and Easter, besides intercessions before events and thanksgiving after them. One of the most celebrated is 'Deo gracias Anglia', which was composed after Henry V's victory at Agincourt in 1415.[28] Judging by the ceremonial nature of some of the earlier carols, and by the secular nature of many of the later ones, there is every reason to suppose that instruments were often used in their performance, and sometimes even without voices.

We have already seen that singers sometimes accompanied themselves on bowed instruments in music that is basically monophonic, and it would therefore have been natural for them to do the same in polyphony. The extent to which it happened would have depended on the complexity of the music and the accomplishments of the musician. A very simple piece for such treatment is the thirteenth-century two-part hymn 'Edi beo thu', where the lower voice consists of only three notes which move up and down in accompaniment to the melody above.[29]

Completely secular polyphony is rare in English sources dating from before c.1400. No great collections of music have survived to show us that any English composer was as celebrated as Machaut, Landini, and Wolkenstein were in France, Italy, and Germany respectively. Even John Dunstable (c.1390–1453), the first really great composer of this country whose name has come down to us, seems to have spent most of his working life abroad, and he left very few secular compositions.

The earliest known completely secular English part-songs date from the thirteenth century. Although instruments could have taken part in all of them, they have nothing to suggest that any one line was written especially for an instrument, and in each case the words start right at the beginning of the music. Two contrasting pieces can serve as examples. One is the somewhat mournful 'Foweles in the frith',[30] in which the expressive quality of the fiddle is very appropriate as an accompaniment in the lower part to the voice above. Alternatively the voice could sing the lower line and the fiddle the upper part. The other song is the six-part 'Sumer is icumen in',[31] a very lively and joyful piece. Its four upper voices in canon over a two-part *pes* can be played on a variety of instruments, including bowed ones. There are unending ways of 'orchestrating' this song. Apart from its original setting for voices alone, it can be sung by voices and doubled by instruments, or just played on instruments alone. If there were not enough singers for the main canonic melody, it could, for instance, be sung by two voices and played on two instruments, while the *pes* could be performed on whatever was available. The crowd might even be a suitable instrument for this part, given an appropriate tuning. If a rendering of this work includes both a rebec and a fiddle, any potential jarring between their sounds should be offset by instruments of a different kind, such as a harp or psaltery or pipe.

From the late fourteenth century there survive several songs with a textless lower part which is well suited to a fiddle. Such an example is 'Ye have so longe keepyt O',[32] where a mention in the text of 'pypis' and the keeping of sheep suggests that a pipe or recorder would be suitable to double the voices, or even to take its place if so desired. The song 'Thys Yool, thys Yool', which may have been composed by a clerk called Edmund during the 1390s at Winchester, actually starts with a short instrumental introduction in the lower part at the beginning of the two main sections.[33] 'Wel wer hym that wyst' is a song in three parts, the words being in the treble and accompanied by two instrumental parts below.[34] Certainly both of these could be played on fiddles, but an alternative setting would be for one of the lines to be played by a harp or a lute. In this case the fiddle should take the lower part, as it contains the final harmony note. If this note were plucked instead of bowed, its sound would fade out quickly, leaving the voice and fiddle on an awkward fourth. The anonymous composer of this song seems to have known about the French manner of composing,[35] and indeed, Chaucer in *The Parliament of Fowls* precedes the roundel text 'Now welcome, somer' by saying 'The note, I trowe, imaked was in Fraunce'. It is thought that he may have intended it to be sung to music by Guillaume de Machaut, whom he may have met during his travels in France.[36]

Moving into the fifteenth century, we find an introduction for three instruments in Dunstable's 'O Rosa bella',[37] a song that was so popular that it has survived in more than a dozen manuscripts. However, none of them are English, and it is not known to what extent the piece was performed in England, as Dunstable spent most of his working life abroad. In fact, as far as the use of bowed instruments is concerned, the same conditions applied on the Continent as in England. By far the best choice is a fiddle, perhaps in company with a lute and portative organ or recorder, but a rebec of good tone could also have been used. (Consorts of rebecs in different sizes, such as those mentioned by Agricola and Gerle, had not yet become fashionable, and the Renaissance viol was only just beginning to emerge in Spain at about the time of Dunstable's death in 1453.)

If, as in 'O Rosa bella', there is a textless part before the voice comes in, there is good reason to believe that it is instrumental. If, however, a phrase *ends* with a long melisma, then there is room for speculation in certain cases, or at least room for choice. Such an example is the three-part 'Tappster, dryngker', dating from c.1450.[38] Its text starts simultaneously with the music, but three phrases end with a melisma after the last syllable has been written. If the singers did not continue right through the piece, but gave themselves an occasional break, the instruments would have played alone after the words 'God sende us good ale' and 'here is good ale y founde'. However, in the final phrase, ending 'lette the coppe goo rounde', it would be frustrating to both the singers and the audience (who would not be sitting in rows in a concert hall, but being entertained in *situ* at or after a feast, or perhaps sitting on tables drinking in a tavern) if the voices stopped short at this point, so they would probably have continued through to the end. Of course the song could be sung totally without instruments, or played without singers, and in this latter case a most suitable instrument to take part would be the rebec, judging from its average sound and its frequent performance in taverns (pp. 102–3). A full-scale tavern performance with voices and instruments might well have included the rhythmic banging of barrels and platters, and it could also have been a time when the bellows-and-tongs skit came to life (p. 71).

Part-songs of the early sixteenth century are well represented in the so-called *Henry VIII's Manuscript* (BL Add. MS 31922), dating from *c*.1510–20.[39] These songs, which include not only English but also French, Flemish, and Latin examples, would often have been sung without instruments. However, if bowed instruments among others were sometimes used to double the voices, then their selection would have depended to a great extent on the range of the music. By this period the bass voice had been established, and several of the songs in question go down to *D*. Hence these bottom parts could not have been played on the average fiddles or rebecs which were used in England at that time (unless all the instruments doubled the voices an octave higher, in which case some of the upper parts would have been too high). The only bowed instrument capable of playing to such a depth was the bass viol, and at the period when *Henry VIII's Manuscript* was written, the viol family was only just appearing in England for the first time (p. 73). It is likely, therefore, that at first these songs may have included one or more fiddles or rebecs to join the voices in the upper parts, with different instruments below. Gradually there would have been more use of viols, and by the end of the reign a performance on a whole consort of viols, or on a broken consort including one or more viols, would have been quite normal. Even the violin might occasionally have been used in the latest part of the period. Whether any of these bowed instruments were ever combined in such a performance would have depended on the sonorities of the instruments concerned, and on the nature of the pieces. Other instruments with which they could have played at this time include the harp, lute, dulcimer, harpsichord, positive organ, recorder, flute, crumhorn[40] (these last two newly established in England), and any other reed instrument which was not too loud to balance the rest of the ensemble.

THE USE OF BOWED INSTRUMENTS IN DANCES AND OTHER INSTRUMENTAL PIECES

Just as today the violin is one of the best instruments for playing traditional dance music, so were its ancestors among the best for playing the dances of the Middle Ages. The rebec must have taken part in the dance songs of the twelfth century, such as the French rondeau 'Tuit cil qui sunt enamourat',[41] which would almost certainly have been known to the minstrels of the Plantagenet kings. From the period after 1200, when the larger fiddle had become established, there survive in English sources a monophonic *estampie*[42] and three two-part examples of the *ductia*,[43] and they could all have been played on either of these two basic types of instrument. The estampie, which can be played on an instrument with built-in drones, actually divides into three parts for a short time, implying that its performance was not restricted to one instrument alone. The ductias would not normally have been played on a duet of rebec and fiddle (p. 40) unless two such instruments were found which happened to blend well together. They might, however, have been played by two rebecs or two fiddles, or by either in combination with a harp, psaltery, gittern (citole), shawm, or pipe. Reinforcement could have been provided by a horn, and rhythmic emphasis by a tabor or cymbals, or, at the end of the thirteenth century, by a timbrel, or by the clappers sometimes known today as 'bones'. The fiddle and gittern (citole) can be seen playing together for an estampie in the BL MS Egerton 1151, fo. 47 (plate 44), but this does not necessarily imply that their music was composed specifically for two parts. The gittern (citole) might be playing drone chords to accompany the melody on the fiddle, a method which works very well in one of the surviving ductias,[44] where the upper part is perfectly self-sufficient without the lower one, and a chordal drone accompaniment would provide a variety to its treatment.

The mediaeval viol seems not to appear as a soloist in pictures of dancing, but it is reasonable to suppose that it sometimes took part when dance music was being played by a group of musicians. What is certain is that as it went out of fashion in England in the early fourteenth century, it would not normally have been used for dances after that time.

During the fourteenth century the estampie continued to be performed, but no English examples survive from that time in monophonic settings or as duets for two instruments. There are, however, three of continental origin, written for organ in the so-called *Robertsbridge Fragment* of *c*.1325–50,[45] and these can give a good idea of their style at that period. Experiments have been made to play these and similar pieces as a duet on a portative organ and fiddle, but the result is not satisfying. Certainly those instruments can blend well together in their general sound, but the co-ordination of the parts in these compositions is better when they are being controlled by one mind rather than two. The continental solo *saltarelli* and other dances from this period are eminently suitable for a fiddle or a rebec, some with drones and some without, and the percussion instruments mentioned above could now be joined by the newly-arrived triangle.

Alongside the lively ductia and the estampie, there existed the dance known as the *carole*.[46] While no surviving instrumental piece is specified as being a carole, we do know that it was a dance-song, and sung by the dancers themselves, either with or without instruments. This was a dance with a gliding motion, and it gradually gave way, during the late fourteenth century, to the similarly dignified *basse-danse*.[47]

During the fifteenth and early sixteenth centuries the basse-danse was the most fashionable dance in England as well as in France. Its basic melody was often a well-known tune which could be played in long notes on one instrument while another improvised a faster part against it. Sometimes the second part was written out, and some examples survive of the dance in three parts. A possible two-part basse-danse from an English source is 'Quene Note' from the Bodl. MS Digby 167, fo. 31ᵛ, dating from the third quarter of the fifteenth century. In keeping with the style of the dance, the tenor appears in long notes while the upper part, added by a different hand, is more florid. As the bottom note of the tenor is *g* and the top of the superius is *c"*, this could be a good duet for two fiddles.[47]

Several of the other basse-danse melodies known in England were listed, after 1500, on the fly-leaf of the *Catholicon* by Johannes Balbus de Janua (1497) which is now in the library of Salisbury Cathedral. Besides an English title, 'The Kings Basse Dance', they include both 'Le petit Rouen' and 'Filles a marier' which were among the best-known examples in France.[48] They and others were also mentioned by Robert Coplande in *The Maner to daunce Bace Daunces* (1521). A setting of 'Taunder naken' (originally a Low-German song but later much used in Flanders) appears in *Henry VIII's Manuscript* as composed by the King himself.[49] He set the original melody in the middle part, and added a much more florid one above. The bottom part starts in a similar rhythmic pattern to that of the tenor, but then gets gradually more elaborate towards the end. The cantus firmus descends to *c*, the superius to *c'*, and the bassus to *F*. Bearing in mind that a performance on loud wind instruments was the most likely, particularly out of doors, we must also consider how the piece might have been played on bowed instruments. While the tenor part, the main melody, is too low for the average English rebec, it could just have been within the range of certain fiddles. However, experience shows that the lowest string on these instruments, being of thick gut, is not suitable for the performance of strong melodies, although both the fiddle and the rebec could have played the top line if instruments of different types played the lower parts. The only bowed instruments which could successfully have played the tenor and bass parts at their written pitch were viols, but, as we have already seen, these were only just becoming established at the English Court when the manuscript was being compiled (p. 114). However, as in all the pieces of the book, the tenor and bass parts would have been played more and more on viols towards the end of the reign, assuming that the pieces were still in the current repertoire. By that time there was also the possibility of performance on members of the violin family. There remains the possibility of transposition. If the piece were transposed up an octave, the top line would almost certainly have been too high for the bowed instruments available between 1510 and 1520, but transposition up a fifth would have rendered the piece much more suitable for the rebec or the fiddle. Indeed, it is just possible that the piece might occasionally have been played this way on a trio of fiddles, although there is no evidence that it actually happened.

One of the four-part instrumental pieces in the same manuscript (no. 91) has been identified by John Ward as a setting of a basse-danse already well known in Spain.[50] Here the cantus firmus, greatly decorated, is again in the tenor part of the piece, which is the only one in the whole manuscript where the bassus descends to *C*. One of the tantalizing questions raised by Professor Ward is whether this setting was ever intended to be danced to, or whether it was just an instrumental piece based on a dance tune. Many other instrumental pieces appear in the manuscript, several of them attributed to Henry VIII himself, and in all of them the use of bowed instruments would have been subject to the conditions discussed in connection with 'Taunder naken'. The other instruments which could have been used in a broken consort have already been mentioned on p. 114.

Gradually, however, the basse-danse was being superseded by other dances such as the galliard, which was performed in *Wyt and Science*, and also by 'bargenettes, pauyons, turgions and roundes' which are named in *The Boke named the Gouernour* 'deuysed by Syr Thomas Elyot knight' (1531).[51] English examples of some of these, and other instrumental pieces, can be found in the BL MS Royal Appendix 58 (*c.* 1530), where some are set for lute and others for keyboard. However, several of the latter originated as consort works, and, being written in three parts, can still be played by different instruments together. These are 'La Bell Fyne', 'The Empororse Pavyn', 'A Galyarde', 'Kyng Harry the VIIIth Pavyn', 'The Crocke', 'The Kyngs Marke' and 'A Galyard'. While performance involving the rebec or fiddle is possible (bearing in mind the conditions given above), these pieces come from the period when the consort of viols was well established, and they may even have been played on some of the 'xix Vialles great and small' from the inventory of Henry VIII's instruments in 1547. It can perhaps safely be assumed that such publications as Pierre Attaingnant's *Neuf basses dances deux branles vingt et cinq Pauennes auec quinze Gaillardes en musique a quatre parties* (Paris, 1530) were also known at the English Court.

The use of bowed instruments in dance music is well documented up to the late fourteenth century, not only by literary references, but also by the visual arts. From that time onwards, however, English pictures of dances become very rare, largely due to the changing artistic convention by which artists in this country virtually ceased to fill the margins of their manuscripts with pictures of people, animals, and grotesques doing different things, including dancing, which had been so commonplace in margins before (p. 3). Fortunately, though, instruments are mentioned in several descriptions of dances that actually took place at the Court of Henry VIII, and from these it becomes apparent that, at least in court circles, the most popular bowed instrument for dancing was the rebec. We know, for instance, that it played for the dancers of 'the Ryche Mount' (p. 94), and for the Christmas mummery of 1514 when the King himself was involved (p. 94). Syr Thomas Elyot takes it for granted as a dance instrument in his somewhat anachronistic descriptions of dance music in ancient Rome:

At Rome, in the tyme of Nero, there was a philosopher called Demetrius, whiche was of that secte, that for as moche as they abandoned all shamefastenes in theyr wordes and actes, they were called Cinici in englishe doggyshe. This Demetrius often reprouinge daunsynge, wolde saye that there was nothynge therin of any importaunce, and that it was none other, but a counterfaytyng with the feete and handes, of the armonye that was shewed before in the rebecke, shalme, and other instrument, and that the motyons were but vayne and seperate from all vnderstandyng, and of no purpose or efficacie.[52]

Returning to 1514, the rebec may have been one of the instruments which played at a ball where Henry VIII and the Duke of Buckingham danced with the ladies nearly all night. The Italian account of the event lists the relevant instruments as 'piva, violetta, un certo pifaretto, cithara', which are translated by John Stevens as 'shawm, rebec, small pipe (and tabor?) and lute (or gittern)'.[53] In view of the occasions mentioned above, the rebec seems to be a reasonable rendering of 'violetta', a word which has had many different meanings throughout a long history. (The word 'cithara' might in fact have meant a harp.)

If the rebec was the favourite bowed instrument for dances at the royal Court, we must not forget that the mediaeval-type fiddle was still being played throughout the country well into the sixteenth century. Pictures of it being used for dancing are extant, but rare, with two of them featuring that most enigmatic animal, the cat. On a misericord at Beverley Minster a cat fiddles while four kittens dance (plate 143), and on a benchend at Fawsley the fiddling cat plays for two long-eared dancing kittens (plate 141). Turning to human beings, it is worth speculating that the two fiddlers on the *Mary Rose* were accustomed to playing nautical dances together, perhaps in company with the pipes and tabor which were also found on board.[54]

It would be tempting Providence too far to guess at the type of 'stick and fidle' which played 'a new dance called hey-didle-didle' in 1569. By that time the violin too was well established in England, as can be seen in a painting of about that year, Joris Hoefnagel's *A Fête at Bermondsey* (plate 152), which is kept at Hatfield House.[55] The young Netherlandish artist visiting England shows an unmistakably English scene, with the River Thames and the Tower of London in the distance, a church just visible from behind some trees, and in the foreground an open-fronted house where tables are are being set for a feast. Well-dressed guests arrive on foot and on horseback, and while the food is being got ready, dancers perform to the music of four musicians arranged in pairs, one in each pair playing a violin and the other a viola (plate 153). The picture was for some time believed to show a wedding feast, but there is now some doubt about the reason for the celebration. It is certain, however, that it is one of the most beautiful paintings of Elizabethan England, and it is also one of the very earliest in this country to show the family of the violin, a new kind of *fiddle*, and one which has never been surpassed.

Notes

❦

CHAPTER I: THE SOURCES

1. *Laȝamon: Brut*, ed. G. L. Brook and R. F. Leslie 2 vols., *EETS: OS* 277 (1978), ii. 592.
2. Illustrated by Crane, *Extant Medieval Musical Instruments*, p. 80, fig. 11.
3. Described and illustrated by Winternitz in *Musical Instruments of the Western World*, pp. 48, 51, where it is listed as a fiddle.
4. Remnant, 'Bowed Instruments in England', plates 137–9.
5. Ibid., plate 116.
6. Disertori, *passim*; Cervelli, p. 19; Crane, op. cit. p. 17; Tiella, 'The Violeta', *passim*; queries by Edgar Hunt in *GSJ* xxix (1976), 143, and reply by Tiella in *GSJ* xxxi (1978), 146.
7. For an English carving of remarkably similar shape, see that at Broad Chalke, plate 117 and p. 64.
8. Baines, *European and American Musical Instruments*, plate 8, where it is dated *c.* 1500. However, Witten, in 'Apollo', p. 38, gives the date of *c.*1535–50 for this instrument.
9. Remnant, *Musical Instruments*, p. 54, plate 42.
10. Baines, *European and American Musical Instruments*, plate 1.
11. Ibid., plates 2–4; Boyden, *The Hill Collection*, plate 8; Witten, in 'Apollo', p. 46, dates this instrument to *c.*1575–90, as opposed to *c.*1525 as given by Boyden.
12. Baines, op. cit., plates 76–9; Boyden, op. cit., plate 1, dates this instrument as probably between 1500–25, whereas Witten, op. cit., gives the period from 1560.
13. Baines, op. cit., plate 87. This instrument is described in detail by Edmunds in 'Reconstructing 16th-century Venetian Viols', p. 521, where he gives its date as being not later than 1550.
14. Emsheimer, 109 ff.
15. Agricola (1528/9), fo. 1vᵛ; ibid. (1545), ff. 48, 49; Hayes, *The Viols*, p. 22.
16. Remnant, 'The Use of Frets', pp. 148–51. The author now has doubts as to whether after all frets are intended to be present on the rebec in Gerard David's *The Virgin and Child with Saints and Angels* (Rouen, Musée des Beaux Arts).
17. A notable left-handed professional violinist of today is James Barton of Barry, Glamorgan, to whom the author is most grateful for information on this subject.
18. The Jerusalem Bible, ed. Alexander Jones (London, 1966), pt. 2 (New Testament), pp. 434–5.
19. *The Cambridge History of the Bible*, ed. G. W. H. Lampe, 3 vols. (Cambridge 1963–70), ii. 332.
20. Illustrated in Manuel Chamoso Lamas, *La Catedral de Santiago de Compostela* (León, 1976), pp. 36–7; López-Calo, *La Música Medieval*, pp. 89–100; Remnant, 'The Diversity', plates 5, 6.
21. Bachmann, *The Origins*, plate 64.
22. Wiltshire, 'Medieval Fiddles', p. 144; Philip Mainwaring Johnston, 'Hardham Church

and its Early Paintings', *Sussex Archaeological Collections* lxiv (1901), 83; Clive Bell, *Twelfth-Century Paintings at Hardham and Clayton*, pub. and ed. Frances Byng-Stamper and Caroline Lucas (Lewes, 1947), p. 10.

23. An exception was when he was illustrating the so-called letter from 'Jerome to Dardanus', which was forged not later than the ninth century, so does not directly concern bowed instruments. For further information see Page, 'Biblical Instruments', *passim*.

24. López-Calo, 'El Pórtico de la Gloria', p. 168.

25. Zarnecki, *Later English Romanesque Sculpture*, pp. 12–13.

26. The angelic band in the Beauchamp Chapel, Warwick, is a special case, as seen on p. 7.

27. Remnant and Marks, 'A Medieval "Gittern" ', p. 91.

28. The present writer, for instance, owns two rebecs. One has three strings and a curved bridge, and makes a fairly thin sound, while the other, which is a good deal larger, has four strings and a combination of flat bridge and tailpiece, which enables all the strings to be sounded together; this instrument is capable of making a loud sound.

29. Wickham, *Early English Stages*, p. 107.

30. This point is emphasized by Christopher Woodforde in *The Norwich School of Glass-Painting*, p. 145.

31. Anderson, *Drama and Imagery*, pp. 89–90.

32. Wickham, *Early English Stages*, p. 188.

33. Ibid.

34. This building is one of the most important decorated mediaeval houses to have survived in England. It is described by E. Clive Rouse and A. Baker in 'The Wall-Painting at Longthorpe Tower', *Archaeologia* xcvi (1955), 1–57, plates I–XXV.

35. A description of the instruments represented in this exhibition can be seen in Remnant, 'Opus Anglicanum'.

36. *Opus Anglicanum* catalogue (Victoria and Albert Museum), p. 30, exhibit 53, plate 10.

37. Ibid., pp. 40–1, exhibit 83.

38. In this case the original colour can be checked by looking at the reverse of the page. If the relevant shape appears there as a greasy mark, the paint will have been silver.

39. Gov. Pownall, '*Observations on Ancient Painting in* England: *In a Letter from Gov.* Pownall, *to the Rev.* Michael Lort, *D.D.V.P.A.S.*', *Archaeologia* ix (1789), 141–56. The paintings in the roof at Peterborough Cathedral were subsequently described by C. J. P. Cave and Tancred Borenius in 'The Painted Ceiling in the nave of Peterborough Cathedral', *Archaeologia* lxxxvii (1937), 279–309. (The author is most grateful to Canon J. L. Cartwright of Peterborough Cathedral for information about these articles.)

40. The carvings at Beverley and Baker's work on them have now been described by Gwen and Jeremy Montagu in 'Beverley Minster reconsidered'.

41. For an outline of English musical history during the Middle Ages, see *Music from the Middle Ages to the Renaissance*, ed. F. W. Sternfeld, Chapter 6, 'England: From the Beginnings to *c*.1540' by Ernest H. Sanders.

42. Some of these pictures can be seen in the facsimile of Escorial MS j.b.2 in the edn. by Anglés, *La Música de las Cantigas*, vol. i.

43. Pächt and Alexander, in *Illuminated Manuscripts* i. 22–3, say that the scribe finished his work in 1338 and the illuminator, Jehan de Grise, in 1344.

44. Laurence Wright's 'The Medieval Gittern and Citole' points to such problems.

45. This was reproduced in Gerbert, *De Cantu*, ii, plate XXXII, but the original source was subsequently destroyed.

46. Herrad of Hohenbourg, *Hortus Deliciarum*, dir. Rosalie Green, 2 vols. (London, 1979), ii. 57; the close connection between this and the St. Blasius picture is discussed by Page in 'The Medieval *Organistrum* and Symphonia 2', pp. 78–82.

47. Evidence for this comes from archaeological sources, such as the lyre discovered in the seventh-century ship burial at Sutton Hoo (now in the British Museum). Crane, in *Extant Medieval Musical Instruments* refers to several other lyres, but to no harps (as we know them) excavated from the Anglo-Saxon period.

48. *Aelfrics Grammatik und Glossar*, ed. Julius Zupitza (Berlin, 1880), p. 302. A twelfth-century version of Aelfric's work is in Thomas Wright, *A Volume of Vocabularies*, i. 88, and Wright, *Anglo-Saxon and Old English Vocabularies*, ed. Wülcker, i. 539ff.

49. *Otfrids Evangelienbuch*, ed. *Oskar Erdmann* (Tübingen, 1957), p. 259. (See p. 123 n. 1 for Bachmann's latest views on the origins of bowing.)

50. Thomas Wright, *A Volume of Vocabularies* (privately printed, 1857), i. 133, 137.

51. *Polychronicon Ranulphi Higden Monachi Cestrensis; together with the English translations of John Trevisa and an Unknown Writer of the fifteenth century*, ed. Churchill Babington, *RS* 41, 9 vols. (London, 1865–86), i. 408–9.

52. Ibid., pp. 354–5.

53. *Giraldus Cambrensis, Opera Omnia*, ed. J. Brewer, *RS* 21, 8 vols. (London, 1861–91), vi. 187, Cap. XII.

54. Higden, op. cit., p.337. The square brackets in this quotation denote part of a different MS from that in the main text of *RS* 41. i.

55. William Caxton, *The Pilgrimage of the Sowle* (1483), v. viii. 99.

56. *The Psalter and Psalms of David, translated by Richard Rolle*, ed. Revd H. R. Bramley (Oxford, 1884), p. 490.

57. Robert Manning of Brunne, *The Story of England*, ed. F. J. Furnivall, *RS* 87, 2 vols. (London, 1887), i. 398.

58. Bullock-Davies, *Menestrellorum*, pp. 156–8.

59. Ibid.

60. Revd John Webb (ed.), *A Roll of the Household Expenses of Richard de Swinfield, Bishop of Hereford, during part of the Years 1289 and 1290, CSP:OS* (1854), p. 148.

61. Galpin, *Old English Instruments*, pp. 215–22.

CHAPTER II: THE INGREDIENTS OF BOWED INSTRUMENTS

1. Bachmann, *The Origins*, p. 50.

2. Baines, 'Fifteenth-century Instruments', p.23.

3. Bachmann, op. cit., p. 86.

4. For the bow apparently used by St. Caterina de'Vigri, see p. 2.

5. Remnant, *Musical Instruments*, p. 47, plate 34.

6. Boyden, *The History of Violin Playing*, p. 208.

7. A. Borgnet (ed.), *De vegetalibus*, B[eati] Alberti Magni ... opera omnia (Paris, 1891), x. 161. F. Pfeiffer (ed.), *Das Buch der Natur von Konrad von Megenberg* (Stuttgart, 1861), p. 314. English translation from Bachmann, *The Origins*, p. 72, n. 13. The German text appears in the original German edition of Bachmann, p. 87. Page, 'German musicians', pp. 195, 196, n. 19.

8. F. Pfeiffer, op. cit., p. 16. Translation from Bachmann, op. cit., p. 73.

9. Ibid., p. 73.

10. Ibid., p. 73.

11. Remnant and Marks, 'A Medieval "Gittern"', plates 76–80.

12. Bachmann, op. cit., p. 71. Stevens, in *Music and Poetry*, p. 313, suggests that this practice was unusual by the late Middle Ages. However, the bad results from some non-playing fiddle-makers of today, together with the knowledge that nearly all mediaeval fiddle designs were different, go to show that only experienced and expert players would have known how to perfect their instruments.

13. For detailed information concerning the acoustical properties of soundholes, see David D. Boyden, 'Soundhole', *Grove 6*.

14. Anglés, *La Musica de las Cantigas*, i, fo. 118; Remnant, 'The Use of Frets', plate XVIId.

15. Bachmann, op. cit., p. 78 ff.

16. Page, 'References to String Materials', p. 34.

17. BL Add. MS 27944, fo. 142^v; John Trevisa, *On the Properties of Things. John Trevisa's translation of Bartholomaeus Anglicus' De Proprietatibus Rerum*, gen. ed. M. C. Seymour, 2 vols. (Oxford, 1975), i. 606.

18. J. Handschin, 'Aus der alten Musiktheorie: V. Zur Instrumentenkunde', *AMl* xvi/xvii (1944–5), 1–2.

19. For recent research on the making of early strings, see articles by Abbott and Segerman.

20. For examples see p. 2 and also Witten, 'Apollo', *passim*.

21. The lute's earliest known documentation in an English source dates from 1285, at the court of Edward I, so it may have arrived there through the influence of his wife Eleanor of Castile, who would have been familiar with it in Spain. (Bullock-Davies, *Menestrellorum*, p. 34.) However, its earliest known English picture is apparently in the Steeple Aston Cope (*c*.1310–40), now in the Victoria and Albert Museum. This was reproduced in Remnant, 'Opus Anglicanum', plate XIIb and on the cover of *EM* iii, 2 (April 1975).

22. For further examples see Remnant, 'Rebec, Fiddle and Crowd in England: Some Further Observations', and the cover of Remnant, *Musical Instruments*.

23. For continental curved bridges see Remnant, 'The diversity of medieval fiddles', plates 7, 10.

24. A similar system is described by Segerman and Abbot in 'Jerome of Moravia and bridge curvature', p. 34.

25. Further suggestions have been put forward by Andrew Hughes in 'Viella: facere non possumus', p. 455.

26. Grocheo, *Concerning Music*, pp. 19–20. (The present writer has substituted the word 'fiddle' for the 'vielle' of the published translation.) Gushee, in 'Two Central Places', pp. 143–4 suggests that as Grocheo only refers to instruments in the context of solo minstrelsy, he implies that they were not used in the performance of polyphony.

27. Grocheo, *Der Musiktraktat*, ed. E. Rohloff, p. 52.

28. Baines, 'Fifteenth-century Instruments', p. 23.

29. Anthony Rooley, 'The Problem of Double Bridges', p. 3. Ravenel, '*Vièles à archet*', i. 71^v–73.

30. Remnant, 'The Use of Frets', pp. 147, 149.

31. Remnant and Marks, 'A Medieval "Gittern"', plate 50. Frets can also be seen on long-necked lutes from Egypt, *c*.1400 BC.

32. Remnant, 'The Use of Frets', plate XVIIb.
33. Ibid., plate XVIIa.
34. Harwood, 'An introduction to renaissance viols', p. 237.
35. Tiella, 'The Violeta', *passim*.

CHAPTER III: THE REBEC

1. Bachmann, *The Origins*, pp. 55, 50 The present writer is most grateful to Dr Bachmann for his subsequent opinion that the origins of bowing probably go back further than his book suggests. More speculation on the origins of bowing can be found in Laurence Picken, *Folk Musical Instruments of Turkey* (Oxford, 1975), p. 323.
2. Bachmann, op. cit., pp. 34–5.
3. Ibid., pp. 24–5.
4. Joseph Hall (ed.), *King Horn* (Oxford, 1901), p. 87.
5. John Lydgate, *Reson and Sensuallyte*, ed. Ernst Sieper, *EETS:ES* 84 (1901), p. 146.
6. Thomas Wright and James Halliwell (eds.), *Reliquiae Antiquae* (London, 1845), p. 81.
7. Remnant, 'Kit', *Grove 6*, *passim*.
8. Bachmann, *The Origins*, p. 137.
9. Julius Zupitza (ed.), *Sammlung englischer Denkmäler* (Berlin, 1880), i. 302.
10. Dodwell, *The Canterbury School of Illumination*, p. 120.
11. Garofalo's painting of a violin, dating from 1505–8 in the Palazzo di Ludovico il Moro at Ferrara, is illustrated in Remnant, *Musical Instruments*, p. 58, plate 45, and David D. Boyden, 'Violin', *Grove 6*.
12. The author is most grateful to Mr Dennis King of Messrs G. King and Son of Norwich, for the view of this glass while it was in his studio for repairs.
13. Remnant, 'The Use of Frets', pp. 148–50.
14. For other jokes concerning bowed instruments, see p. 71.
15. Ferd, J. de Hen, 'Folk Instruments of Belgium, Part I', *GSJ* xxv (1972), 110–11.
16. Remnant, 'Kit', plate 2(d).
17. Virdung, in *Musica Getutscht*, does not give tunings for the rebec.
18. Page, 'Jerome of Moravia', pp. 82, 88–9.
19. For Agricola's tuning of a four-stringed rebec, see p. 36.
20. Agricola (1545), ff. 46, 47, 47ᵛ; (facsimile) pp. 211, 213, 214.
21. Bachmann, *The Origins*, plate 64.
22. No mediaeval instrument had a chinrest. This device was invented by the violinist Ludwig Spohr, *c*.1820.
23. Many seventeenth-century Dutch paintings show the violin being plucked like a guitar, and a well-known eighteenth-century French example is in Chardin's portrait of Rameau, now in the Musée des Beaux Arts, Dijon.
24. Arcipreste de Hita, *Libro de Buen Amor*, ed. Manual Criado de Val and Eric W. Naylor (Classicos Hispanicos, 1965), p. 379.
25. Domino Du Cange, *Glossarium*, under 'Baudosa'.
26. F. N. Robinson (ed.), *Chaucer*, p. 92.
27. Revd A. Dyce (ed.), *The Poetical Works of John Skelton*, 2 vols. (London, 1843), i. 111.
28. Baines, 'Fifteenth-century Instruments', pp. 24–5.
29. Anglés, *La Musica de las Cantigas*, i, fo. 118.
30. Nevertheless, it must be acknowledged that as most mediaeval instruments were different

from each other even within one basic type, the variants in tone quality would change from one case to another. Even so, this does not minimize the fact that these combinations are almost non-existent in the visual arts.

31. The word *pipe* is used here in its generic sense, to cover instruments which cannot be precisely identified.
32. N. F. Robinson (ed.), *Chaucer*, p. 49.
33. H. N. MacCracken (ed.), *Minor Poems of John Lydgate*, 2 vols., *EETS:OS* 192 (1934), ii. 695.
34. Remnant, 'Kit', *Grove 6*.
35. For this reference the author is most grateful to Mr Geoff Ralph.

CHAPTER IV: THE CROWD

1. Bruce-Mitford, 'The Sutton Hoo Lyre', *passim*; Remnant, *Musical Instruments*, p. 20, plate 2.
2. Stauder, *Alte Musikinstrumente*, p. 78, plate 111b.
3. Ibid., p. 78, plate 110a; Galpin, *Old English Instruments*, plate 2.
4. Panum, *Stringed Instruments*, p. 96, fig. 82.
5. Bragard and De Hen, *Musical Instruments*, plate II, 3.
6. Myrtle Bruce-Mitford, 'Rotte ii', *Grove 6*.
7. Galpin, *Old English Instruments*, p. 2.
8. Ibid., p. 3.
9. Ibid., p. 5; Myrtle Bruce-Mitford, op. cit.; Steger, *Philologia*, Ch. VII.
10. *Laȝamon: Brut*, ed. G. L. Brook and R. F. Leslie, 2 vols., *EETS:OS* 250 (1963), i. 182.
11. N. F. Robinson (ed.), *Chaucer*, p. 19.
12. Sir Walter Scott (ed.), *Sir Tristrem* (Edinburgh, 1804), p. 108.
13. Roslyn Rensch, *The Harp* (London, 1969), plate 27b.
14. J. Ritson (ed.), *AEMR* ii. 7, 75.
15. Mary Remnant, 'Chorus ii', *Grove 6*.
16. Du Cange, *Glossarium*, 'Baudosa'.
17. Galpin, *Old English Instruments*, p. 59.
18. This instrument is sometimes known as the Foelas (pronounced *Voylas*) Crwth, as for many years it belonged to the Wynn family at Foelas Hall in the village of Pentrefoelas, North Wales. The author is most grateful to Mr Roy Saer for this information.
19. Jones, *Musical and Poetical Relicks*, p. 115; Daines Barrington, 'Two Musical Instruments', plate VII.
20. William Bingley, *North Wales*, 2 vols. (London, 1804), ii. 332.
21. Galpin, *Old English Instruments*, p. 58.
22. Bevil, 'The Welsh Crwth', pp. 35–6; Jones, *Musical and Poetical Relicks*, p. 42.
23. Jones, op. cit., p. 115.
24. Bingley, op. cit., p. 331.
25. Jones, op. cit., p. 85.
26. Illustrated in Crossley-Holland, *Music in Wales*, p. 18; Peter Crossley-Holland, 'Wales: Instruments', *Grove 6*.
27. Bevil, 'The Welsh Crwth', pp. 28–35.
28. One of the nineteenth-century roof bosses at the Fitzalan Chapel, Arundel, shows a rectangular crowd. While this could be ignored because of its date, there is a possibility

that it may have been based on one of the earlier bosses, in view of the copying of an earlier boss containing a fiddle. Cave, 'The Wooden Roof Bosses'.

29. The crowd which used to be at St. Mary's Church, Shrewsbury, was destroyed when the church spire collapsed in a gale on the night of 11 February 1894. Fortunately it had been photographed, and its picture was published in the first edition of Galpin's *Old English Instruments* (1910), p. 75. The photographic block was in turn lost during the Second World War (for this information the author is indebted to Mr Brian Galpin), and the subsequent revision of the book by Thurston Dart in 1965 shows in its place (p. 57) the carving which was substituted for the original. While giving a good picture of a crowd, it is not itself mediaeval, so the older photograph (taken from Galpin's book) is shown here.

30. Bragard and De Hen, *Musical Instruments*, plate II. 3.

31. Bachmann, *The Origins*, plate 91.

32. Ibid., plates 89, 94.

33. Galpin, *Old English Instruments*, p. 225.

34. Andersson, *The Bowed-Harp*, pp. 254–5; Mette Müller (ed.), *From Bone Pipe and Cattle Horn to Fiddle and Psaltery* (Copenhagen, 1972), p. 33; Ilkka Kolehmainen, 'Finland, II', *Grove 6*; here the instrument is referred to as the 'jouhikko' or 'jouhikannel'.

35. Jones, *Musical and Poetical Relicks*, p. 115. This includes the Welsh text.

36. Andersson, *The Bowed-Harp*, p. 221.

37. Victoria and Albert Museum, *Catalogue of Musical Instruments*, ii. 19–20, plates 22–3.

38. Andersson, op. cit., p. 222.

39. Bevil, 'The Welsh Crwth', p. 147.

40. Ibid., pp. 6, 5; Engel, *Researches into the Early History of the Violin Family*, p. 28.

41. Bevil, op. cit., p. 6.

42. *The Psalter and Psalms of David*, trans. Richard Rolle, ed. Revd H. R. Bramley (Oxford, 1884), pp. 490, 492–3.

43. Jones, *Musical and Poetical Relicks*, p. 114.

44. D. Roy Saer, *The Harp in Tudor Wales*. The author is most grateful to Mr Saer for the relevant information before he had published it.

45. Revd Josiah Forshall and Sir Frederic Madden (eds.), *The New Testament in English according to the version by John Wycliffe about AD 1388* (Oxford, 1879), p. 156.

46. Revd Josiah Forshall and Sir Frederic Madden, (eds.), *The Holy Bible made from the Latin Vulgate by John Wycliffe and his followers* (Oxford, 1850), p. 648.

47. *Brut Y Tywysogyon or The Chronicle of the Princes*, trans. Thomas Jones, Board of Celtic Studies, University of Wales History and Law Series (1952), xi. 71; W. O. Hassall (ed.), *They Saw it Happen* (Oxford, 1957), p. 90.

48. Stephen Hawes, *The Passetyme of Pleasure*, ed. William Edward Mead, *EETS:OS* 173 (1928), p. 61.

49. Galpin, *Old English Instruments*, p. 59; Bullock-Davies, 'Welsh Minstrels', pp. 114–15.

50. G. G. Coulton (ed.), *Social Life in Britain from the Conquest to the Reformation* (Cambridge, 1956), pp. 406–7. Coulton's footnote describes the term 'livery' as 'i.e. *corrody*; a daily allowance of the necessaries of life'.

CHAPTER V: THE MEDIAEVAL VIOL

1. Illustrated in: Reese, *Music in the Middle Ages*, plate VI; Richard Hunt, 'The Sum of Knowledge', *The Flowering of the Middle Ages*, ed. Joan Evans (London, 1966), p. 182.

2. Bachmann, *The Origins*, plate 64.

3. Ibid., plate 61.

4. Ibid., plate 61.

5. Remnant, 'Bowed instruments', p. 108.

6. The problem of the crowd is different in this respect, as it did survive for several hundred years, even though its activities were restricted.

7. Victoria and Albert Museum, *Opus Anglicanum* catalogue, p. 30, entry 53, plate 10.

CHAPTER VI: THE FIDDLE

1. Bachmann, *The Origins*, plate 11.

2. Not all the fiddles at Santiago show this characteristic, and, those that do, display it better in some light effects than in others. A close-up examination is needed to make a final assessment on the matter.

3. The author is very grateful to Mr Alan Crumpler for information about the instrument carvings at Broad Chalke.

4. Seven and eight strings can be found in continental examples, but at present the author does not know of any English ones.

5. Page, 'Jerome of Moravia', pp. 82 ff.

6. Ibid., p. 97.

7. Ibid., pp. 83–4.

8. Tinctoris also used the word 'viola' for an instrument of the guitar type. Baines, 'Fifteenth-century Instruments', p. 22.

9. Ibid., pp. 22–3.

10. Page, op. cit., p. 84. Latin text in: Gerbert, *Scriptores* iii. 214.

11. Page, 'Fourteenth-century Instruments', pp. 26–7, plate II.

12. Remnant and Marks, 'A Medieval "Gittern"', *passim*.

13. Bachmann, *The Origins*, plates 65, 67, 68.

14. The author is most grateful to Mr Philip Astle and Mr Paul Williamson for the information about this source.

15. Bachmann, *The Origins*, plate 65.

16. Puccianti, 'La Descrizione della *Viella*', p. 233.

17. J. Ernst Wülfing (ed.), *The Laud Troy Book*, 2 vols., *EETS:OS* 121 (1902), i. 282.

18. Thomas Wright (ed.), *The Metrical Life of St. Brandan*, PSP (London, 1844), p. 40.

19. Bachmann, *The Origins*, p. 133.

20. An Italian example is in Sano di Pietro's *Virgin and Child with Angels* at the Pinacoteca Nazionale, Siena.

21. E. W. Safford, 'An Account of the Expenses of Eleanor', p. 132.

22. Rastall, 'Secular Musicians', ii. 40.

23. Ibid., p. 171.

24. Ibid., p. 183.

25. Ibid., p. 39.

26. S. Bentley (ed.), 'Extracts from the Privy Purse Expenses of King Henry the Seventh', *Excerpta Historica* (London, 1831), p. 85.

CHAPTER VII: THE RENAISSANCE VIOL

1. Woodfield, 'Viol', *Grove 6*; *The Early History of the Viol*, pp. 61, 81, 95–6.

2. As opposed to forms of the word *fiddle*, of which he gives many examples.

3. M. V. Offord (ed.), *The Book of the Knight of the Tower*, trans. William Caxton, *EETS:SS* 2 (1971), p. 153. This is a later version of the work cited on p. 81 of the present book, and the names of the instruments have been changed to more modern ones.

4. (van Wilders), Holman, 'The English Royal Violin Consort', p. 39; (1517 expenses), *L & P*, i, pt. 3, pref., p. lxv, n. 1.

5. BL MS Eg. 2604, fo. 1; Woodfill, *Musicians in English Society*, p. 297; Pulver, 'The Viols in England', p. 4. Holman, op. cit., p. 40.

6. Woodfield, *The Early History of the Viol*, pp. 207–8.

7. Woodfill, op. cit., p. 297. Holman, op. cit., *passim*

8. Hayes, *The King's Music*, p. 77.

9. Galpin, *Old English Instruments*, pp. 218, 220.

10. Woodfield, op. cit., pp. 206–7.

11. J. B. Trapp and Hulbertus Schulte Herbrüggen, *Sir Thomas More*, pp. 84–6; Jane Roberts, *Holbein* (London, 1979), p. 41. For an outline of the music and instruments in the life of Sir Thomas More, see Nan C. Carpenter, 'A Song for All Seasons'.

12. Angela Lewi, *The Thomas More Family Group*, pp. 5–7.

13. Geraldine Norman, 'How Holbein hid a royal secret', *The Times* (25 March 1983), p. 12.

14. Woodfill, op. cit., p. 267.

15. Ibid., p. 268.

16. Price, *Patrons and Musicians*, p. 122.

17. *L & P*, xv. 449, no. 905.

18. Hayes, *The Viols*, p. 83; Woodfield, op. cit., p. 209.

19. Harwood, 'An introduction to renaissance viols', p. 237.

20. Agricola, *Musica Instrumentalis* (1528), ff. xlv^v, xlvi (pp. 90, 91).

21–3. Ganassi's work is discussed in detail by Woodfield in 'Viol playing techniques'.

CHAPTER VIII: THE TRUMPET MARINE?

1. Stauder, *Alte Musikinstrumente*, p. 91, plate 133.

2. Other offshoots from the monochord, such as the *tambourin de Béarn* and the *Scheidtholt*, do not come within the scope of this book.

3. Wangermée, *Flemish Music*, p. 80, plate 25.

4. Praetorius, *Syntagma Musicum* ii. 59; Blumenfeld, *The Syntagma Musicum*, p. 59.

5. Wangermée, *Flemish Music*, p. 188, plate 68; Staude, *Alte Musikinstrumente*, plate V; Montagu, *The World of Medieval and Renaissance Musical Instruments*, p. 78, plate VIII.

6. Heinrich Glarean, *Dodecachordon* (Basle, 1547), trans. and ed. Clement A. Miller, 2 vols., *MSD* 6 (AIM 1965), i. 87.

7. Bärenreiter calender, *Musica* (1970).

8. Glarean, op. cit., p. 87.

9. Philip Nelson, *Ancient Painted Glass in England* (London, 1913), pp. 41–2. H. R. Hosking, *The Collegiate Church of St. Mary, Warwick* (Warwick, 1978), p. 9.

CHAPTER IX: FIDDLERS

1. Bachmann, *The Origins*, p. 122.

2. Ibid.

3. Wilhelm Keller, 'Das Sirventes "Fadet Joglar" ', *Romanische Forschungen* xxii (1906), 144 f.

4. For Thomas of Chobham's analysis of good and bad minstrels, see *Thomae de Chobham Summa Confessorum*, ed. Revd F. Broomfield (Louvain and Paris, 1968), pp. 291–2.

5. Page, 'Jerome of Moravia', p. 80.

6. Holmes, 'The Mediaeval Minstrel', p. 157.

7. Robert Manning of Brunne, *The Story of England*, ed. F. J. Furnivall, 2 vols., *RS* 87 (London, 1887), i. 141.

8. M. Mills (ed), *Lybeaus Desconus, EETS:OS* 261 (1969), pp. 82–3 for the two versions.

9. Rastall, 'Secular Musicians', ii. 169.

10. Ibid., p. 171.

11. Woodfill, *Musicians in English Society*, p. 297.

12. Bullock-Davies, *Menestrellorum*, pp. 123–4.

13. Ibid., pp. 163–4.

14. Ibid., p. 168.

15. Ibid., p. 122.

16. Ibid., p. 168.

17. Ibid., pp. 84–5.

18. Rastall, 'Secular Musicians', ii. 93.

19. Ibid., ii. 109.

20. (Robert Fytheler), ibid., ii. 143; (Walter le Vyelur), PRO, Personal Seals, i. 69 and plate 23.

21. Stevens, *Music and Poetry*, p. 277.

22. From the front view the plucked instrument might be taken for a cittern, but when seen from the side its back is definitely vaulted, as is that of the lute. It is not, however, a fully-developed lute of the time, such as that in the east end frieze at Hillesden Church. The pipe is now broken off, leaving only the tabor of the pipe-and-tabor combination, but a drawing by Caroline Brereton, dated 1866 (now in the local Museum), shows the pipe in place. It was still there in 1894, when R. C. Hope read his paper 'Notes on the Minstrels' Pillar, St. Mary's Church, Beverley' to the East Riding Antiquarian Society. (The author is most grateful to Mr Michael Boardman of the Humberside COunty Council and Mr G. P. Brown of the Local History Library, Beverley, for information on this matter.)

23. Thomas Wright (ed.), *The Book of the Knight of La Tour Landry EETS:OS* 33 (rev. edn., London, 1906), p. 159.

24. See p. 72 for another version of this work.

25. Eugen Kölbing (ed.), *Sir Beues of Hamtoun* 3 vols. *EETS:ES* 46, 48, 65 (1885, –86, –94), i. 182.

26. Rastall, 'Secular Musicians', ii. 92.

27. Ibid., ii. 88.

28. E. W. Safford, 'An Account of the Expenses of Eleanor', p. 135.

29. Thomas Rymer, *Foedera*, 20 vols. (1704–32), ix. 255.

30. John Harvey, *The Plantagenets*, pp. 108–9.

31. Lucy Toulmin Smith (ed.), *Henry, Earl of Derby, Expeditions to Prussia and the Holy Land in the Years 1390–1 and 1392–3, CSP:OS* (1894), p. 113.

32. The Abbey of Las Huelgas was founded in 1187 by King Alfonso VIII of Castile and his

wife Eleanor, who was the daughter of Henry II of England and Eleanor of Aquitaine. The music has been edited by Anglés in *El Codex Musical de Las Huelgas*.

33. John Harvey, *The Plantagenets*, pp. 67–75; on oriental influence, p. 71.
34. Bullock-Davies, *Menestrellorum*, p. 146.
35. Rastall, 'Secular Musicians', ii. 31.
36. Bullock-Davies, op. cit., pp. 106–7.
37. Rastall, op. cit., ii. 46; Bullock-Davies, op. cit., p. 108.
38. Bullock-Davies, op. cit., p. 108.
39. Rastall, op. cit., ii. 39.
40. Ibid., ii. 40.
41. Ibid., ii. 45.
42. Ibid., ii. 88.
43. Edmond Van der Straeten, *La Musique aux Pays-Bas avant le XIXe Siècle*, 8 vols. (Brussels, 1867–88), vii. 160–1; Martin Picker, *The Chanson Albums of Marguerite of Austria* (Berkeley and Los Angeles, 1965), p. 25.
44. Van der Straeten, op. cit., vii. 163.
45. J. E. Hulme, *Symbolism in Christian Art* (London, 1891), p. 180.
46. F. C. Sillar and R. M. Meyler, *Cats Ancient and Modern* (London, 1966), p. 145.
47. Iona and Peter Opie (eds.), *The Oxford Dictionary of Nursery Rhymes* (rev. edn., London, 1952), pp. 203–5.
48. Revd A. Dyce (ed.), *The Works of John Skelton* 2 vols. (London, 1843), i. 391.
49. Opie, op. cit., p. 203. Edmund Creeth (ed.), *Tudor Plays* (New York, 1966), pp. 494–5.
50. For further information of the symbolism of animals, see: H. W. Janson, *Apes and Apelore in the Middle Ages and Renaissance* (London, 1952); Lillian M. Randall, *Images in the Margins of Gothic Manuscripts* (Berkeley and Los Angeles, 1966); F. C. Sillar and R. M. Meyler, *The Symbolic Pig* (London, 1961).

CHAPTER X: BOWED INSTRUMENTS IN ENGLISH SOCIETY

1. Recent changes in the Catholic Church will illustrate this point. During the 1950s it was necessary, in England, to obtain the permission of a bishop to perform a setting of the Mass with orchestra in its proper liturgical context. Now, some thirty years later, such a free rein is given to choir directors that in certain places the liturgy is embellished with music of 'pop' style, together with its attendant instruments such as electric guitars.
2. Rastall, 'Secular Musicians', i. 67 ff.; 'Minstrelsy, Church and Clergy'.
3. Coussemaker, *Scriptorum*, i. 253.
4. Rastall, 'Minstrelsy, Church and Clergy' p. 86.
5. Ibid., pp. 86–7.
6. Ibid., p. 87.
7. Ibid., p. 87.
8. Ibid., p. 87. Rastall, 'Secular Musicians' ii. 114.
9. Ibid., p. 87. The Latin version appears in Safford, 'An Account of the Expenses of Eleanor', p. 132. See also p. 20 here.
10. G. H. Cook, *Old St. Paul's Cathedral* (London, 1955), p. 40. At the time of writing 'Rebec, Fiddle and Crowd in England', the present writer was under the misapprehension that the Cross at the north door was St. Paul's Cross outside the Cathedral (see p. 26 of that article).

11. Bachmann, *The Origins*, p. 122.
12. Bowles, 'Haut et bas', 128 f.
13. Pirro, *La Musique*, p. 20.
14. Ibid., p. 20.
15. Rastall, 'Secular Musicians', i. 67.
16. Frank Harrison, in 'Tradition and Innovation', p. 328, says that 'on the feast of Corpus Christi, especially in Italy and Spain ... the players of instruments from the town or region who had walked in the sacred procession continued with it into the church and played at suitable points in the service'.
17. Bowles, 'Musical Instruments in the Medieval Corpus Christi Procession', *passim*.
18. Ibid., p. 257. Here the relevant footnote in Bowles's article leads to an incorrect source.
19. Lucy Toulmin Smith (ed.), *English Gilds EETS:OS* 40 (1870), p. 148.
20. John Brand, *Observations on the Popular Antiquities of Great Britain*, 3 vols. (London, 1849), ii. 158–9.
21. Eleanor Shipley Duckett, *Anglo-Saxon Saints and Scholars* (New York, 1947), p. 41. Jeff Opland, *Anglo-Saxon Oral Poetry* (Newhaven and London, 1980), p. 121.
22. Revd Alexander Dyce (ed.), *The Poetical Works of John Skelton*, 2 vols. (London, 1843), ii. 433–4. This is the edition of Skelton's works which Bachmann cites in *The Origins of Bowing*, p. 128, although the quotation given there is 'They play on their fiddles and sing in fifts' [*sic*]. This is in fact a translation back into English from the German translation given in the original German edition of the book, *Die Anfänge des Streichinstrumentenspiels*, p. 148: 'Sie spielen auf ihren Fideln und singen in Quinten'.
23. *The Play of Daniel*, ed. W. L. Smoldon, rev. David Wulstan (PMMS, Sutton, 1976), p. 15.
24. Young, *The Drama of the Medieval Church*, ii. 302 ff.
25. Bowles, 'The Role of Musical Instruments', p. 76.
26. Bowles, ibid., pp. 74–5, says that the actors only held their instruments in a playing position, while real musicians played behind them. While this may have happened sometimes, there is no evidence that it was always the case. If being a member of an angelic 'orchestra' demanded no particular acting ability, there is every reason why the minstrels should have taken real parts, particularly if the play were the corporate effort of the whole town.
27. Hardin Craig (ed.), *Two Coventry Corpus Christi Plays EETS:ES* 87, 2nd edn. (1957), p. 19. See p. 72 above for a reference to the 'viallis'.
28. Anderson, *Drama and Imagery*, plate 11g for the Resurrection of the Innocents.
29. Ibid., p. 137.
30. Chambers, *The Mediaeval Stage*, ii. 64–5, 107, 133.
31. W. C. Hazlitt (ed.), *Dodsley's Old English Plays*, 15 vols. (London, 1874–6, 4th edn.), i. 48. The staging of this play is discussed by Richard Southern in *The Staging of Plays*, pp. 201–16.
32. E. Creeth (ed.), *Tudor Plays* (New York, 1966), p. 346.
33. J. Q. Adams (ed.), *Chief Pre-Shakespearean Dramas* (London, 1925), pp. 330, 335.
34. Ibid., p. 342.
35. J. S. Brewer (ed.), *L & P* 2, ii. 1499, 1501.
36. Ibid., 2, ii. 1501. The word 'pageant' is used here in its sense of a moveable stage.
37. Wickham, *Early English Stages*, i. 17.
38. Ibid., 69 f. The author also quotes the original Latin of part of the poem.

39. W. P. Ker and W. E. Henley (eds.), *J. Froissart, Chronicles* (London, 1901), i. 65.

40. See p. 40 for a suggestion that the latter instrument might also be intended to be accompanied by a tabor.

41. Auvo Kurvinen (ed.), *Sir Gawain and the Carl of Carlisle in two Versions* (Helsinki, 1951), p. 154 (A version).

42. Ibid., p. 157 (B version).

43. A. J. Bliss (ed.), *Sir Orfeo* (2nd edn., Oxford, 1966), p. 44.

44. Edith Rickert (ed.), *The Romance of Emaré EETS:ES* 99 (1906), p. 13.

45. A celebrated event involving another noble bird was the Feast of the Pheasant, held by Philip the Good, Duke of Burgundy, on 17 February 1454. This has been described, not altogether accurately, by Edmund Bowles in 'Instruments at the Court of Burgundy (1363–1467)', *GSJ* vi (1953), 41–51.

46. Baines (ed.), 'Fifteenth-century Instruments', p. 24.

47. See p. 79, n. 4. Chambers, *The Mediaeval Stage*, ii. 262–3.

48. The list is printed by Bullock-Davies in *Menestrellorum*, pp. 1–6. The exact number of minstrels and their instruments cannot be known, because the accounts are sometimes restricted to a performer's name, with no reference to an instrument. Also, there are lists of payments written in French and in Latin, and while they are by no means identical, there is a certain degree of overlapping in their contents.

49. Ibid., pp. 1–6.

50. Rastall, 'Secular Musicians', ii. 74.

51. Bullock-Davies, op. cit., pp. 140–1.

52. Ibid., pp. xxix–xxx.

53. Ibid., p. xxx.

54. Thomas Percy (ed.), *The Regulations and Establishment of the Household of Henry Algernon Percy, the Fifth Earl of Northumberland, at his Castles of Wresill and Lekinfield in Yorkshire* (London, 1770), pp. 343–4.

55. Carl Horstmann (ed.), *Seint Thomas, Early South English Legendary EETS:OS* 87 (1887), p. 379.

56. *Launfal, AEMR* i. 199.

57. *The Squyr of Lowe Degre, AEMR* iii. 189–90.

58. Wickham, *Early English Stages*, i. 17.

59. Galpin, 'Old Instruments of Music . . . of Essex', p. 22.

60. Derek Pearsall (ed.), *Piers Plowman by William Langland (C Text)* (London, 1978), p. 126.

61. Robinson (ed.), *Chaucer*, p. 61.

62. John Lydgate, trans. from the French of Guillaume de Deguileville, *The Pilgrimage of the Life of Man*, ed. Frederick J. Furnivall, 3 vols., *EETS:ES* 77, 83, 92 (1899–1904), 317.

63. John Lydgate, *Reson and Sensuallyte*, ed. Ernst Sieper, *EETS:ES* 84 (1901), p. 146.

CHAPTER XI: THE USE OF BOWED INSTRUMENTS IN MUSIC

1. For a few exceptions to this rule, see Remnant, *Musical Instruments*, pp. 197–8.

2. Transcribed in *Compositions of the Bamberg Manuscript*, ed. Gordon A. Anderson, *CMM* 75 (AIM 1977), from the MS Bamberg, Staatsbibliothek, Lit. 115 (*olim* Ed. IV. 6), p. 138, no. 105.

3. *LU*, p. 957. While belonging particularly to the feast of Corpus Christi, this hymn can be

sung on many occasions throughout the year. It is 'Pange lingua ... mysterium' as opposed to Pange lingua ... certaminis', which is from the liturgy of Good Friday.

4. Ibid., p. 780.

5. Ibid., pp. 40–2.

6. Ibid., pp. 62–3.

7. Ibid., p. 276.

8. Ibid., pp. 1832–7.

9. Chaytor, *The Troubadors and England*, pp. 34 ff.

10. Transcriptions in J. B. Trend, 'The First English Songs', *M & L* (1928), pp. 120–3; Dobson and Harrison, *Medieval English Songs*, pp. 228–9, with commentary on pp. 103–9, 295–6. On the life of St. Godric, see also Brian Trowell, 'Godric', *Grove 6*.

11. Transcription in *HAM* i. 16, no. 19a.

12. Cambridge University Library Add. MS 710, fo. 127. Transcription in Dobson and Harrison, *Medieval English Songs*, p. 261; facsimile in Dom Hesbert, OSB, *Le Tropaire-Prosaire de Dublin, MMS* iv (Rouen, 1970), plate 186.

13. BL MS Arundel 248, fo. 254. Transcription in Dobson and Harrison, op. cit., p. 263.

14. Transcriptions in *NOHM* iii. 113; Dobson and Harrison, op. cit., p. 269.

15. Transcriptions in *NOHM* ii. 251; Dobson and Harrison, op. cit., pp. 244–5.

16. Guilelmi Monachi, *De Preceptis Artis Musicae*, ed. Albert Seay, *CSM* 11 (AIM, 1965), pp. 38–9.

17. The author speaks here from experience, having once taken part in a performance of this piece which was transposed down a tone to suit the voice of the singer. It meant droning with the third finger on the bottom string of a five-stringed fiddle for about ten minutes, which seemed to be a very long time in the circumstances. Facsimile in *EEH* i, plates 12–17.

18. Bachmann, *The Origins*, p. 88.

19. Ibid., p. 126.

20. *Dan Michel's Ayenbite of Inwyt*, ed. Richard Morris, *EETS:OS* 23 (1866), p. 105.

21. John Lydgate, trans. from the French of Guillaume de Deguileville, *The Pilgrimage of the Life of Man*, ed. F. J. Furnivall, 3 vols., *EETS:ES* 77, 83, 92 (1899–1904), 577. This is a different version from the text in the BL MS Cott. Tiberius A. vii, fo. 79ᵛ, where the margin contains a picture of an angel playing a rebec. See p. 15 above.

22. Such an example is in Hugo von Montfort's 'Fraw, wilt du wissen', transcribed in Erwin Leuchter (ed.), *Florilegium Musicum* (Buenos Aires, 1964), p. 11.

23. Bachmann, *The Origins*, p. 126.

24. Luther Dittmer (ed.), *The Worcester Fragments, MSD* ii (AIM, 1957), pp. 2–4.

25. *LU*, p. 16.

26. Andrew Hughes and Margaret Bent (ed.), *The Old Hall Manuscript, CMM* 46 (AIM, 1969–73), i. 93 ff.

27. *Leonel Power Complete Works*, ed. Charles Hamm, *CMM* 50 (AIM, 1969), pp. 2–3.

28. Stevens, *Medieval Carols*, p. 6.

29. Transcriptions in *NOHM* ii. 342; Dobson and Harrison, op. cit., p. 258.

30. Transcriptions in *NOHM* ii. 343; Dobson and Harrison, op. cit., p. 246.

31. Transcription in ibid., pp. 246–50.

32. Transcription in ibid., p. 276.

33. Transcription in ibid., pp. 282–3.

34. Transcription in ibid., p. 284.

35. Harrison, however, points out that the composer was somewhat old-fashioned in his use of consecutive fifths, which by that time were out of date in France. Ibid., p. 311.

36. Robinson (ed.), *Chaucer*, p. 318. On p. 796, n. 677, Robinson points out that in several MSS the words 'Qui bien aime a tard oublie' indicate the probable melody, although other composers than Machaut have set that text to music. David Wulstan, however, considers that 'Now welcome sumer' should be sung to the music of Machaut's 'Dame, qui vous n'avez aperceu'. David Wulstan, *An Anthology of Carols* (London, 1968), pp.47–8 and n. 31.

37. Transcriptions in *HAM* i. 65–6, no. 61.

38. Transcription in ibid., pp. 89–90, no. 85.

39. Stevens, *Music at the Court of Henry VIII*, xvii ff. This source has become known as *Henry VIII's Manuscript* because it contains several compositions by that King, but there is no evidence that it belonged to him.

40. The crumhorn is another instrument which apparently came to England during the reign of Henry VIII, who was sent thirteen of them in 1515 by Pierre Van den Hove, known as 'Alamire', a music scribe working at the court of Marguerite of Austria at Malines. He (Alamire) was also involved in espionage on behalf of Henry VIII, reporting to him the activities of certain Englishmen living abroad. As a cover for his spying, he sent manuscripts to England, and also instruments. Martin Picker, *The Chanson Albums of Marguerite of Austria* (Berkeley and Los Angeles, 1965), p. 34.

41. Transcription in *NOHM* ii. 245–6.

42. Transcription in *HAM* i. 43, no. 40c.

43. Transcription in Dom Anselm Hughes (ed.), *Early Medieval Music up to 1300, HMS* ii (London, 1960), pp. 45–7.

44. Ibid., pp. 45–6.

45. The keyboard dances are transcribed in Willi Apel, *Keyboard Music of the Fourteenth and Fifteenth Centuries, CEKM* i (AIM, 1963), 1–3.

46. John Stevens, 'Carole', *Grove 6*; Ingrid Brainard, 'Dance III. 2', *Grove 6*.

47. Daniel Heartz, 'Basse-danse', *Grove 6*; Ingrid Brainard, 'Dance III. 2', *Grove 6*. For 'Quene note' see Crane, *Basse Danse*, pp. 15, 64–5, 105.

48. Heartz, 'The Basse-Danse', pp. 309–11. Crane, op. cit., p. 24.

49. Transcription in Stevens, *Music at the Court of Henry VIII*, pp. 58–60. For the melodic origin see Crane, op. cit., p. 105.

50. Ward, 'The manner or dauncying', *passim*, including transcription. Another transcription in Stevens, op. cit., pp. 68–9.

51. Syr Thomas Elyot, *The Boke named the Gouernour* (London, 1531), fo. 77. The pieces from MS Roy. App. 58 are published in *Ten Pieces by Hugh Aston and others* (Schlott's *Anthology of Early Keyboard Music*, i), ed. Frank Dawes (London, 1951).

52. Elyot, op. cit., fo. 75. The spelling here is from the 1537 edition.

53. Stevens, *Music and Poetry*, pp. 262, n. 50, 245.

54. Palmer, 'Musical Instruments', pp. 57–8.

55. Colour illustration in Neville Williams, *The Life and Times of Elizabeth I* (London, 1972), pp. 82–3.

1 (*above*) Asaph playing the crowd among David's minstrels in the Winchcombe Psalter, *c*.1030–50.

2 (*right*) David plays the harp and his minstrels play a wind instrument, rebec, and horn, together with a juggler; from the Tiberius Psalter, *c*.1050.

3 Rebec-player on a counter from the Gloucester Tables Set, an early form of Backgammon discovered in 1983, late 11c.

4 David harping with a rebec-player and juggler in the *Beatus* initial from St. Augustine's *Commentary on the Psalms*, *c*.1070–1100.

5 (*above*) Rebec played by an animal near the *Beatus* initial of a Psalter, 12c.

6 (*right*) Rebec-player from an illustration to *Lives of the Saints*, c.1100–20.

7 Crowd, illustrating 'Lira' in a book about the constellations, c.1100–20.

8 Mediaeval viol played in St. Jerome's *Commentaries on the Old Testament*, c.1120.

9 An early example of angels playing a mediaeval viol and primitive fiddles; from
St. Augustine's *De Civitate Dei*, *c*.1120.

10 David playing a mediaeval viol in the St. Albans
Psalter, *c*.1120–30.

11 David playing a mediaeval viol, while two of his
minstrels play horns and gongs, two play harps, and
two play chimebells; from the St. Albans Psalter,
c.1120–30.

12 Minstrel playing a fiddle or rebec on an exterior corbel-table, Romsey Abbey, c.1120–40.

13 Rebec and shawm played by a devil and horned animal on a capital, Canterbury Cathedral, before 1130.

14 David plays the harp and his minstrels the rebec and horn (note the studs on the tailpiece of the rebec); from a Bible, c.1130.

15 Two of David's minstrels play a rebec and harp, while the third, dressed as a bear, wears bells on his costume and strikes a tabor; from the *Beatus* initial of the Shaftesbury Psalter, c.1130–40.

16 One of David's minstrels playing a rebec in the *Beatus* initial of the Winchcombe Bible, *c.*1130–40.

17 Grotesque rebec-player from a Romanesque corbel-table, Church of St. Mary and St. David, Kilpeck, *c.*1140.

18 Fiddler wearing a grotesque head in the Lambeth Bible, *c.*1140–50.

19 Plucked rebec from the Lambeth Bible, *c.*1140–50.

20 David plays a mediaeval viol in the Winchester Psalter, *c.*1150.

21 Rebec-player among David's minstrels in the York Psalter, c.1170.

22 Mediaeval viol player among David's minstrels in the York Psalter, c.1170.

23 Players of the harp, rebec, and mediaeval viol stand by David who holds a psaltery in the Great Canterbury Psalter, c.1180–90.

24 (*left*) Minstrel playing a mediaeval viol above a pillar, Oakham Castle, *c*.1180–90.

25 Elders holding fiddles (the bottom one seems to have two soundposts), Cathedral of Santiago de Compostela, *Pórtico de la Gloria*, *c*.1188.

26 (*above*) David and his minstrels playing a harp, rebec, mediaeval viol, and double pipe in a Psalter, *c*.1190–1200.

27 (*right*) Minstrels playing a rebec (in outer mandorla), pipe, mediaeval viol, panpipes, and harp (in inner roundels) in the south doorway, Church of St. Nicholas, Barfrestone, late 12c.

29 Minstrels play a rebec, psaltery, harp, mediaeval viol, and horn in the *Exultate* initial of a Psalter, *c*.1200–10.

30 Rebec-player in an initial from the Canterbury Psalter (Oxford), *c*.1210–20.

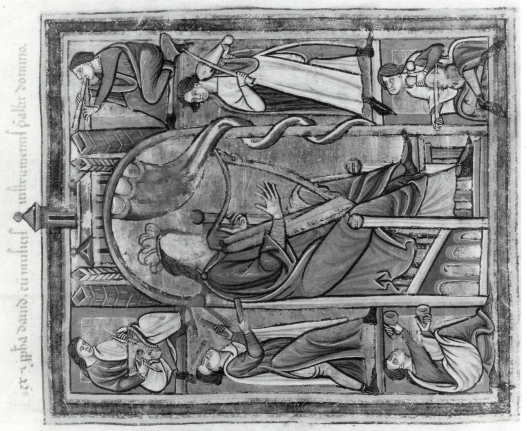

28 David harping, with minstrels playing handbells, psaltery, double pipe, rebec, and mediaeval viol, and a juggler; from a Psalter, late 12c.

31 A nineteenth-century 'restoration' turning a thirteenth-century painted fiddle into a violin, nave roof, Peterborough Cathedral.

32 Rebec and panpipes played together in a spandrel carving, Bristol Cathedral, *c*.1215–34.

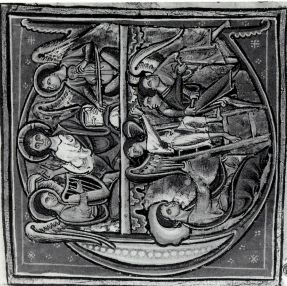

34 Angels playing harp and mediaeval viol in the *Exultate* initial of a Psalter, *c.*1220–30.

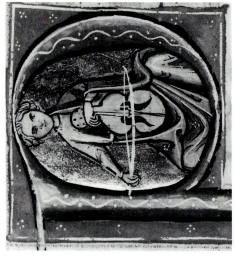

35 Mediaeval viol played in a Psalter, *c.* 1220–30.

33 David the harpist with minstrels playing a fiddle, mediaeval viol, psaltery, and organistrum in the Lindesey Psalter, before 1222.

37 Mediaeval viol played in a roundel from the Brailes Psalter, illuminated by William de Brailes, *c.*1230–40.

38 One of several musical angels in Gothic arcading, Westminster Abbey, mid 13c. The angel plays a mediaeval viol.

36 David the harpist is joined by animals playing panpipes, psaltery, rebec, harp, mediaeval viol, and cymbals, with a juggler and other performers; from the *Beatus* page of a Psalter, *c.*1220–30.

40 Mediaeval viol played in an initial of the Amesbury Psalter, *c.*1240–60.

39 Elders with a gittern (citole) and harp, and a fiddle with a curved bridge; from the Lambeth Apocalypse, mid 13c.

prés ico 10 01 aufi cum une grauor uois de
nuttef bufinef. en le cel difaunf. alleluia . lo

uelura est lu eltre chaunce eine ftz de fer uois.
A la premæ ftz e a la feunde. de la uois de

41 Minstrels playing a fiddle and harp in the Trinity College Apocalypse, *c.*1250–60.

42 (*left*) Three rebecs on the Seal of
Walter le Vyelur, *c*.1256–7.

43 Elders with crowd and organ, from an Apocalypse,
c.1260–70.

44 Dancers perform to the sound of a fiddle and gittern
(citole) in a Book of Hours, *c*.1260–90.

45 Singers and a rebec-player in the *Cantate* initial of the
Venice Psalter, *c*.1270.

46 A member of the Angel Choir playing a fiddle, Lincoln Cathedral, c.1280.

47 David plays chimebells with a fiddler and an acrobat in the Huth Psalter, c.1280–90.

48 Fiddler with animals playing a gong and bagpipes in the Alfonso Psalter, c.1281–4.

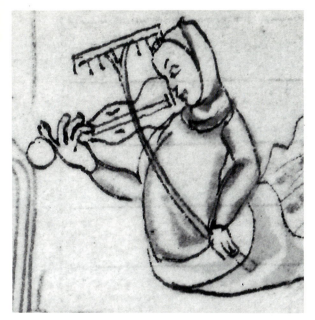

49 Fiddle bowed with a rake, from a Royal Roll, late 13c.

50 Minstrels playing a fiddle and mediaeval viol below Christ in majesty, from a Psalter, late 13c.

51 Grotesque rebec-player from the Bird Psalter, late 13c.

52 An angelic fiddler running, from a Flemish Book of Hours, c.1300.

53 Angelic fiddler on a roof boss (the bow is broken at its point), Exeter Cathedral, *c.*1300–2.

54 Fiddle played by a pig on a misericord, where it is accompanied by a double shawm, Winchester Cathedral, *c.*1305.

55 Rebec played on a misericord, where it is accompanied by a double shawm, Winchester Cathedral, *c.*1305.

56 David and his minstrels play a harp, fiddle, and gittern (citole), from the Peterborough Psalter, *c*.1299–1318.

57 Fiddler from a margin in the Peterborough Psalter, *c*.1299–1318.

58 Minstrels playing a fiddle, harp, gittern (citole), portative organ, trumpet, rebec, and pipe-and-tabor in the Peterborough Psalter, *c*.1299–1318.

60 David plays a fiddle with a trumpeter, in procession by the Ark of the Covenant; from the Tickhill Psalter, c.1303–13.

62 The Seal of Roger Wade the Crowder, early 14c.

59 Grotesque fiddler from the Tickhill Psalter, c.1303–13.

61 David carries Goliath's head, with minstrels (behind) playing two rebecs and two trumpets, and (in front) a fiddle, gittern (citole), and two trumpets: from the Tickhill Psalter, c.1303–13.

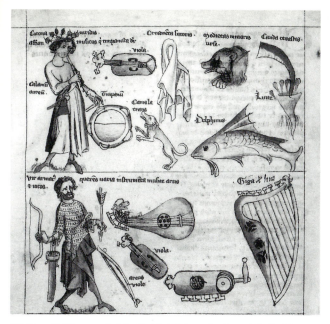

63 Two fiddles, each labelled 'viola', and a bow labelled 'arcus viole', besides a shawm, timbrel, citole, symphony, and harp, in a Flemish book of astrology, early 14c.

64 A cat fiddles while a goat plays a mandora (gittern) or plucked rebec, on a misericord, Hereford Cathedral, early 14c.

66 (*above*) Singers and a fiddler in the *Cantate* initial of the Vaux Psalter, *c.*1300–25.

65 (*left*) Minstrels playing a gittern (citole) and fiddle on a roof boss, Norwich Cathedral, early 14c.

67 A fiddler precedes the food to a feast in the Queen Mary Psalter, c.1310–20.

68 Angels with fiddle and gittern (citole) play for St. Catherine in prison, from the Queen Mary Psalter, c.1310–20.

70 An ape fiddles for a dancing lion in the Gorleston Psalter, c.1310–25.

69 David playing chimebells with a bagpiper and fiddler in the Howard Psalter, c.1309–26.

71 David playing a harp, while his minstrels play a portative organ, trumpet, fiddle, gittern (citole), psaltery, and timbrel; from the Gorleston Psalter, c.1310–25.

72 Angelic fiddler from the Ormesby Psalter, c.1310–25.

73 Bellows-and-tongs played by a grotesque minstrel in the Ormesby Psalter, c.1310–25.

74 Fiddle played by a centaur in stained glass, Church of St. Peter, Ringland, c.1310–25.

75 Fiddle with cross-shaped soundholes, on a corbel, Exeter Cathedral; the carving dates from c.1310–25, and the present paint from the mid 14c.

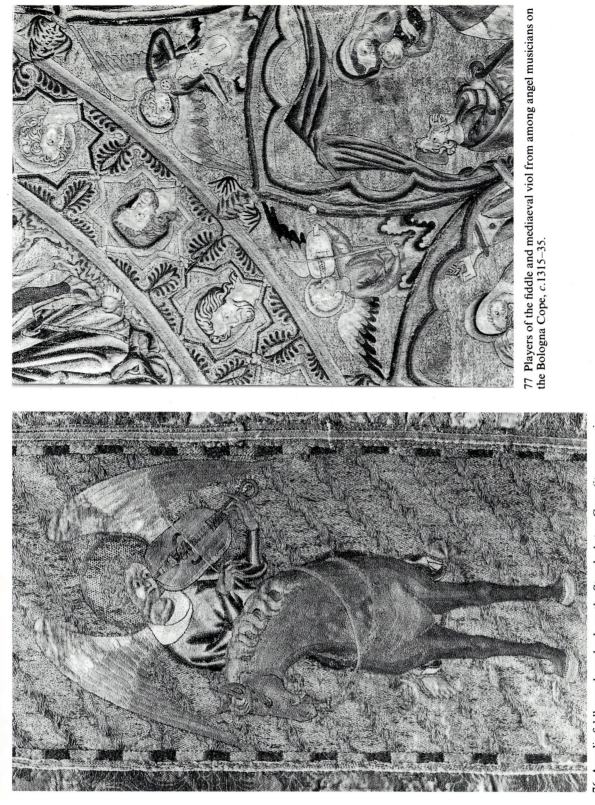

77 Players of the fiddle and mediaeval viol from among angel musicians on the Bologna Cope, c.1315–35.

76 Angelic fiddler on horseback on the Steeple Aston Cope (its companion plays the earliest known English picture of a lute), c.1310–40.

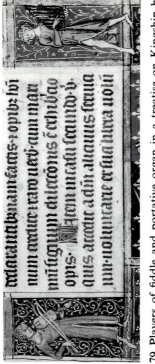

78 (*left*) The minstrels who should entertain a king, according to a treatise by Walter de Milemete, 1326; their instruments are bagpipes, timbrel, gittern (citole), fiddle, double pipe, shawm, crowd, pipe-and-tabor, gong (or juggling?), portative organ, harp, and positive organ.

79 Players of fiddle and portative organ in a treatise on Kingship by Walter de Milemete, 1326.

80 Detail of crowd from plate 78.

81 Organ and fiddle played together in the border of a manuscript made for Edward III by Walter de Milemete, 1326–7.

82 A woman dances to the sound of pipe-and-tabor and fiddle in an account of the possessions of Battle Abbey, 14c.

83 Minstrel fiddling on a corbel, Church of St. Peter, Navenby, 14c.

84 Grotesque rebec-player from the
Smithfield Decretals, *c*.1325–50.

85 A mermaid fiddles in the Smithfield Decretals, *c*.1325–50.

86 Fiddle (its neck is modern) played by one of
twelve angels on the Minstrels' Gallery, Exeter
Cathedral, *c*.1325–50.

87 Angel fiddler from the Psalter of Robert de
Lisle, *c*.1330–9.

88 Cat and fiddle on a misericord, Wells Cathedral, *c.*1330–40.

89 Grotesque rebec-player from a margin in the Luttrell Psalter, *c.*1335–40.

90 Fiddle and trumpet (broken) are played together on a misericord designed by Hurley, Ely Cathedral, 1339–41.

91 The game of *barriers* enlivened by fiddle and shawm in the border of a Psalter (note the curved bridge on the fiddle), *c*.1340.

92 An elderly fiddler above a capital, Church of St. Peter, Hanwell, *c*.1340.

93 Fourteenth-century fiddler in a margin of a twelfth-century copy of St. Augustine's *De Civitate Dei*, mid 14c.

94 A fiddling sheep on a roof corbel, Church of St. Mary the Virgin, Cogges, mid 14c.

95 A damaged Minstrels' Pillar, showing the remains of a fiddle, Beverley Minster, c.1308–49.

97 Plaster cast of an angel fiddling on a roof boss, Tewkesbury Abbey, mid 14c.

96 Angel fiddling on a roof boss, Gloucester Cathedral, c.1350.

99 Grotesque minstrel holding a fiddle on which the combination of bridge and tailpiece is curved, enabling the strings to be sounded separately; from the Bohun Psalter (London), *c*.1370–80.

98 David plays the harp, while near him are two rebecs—one may be a mandora (gittern)—with a bow, and a psaltery. The rebec on the left has a crennellated bridge. From a French Psalter, 14c.

100 Singers and a fiddler from the *Cantate* initial of a Psalter, *c*.1350–75.

101 Minstrels with fiddle, mandora (gittern), shawm, and two trumpets at the Peacock Feast on the Braunche brass (made in Flanders) Church of St. Margaret, King's Lynn, 1364.

102 Fretted fiddle played in a border of the Bohun Psalter (London), *c.*1370–80.

103 Angels play a fiddle, psaltery, and mandora (gittern) in the Bohun Psalter (London), *c.*1370–80.

104 Angel fiddler from the Litlyngton Missal, 1383–4.

105 Fiddler in a border of the Litlyngton Missal, 1383–4.

106 Elders with (left) two fiddles, psaltery, and trumpet, and (right) a harp, portative organ, cymbals, and crowd, from an Apocalypse, *c*.1380–95.

107 St. John listening to players of the harp, fiddle, and psaltery in an Apocalypse, *c*.1380–95.

108 Angel playing a crowd on a misericord, Worcester Cathedral, *c*.1397.

109 Rebec and psaltery played on a misericord, Worcester Cathedral, *c*.1397.

[Conway Library, Courtauld Institute of Art and Canon M. H. Ridgway.]

110 Rebec played by a roof angel (before restoration), St. Mary's Hall, Coventry, late 14c.

111 Elders of the Apocalypse with fiddle and crowd in wall-paintings by Brother John of Northampton, Westminster Abbey, *c*.1400.

112 Rebec-playing angel in a stained glass roundel from Bury St. Edmunds, *c*.1400.

113 Fiddler in attendance in a stained glass scene when Herod receives the head of St. John the Baptist (the fiddle's scroll is not original), York Minster, *c*.1414.

114 Angels from the Celestial Hierarchy playing a portative organ, psaltery, symphony, gittern (citole), fiddle, harp, rebec, mandora (gittern), lute, triangle, (?) psaltery, and timbrel in the Sherborne Missal, designed by John Siferwas, *c*.1400–6.

115 Fiddler in a border of the Hours of Elizabeth the Queen, illustrated by Johannes, *c.*1420–30.

116 Angel fiddling in a stained glass roundel, St. Mary's Church, Saxlingham Nethergate, *c.*1420–50.

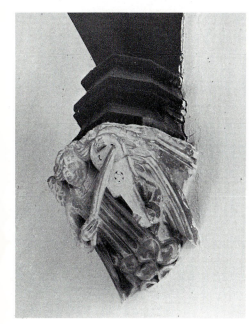

117 Angel fiddling on a roof corbel, Church of All Saints, Broad Chalke, 15c.

118 Lydgate's Pilgrim is approached by the bird-man 'Worldly Gladness', who carries a rebec; from *Pilgrimage of the Life of Man*, after 1426.

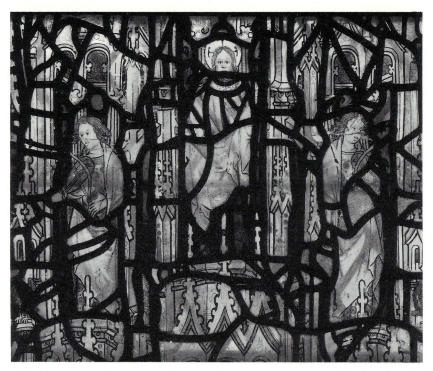

119 Fiddles played by two angels in the St. Cuthbert window, York Minster, after 1443.

120 Rebec-player on an arm-rest, St. Mary's Church, Beverley, 1445.

121 Rebec played by a roof angel, before restoration, Church of All Saints, York, 15c.

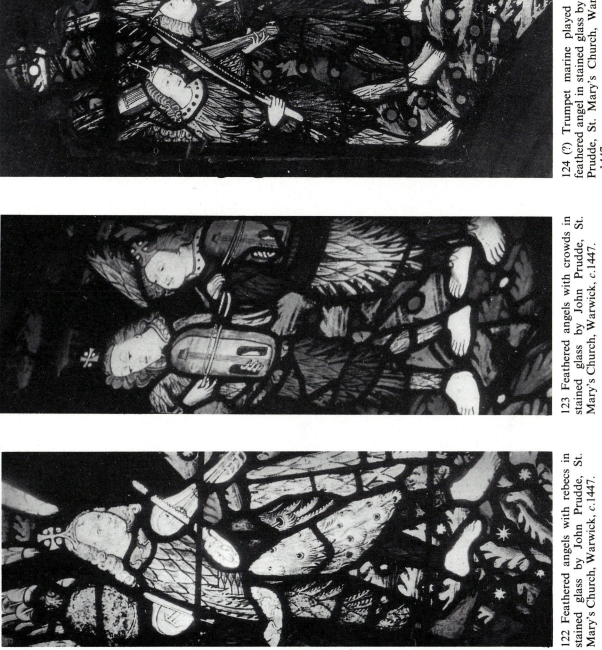

124 (?) Trumpet marine played by a feathered angel in stained glass by John Prudde, St. Mary's Church, Warwick, c.1447.

123 Feathered angels with crowds in stained glass by John Prudde, St. Mary's Church, Warwick, c.1447.

122 Feathered angels with rebecs in stained glass by John Prudde, St. Mary's Church, Warwick, c.1447.

125 Feathered angels in stained glass playing bagpipes and fiddle at the Annunciation, Church of St. Peter Hungate, Norwich, 15c.

126 Minstrels play a lute and rebec in stained glass, Church of All Saints, Besthorpe, 15c.

127 A roof angel with a rebec, Ely Cathedral, 15c.

128 Rebec played by a roof angel, Church of St. John, Stamford, 15c.

129 Fiddle with its stringholder at the lower end, York Minster, before 1472.

130 A fiddle played in the downward position (unusual for England) by a roof angel, St. Mary's Church, Buckden, 15c.

131 Feathered angel playing a fiddle in stained glass of the Norwich school, c.1460–80.

132 Angels playing a fiddle and lute by Christ in Majesty in the *Speculum Humanae Salvationis*, late 15c.

133 Rebec and pipe played together at a feast, in the *Speculum Humanae Salvationis*, late 15c.

134 The former crowd (destroyed in a storm of 1894) played by a roof angel, St. Mary's Church, Shrewsbury, late 15c.

135 Minstrels with rebec and pipe (with tabor out of sight?) greet David after he has killed Goliath; from the *Exultate* initial of a Psalter, late 15c.

136 (?) Trumpet marine played by an angel on the choir screen, York Minster, *c*.1475–1500.

137 Angels playing a rebec, harp, and lute, from a frieze which also includes a portative organ, Church of All Saints, Hillesden, *c*.1493.

138 Angels playing a lute, harp, and fiddle, from the opposite frieze, which also contains a portative organ, Church of All Saints, Hillesden, *c*.1493.

139 A feathered angel fiddles in stained glass, Great Malvern Priory, 1501.

140 One of several musical roof angels, playing a fiddle, Church of SS. Peter and Paul, Knapton, 1503.

142 Angels playing a rebec and lute, King's College Chapel, Cambridge, c.1508–16.

141 A cat fiddles while long-eared kittens dance on a pew end, St. Mary's Church, Fawsley, 16c.

143 A cat fiddling for dancing kittens on a misericord, Beverley Minster, 1520.

144 Singing rebec-player on a corbel, St. Mary's
Church, Beverley, early 16c.

145 Minstrels' Pillar, showing a broken pipe-and-tabor and rebec,
with a more complete lute (?) and shawm (the central instrument is
completely destroyed), St. Mary's Church, Beverley, 1520–4.

146 Fiddler on a benchend playing an instrument
similar to those found on the *Mary Rose* (plates
150, 151), Church of St. Nonna, Altarnun, after
1523.

147 Detail of the lute and Renaissance viol from *The More Family Group* by Holbein, 16c. perhaps copied by Rowland Lockey.

148 *The Family of Sir Thomas More* by Hans Holbein II, *c.*1527; a Renaissance viol hangs on the wall, and More's daughter Elizabeth Dauncey holds a lute.

150 Fiddle from Henry VIII's flagship the *Mary Rose*, which sank on 19 July 1545.

151 Fiddle from Henry VIII's flagship the *Mary Rose*, which sank on 19 July 1545.

149 *Apollo and the Muses*; design for the Coronation procession of Anne Boleyn in 1533, possibly by Hans Holbein II, *c*.1533. Apollo plays a harp, while some of the Muses sing and others play a fiddle, crumhorn with bladder, triangle, lute, and pipe-and-tabor.

152 *A Fête at Bermondsey* by Joris Hoefnagel, *c*.1570; on the right are two groups of musicians, each comprising a violin and viola player.

153 Detail of musicians from plate 152.

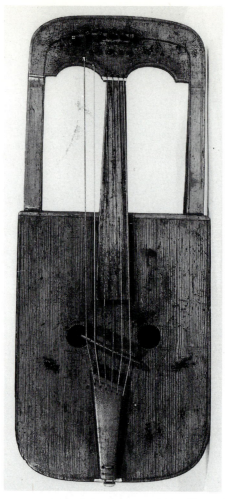

154 Crwth by Richard Evans of Llanfihangel
Bachellaeth, 1742.

155 Yugoslav gusle, modern.

Bowed Instruments and their Accessories in Fifteenth-century Word Lists and Dictionaries

Promptorium Parvulorum by Frater Galfridus, OP, *c.*1440,
ed. Albertus Way, 3 vols., *CSP:OS* (1843–65).

BOWE	Arcus
BRYGGE	Pons
CROWDE, instrument of musyke	Chorus
FYDELARE	Fidicen, vitulator
FYDELIN, or fyielyn	Vitulor
FYDYLL, or fyyele	Viella, fidicina, vitula
FYTHIL, supra in FEDYLLE*	(*there is no FEDYLLE)
[LUTE, instrument of musyke	Viella, samba, lambutum]
PEGGE	Cavilla
RYBYBE	Vitula
STRYNGE	Cordula, instita

Catholicon Anglicum, 1483,
ed. Sidney J. H. Herrtage, *CSP:OS* (1882)

A BOWE	Archus, arculus diminutiuum
A BRYGE	Pons, ponticulus
A CROWDE	Corus sine h litera (sine aspiracione A)
A FIDILLER	Fidulista, vidulista
A FIDYLLE	Vidula, vidella, viella
TO FIDYLLE	Vidulare, viellare
A FIDYLLE STIK	Arculus
[AN HARPER	Citharedo ... fidicen, fidicina, etc.]
A PEGE	Cavilla, cavillula diminutiuum.
A STRYNGE	Corda, cordula diminutiuum.

Nominale A (BL MS Royal 17 C. xvii, fo. 43ᵛ)

[Hec lira	HARPESTRYNG]	p. 216
Hic fidis	FYDELLERE	
Hec viella	FEDYLLE	
Hic arculus	FYDYLSTYK	

Hic corallus	CROWDERE	
Hec coralla	CROWDE	

Another Nominale in the same MS (fo. 21 ff.) contains the following on fo. 27:

[Hec lira	HARPESTRYNG]	p. 202
Hec vetella	RYBYBE	p. 202
Hec viella	FYTHYLLE	p. 202

NOMINALE B (formerly in the collection of Joseph Mayer of Liverpool)

Hic cordex	STRYNG-MAKER	p. 213
[Hec fides	HARPE-STRYNG]	p. 240
[Hec lira	HARPE]	p. 240
Hic vidulator	FYDELER	p. 218
Hec vitula	RYBYBE	p. 240

The above three *nominalia* are published in Thomas Wright's *A Volume of Vocabularies*. As the relevant entries are not alphabetical, their page numbers in Wright are given at the end of the appropriate lines. In Wülcker's revision of Wright's work, the following alterations can be found in *Nominale B*: 'HARPE-STRYNG' becomes 'HARPSTRYNG' (p. 738) and 'STRYNG-MAKER' looses its hyphen (p. 686).

Items in brackets are not bowed instruments but are involved in Appendix B. Attempts to trace the whereabouts of Joseph Mayer's MS have so far been unsuccessful.

Some Contradictions among Fifteenth-century Word Lists and Dictionaries

This list shows only a few of the words which are muddled between the relevant dictionaries and word lists. The crowd is not included here as it remains outside this particular confusion in the dictionaries concerned.

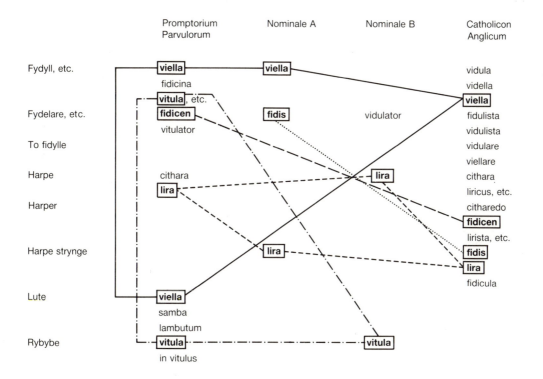

English Representations of Bowed Instruments Quoted in the Text

It had been hoped that this list would contain all the English pictures, carvings, etc., of bowed instruments known to the author. However, such a list would be (a) far too long for this book, and (b) not truly representative of the country as a whole, as it would be limited by the extent of the author's travels, which, even after thirty years, have not managed to penetrate to every corner of the realm. The list includes certain works which were made in England by foreign artists, or made abroad for immediate despatch to England, and the nationality of these is indicated.

A. MANUSCRIPTS, DRAWINGS, AND SEALS

Place	Reference	Date	Folio	Instrument	Plate ref
Alnwick Castle, Northumberland	Sherborne Missal	c.1400–6	p. 276	rebec, fiddle	114
Basel, Kupferstichkabinett	Drawing by Hans Holbein II (German), The Family of Sir Thomas More	c.1527		Renaissance viol	148
Berlin, Staatliche Museen	Drawing, possibly by Hans Holbein II (German). Design for a triumphal arch for Anne Boleyn's Coronation procession	c.1533		fiddle	149
Brussels, Bibliothèque Royale Albert Ier	MS 9961–2, Peterborough Psalter	c.1299–1318	fo. 14	fiddle	56
			fo. 57	fiddle	57
			fo. 74	rebec, fiddle	58
Cambridge, Fitzwilliam Museum	MS 2–1954, Bird Psalter	late 13c.	fo. 38^v	rebec	51
	MS 330, Brailes Psalter	c.1230–40	leaf 5	mediaeval viol	37
			leaf 6	mediaeval viol	
Cambridge, St. John's College	MS K.30	c.1190–1200	fo. 86	rebec, mediaeval viol	26
Cambridge, Trinity College	MS B. 5. 26	1070–1100	fo. 1	rebec	4
	MS B. 10. 2	1380–95	fo. 4^v	crowd, fiddle	106
			fo. 30	fiddle	107
	MS B. 11. 4	c.1220–30	fo. 74^v	fiddle	34
			fo. 85	mediaeval viol	35
			fo. 128	mediaeval viol	

Place	Reference	Date	Folio	Instrument	Plate ref
Cambridge, Trinity College (*cont.*)	MS O. 4. 7	c.1120	fo. 112	mediaeval viol	8
	MS R. 16. 2, Trinity College Apocalypse	1250–60	fo. 22	fiddle	41
Cambridge, University Library	MS Dd. viii. 18	15c.	fo. 110	rebec	135
	MS Ff. 1. 23	c.1030–50	fo. 4ᵛ	crowd	1
Cardiff, Central Library	MS Havod 24 (Welsh)	17c.	p. 358	crwth	
Dublin, Trinity College	MS 53, Winchcombe Bible	c.1130–40	fo. 151	rebec	16
	MS K. 4. 31, Dublin Apocalypse	early 14c.	p. vi	2 fiddles	
Durham, Cathedral Library	MS Hunter 100	c.1100–20	fo. 62ᵛ	crowd	7
Edinburgh, National Library of Scotland	MS Accession 3141, Iona Psalter	c.1210	fo. 7	rebec, mediaeval viol	
Florence, Biblioteca Medicea Laurenziana	MS Pluteus xii. 17	c.1120	fo. 2ᵛ	mediaeval viol, fiddle, fiddle or rebec	9
Glasgow, University Library	MS Hunter 229, York Psalter	c.1170	fo. 21ᵛ	rebec, mediaeval viol	21–2
Hildesheim, Church of St. Godehard	St. Alban's Psalter	c.1120–30	p. 56	mediaeval viol	10
			p. 417	mediaeval viol	11
Leiden, Bibliotheek der Rijksuniversiteit	MS Lat. 76A, St. Louis Psalter	c.1190–1200	fo. 30ᵛ	rebec, mediaeval viol	
Lisbon, Gulbenkian Collection	MS L. A. 139	13c.	fo. 41ᵛ	mediaeval viol, fiddle	

London, British Library

Manuscript	Date	Folio	Instrument	Page
Add. MS 15036 (Welsh)	18c.	fo. 66	crwth	
Add. MS 21926	13c.	fo. 25^v	rebec	
Add. MS 24686, Alfonso Psalter	c.1281–4	fo. 17^v	fiddle	48
Add. MS 28681, Grandison Psalter	13c.	fo. 100	mediaeval viol, fiddle	50
Add. MS 35166	c.1260–70	fo. 4^v	crowd	43
Add. MS 38116, Huth Psalter	c.1280–90	fo. 89	fiddle	47
Add. MS 42130, Luttrell Psalter	c.1335–40	fo. 149	rebec	89
Add. MS 44874, Evesham Psalter	mid-13c.	fo. 7^v	mediaeval viol, fiddle	
Add. MS 47680	1326–7	ff. 6, 9^v, 16^v, 18^v	fiddle	81
Add. MS 49622, Gorleston Psalter	c.1310–25	fo. 35	fiddle	70
Add. MS 50001, Hours of Elizabeth the Queen	c.1420–30	fo. 107^v	fiddle	71
		fo. 7	fiddle	115
MS Arundel 83, (a) Howard Psalter	1309–26	fo. 55^v	fiddle	69
(b) Lisle Psalter	c.1330–39	fo. 134^v	fiddle	87
MS Arundel 91	c.1100–20	fo. 218^v	rebec	6
MS Arundel 157	c.1200–10	fo. 71^v	rebec, mediaeval viol	29
MS Cott. Domitian A. ii	14c.	fo. 8	fiddle	82
MS Cott. Nero C. iv, Winchester Psalter	c.1150	fo. 46	mediaeval viol	20
MS Cott. Tiberius A. vii	15c.	fo. 77	rebec	
		fo. 79^v	rebec	118

Place	Reference	Date	Folio	Instrument	Plate ref
London, British Library (cont.)	MS Cott. Tiberius C. vi	c.1050	fo. 30^v	rebec	2
	MS Egerton 1151	c.1260–90	fo. 47	fiddle	44
	MS Egerton 3277, Bohun Psalter (London)	c.1370–80	fo. 24	fiddle	99
			fo. 29^v	fiddle	102
			fo. 160	fiddle	103
	MS Harley 2027	17c.	fo. 272	rebec ('Kit')	
	MS Harley 2838	late 15c.	fo. 44^v	fiddle	132
			fo. 45	rebec	133
	MS Harley 6563	14c.	fo. 40	fiddle	
	MS Lansdowne 383, Shaftesbury Psalter	c.1130–40	fo. 15^v	rebec	15
	MS Lansdowne 420	c.1220–30	fo. 12^v	rebec, mediaeval viol	36
	MS Royal 1 C. vii	c.1130	fo. 92	rebec	14
	MS Royal 2 B. vii, Queen Mary Psalter	c.1310–20	fo. 125^v	fiddle	
			fo. 174	fiddle	
			ff. 184^v–185	fiddle	67
			fo. 193	fiddle	
			fo. 203	fiddle	
			fo. 282	fiddle	68
	MS Royal 10. E. iv, Smithfield Decretals	c.1325–50	fo. 4	rebec	84
	MS Royal Roll 14 B. v	before 1300	fo. 71	fiddle	85
	Seal lxxxvii. 44, Seal of Roger Wade the Crowder	early 14c.		fiddle and rake	49
				crowd	62

142

London, Lambeth Palace Library	MS 3, Lambeth Bible	c.1140–50	fo. 67	fiddle	18
			fo. 309	rebec (plucked)	19
	MS 209, Lambeth Apocalypse	mid 13c.	fo. 3	fiddle	39
	MS 233, Vaux Psalter	c.1300–25	fo. 145^v	fiddle	66
	MS 563, St. Neot's Psalter	c.1220	fo. 20	mediaval viol	
London, Public Record Office	Seal P832, Seal of Walter le Vyelur	c.1256–7		3 rebecs	42
London, Society of Antiquaries	MS 59, Lindesey Psalter	before 1222	fo. 38^v	mediaeval viol, fiddle	33
London, Westminster Abbey Library	MS 37, Litlyngton Missal	1383–4	fo. 121	fiddle	104
			fo. 221^v	fiddle	105
Lunel, Bibliothèque Municipale	MS I, Lunel Psalter	c.1100–50	ff. 5^v–6	rebec	
New York, Pierpont Morgan Library	MS Glazier 25	c.1225	fo. 5^v	rebec, mediaeval viol	
			fo. 57	2 rebecs	
New York, Public Library	MS Spencer 26, Tickhill Psalter	c.1303–13	fo. 14	fiddle	59
			fo. 17	2 rebecs, fiddle	61
			fo. 64^v	fiddle	60
Oxford, All Souls College	MS 6, Amesbury Psalter	c.1240–60	fo. 16	fiddle	40
			fo. 55^v	mediaeval viol	
Oxford, Bodleian Library	MS 7	c.1322–5	fo. 7	fiddle	
	MS Ashmole 1523, Bromholm Psalter	early 14c.	fo. 99	fiddle	

Place	Reference	Date	Folio	Instrument	Plate ref
Oxford, Bodleian Library (*cont.*)	MS Ashmole 1525, Canterbury Psalter (Oxford)	c.1210–20	fo. 102	rebec	30
	MS Bodley 691	mid 14c.	fo. 1	fiddle	93
	MS Douce 131	c.1340	fo. 20	fiddle	91
	MS Douce 180, Douce Apocalypse	before 1272	p. 37	fiddle	
	MS Douce 366, Ormesby Psalter	c.1310–25	fo. 9^v	fiddle	72
			fo. 24	bellows and tongs	73
			fo. 45	fiddle	
	MS Gough Liturg. 2	late 12c.	fo. 32	rebec, mediaeval viol	28
	MS Liturg. 198	c.1350–75	fo. 91^v	fiddle	100
	MS New College 7 (kept in the Bodleian Library)	13c.	fo. 145^v	fiddle	
Oxford, Christ Church	MS 92	1326	fo. 18^v	fiddle	79
			fo. 29	fiddle	78
			fo. 43	fiddle, crowd	
Oxford, Exeter College	MS Coxe 47, Bohun Psalter (Oxford)	second quarter 14c.	fo. 58	fiddle	
Paris, Bibliothèque Nationale	MS Lat. 8846, Great Canterbury Psalter	c.1180–90	fo. 54^v	rebec, mediaeval viol	23
Venice, Biblioteca Nazionale Marciana	MS Lat. I. 77, Venice Psalter	c.1270	fo. 26^v	fiddle (or rebec)	
			fo.115	rebec	45
Vienna, Nationalbibliothek	MS 1100	12c.	fo. 1	rebec	5

NB: as mentioned above, these sources are those referred to in the text. Many other pictures of bowed instruments can be found in the same manuscripts, and also in the same churches and museums as those listed below.

B. CHURCHES, MUSEUMS, ETC.

Place	Detail	Date	Instrument	Plate ref.
Adderbury (Oxon.), Church of St. Mary	north side carved frieze, exterior	c.1350	fiddle	
Altarnun (Cornwall), Church of St. Nonna	benchend	after 1523	fiddle	146
Audley End (Essex)	stained glass	14c.	rebec	
Barfrestone (Kent), Church of St. Nicholas	south doorway	late 12c.	rebec, mediaeval viol	27
Besthorpe (Norfolk), Church of All Saints	stained glass	15c.	rebec	126
Beverley (Yorks.), Minster (now Humberside)	nave, north side, label stop	1308–49	fiddle	
	Minstrels' Pillar	1308–49	fiddle	95
	misericord	1520	fiddle	143
Beverley (Yorks.), Church of St. Mary (now Humberside)	arm-rest	1445	rebec	120
	vestry (formerly Holy Trinity Chapel), corbel	early 16c.	rebec	144
	Minstrels' Pillar	1520–24	rebec	145
Bologna, Museo Civico	Bologna Cope	c.1315–35	mediaeval viol, fiddle	77
Brinsop (Herefs.), Church of St. George	arch, interior	c.1150–60	rebec	
Bristol (Avon), Cathedral	Elder Lady Chapel, spandrel carving	c.1215–34	rebec	32
Broad Chalk (Wilts.), Church of All Saints	roof corbel	15c.	fiddle	117

145

Place	Detail	Date	Instrument	Plate ref.
Buckden (Cambs.), Church of St. Mary	roof angel	15c.	fiddle	130
Cambridge, King's College Chapel	south porch, exterior	1508–16	rebec	142
Canterbury (Kent), Cathedral	crypt, St. Gabriel's Chapel, capital	before 1130	rebec	13
Castor (Cambs.), Church of St. Kyneburgha	roof angel	mid 15c.	rebec	
Cley-next-the Sea (Norfolk), Church of St. Margaret	nave corbel	mid 14c.	fiddle	
Cogges (Oxon.), Church of St. Mary the Virgin	north wall cornice, interior	mid 14c.	fiddle	94
Cotehele House (Cornwall)	Welsh bed	late 16c.	crwth	
Coventry (West Midlands), St. Mary's Hall	roof angel	late 14c.	rebec	110
Ely (Cambs.), Cathedral	misericord roof angel	1339–41 15c.	fiddle rebec	90 127
Exeter (Devon), Cathedral	choir roof boss Minstrels' Gallery nave, north side, corbel	c.1300 c.1325–50 c.1310–25	fiddle fiddle fiddle	53 86 75
Fawsley (Northants.), Church of St. Mary	pew	16c.	fiddle	141
Gloucester, Cathedral	choir roof boss	c.1350	fiddle	96
Gloucester, City Museum and Art Gallery	backgammon counter	late 11c.	rebec	3
Great Malvern (Worcs.), Priory	north transept, stained glass	1501	fiddle	139

146

Location	Feature	Date	Instrument	Page
Hanwell (Oxon.), Church of St. Peter	figure above capital	c.1340	fiddle	92
Hardham (Sussex), Church of St. Botolph	wall-paintings	early 12c.	rebecs and fiddles	
Hatfield House (Herts.)	Joris Hoefnagel, *A Fête at Bermondsey*	c.1570	2 violins, 2 violas	152–3
Hawkchurch (Devon), Church of St. John	capital	13c.	fiddle (or rebec)	
Hereford, Cathedral	misericord	early 14c.	fiddle	64
Hillesden (Bucks.), Church of All Saints	east end sculptured frieze, interior	c.1493	rebec, fiddle	137 138
Kilpeck (Herefs.), Church of St. Mary and St. David	corbel, exterior	c.1140	rebec	17
Kimberley (Norfolk), Church of St. Peter	stained glass	15c.	2 fiddles	
King's Lynn (Norfolk), Church of St. Margaret	Braunche brass (Flemish)	1364	fiddle	101
Knapton (Norfolk), Church of SS Peter and Paul	roof angel	1503	fiddle	140
Lavenham (Suffolk), Church of SS Peter and Paul	misericord	14c.	bellows-and-tongs (or crutch)	
Lawford (Essex), Church of St. Mary	north-east window carving, interior	c.1330	rebec	
Lincoln, Cathedral	Angel Choir, spandrel carving	c.1280	fiddle	46
	cloister roof boss	14c.	fiddle	
	north transept, stained glass	14c.	fiddle	
London, Victoria and Albert Museum	Steeple Aston Cope	1310–40	fiddle	76
	stained glass, Norwich school	c.1460–80	fiddle	131

Place	Detail	Date	Instrument	Plate ref.
London, Victoria and Albert Museum	stained glass roundel, Bury St. Edmunds,	c.1400	rebec	112
London, Westminster Abbey	north transept, arcade carving	mid 13c.	mediaeval viol	38
	Chapter house, wall-painting	c.1400	crowd fiddle, rebec	111
Longthorpe Tower (Cambs.)	wall-painting	early 14c.	fiddle	
Loughborough (Leics.), Church of All Saints	roof angel	c.1450	fiddle	
March (Cambs.), Church of St. Wendreda	roof angels	c.1500	rebec	
Navenby (Lincs.), Church of St. Peter	south aisle corbel	14c.	fiddle	83
Newark-on-Trent (Notts.), Church of St. Mary Magdalene	Fleming brass (Flemish)	c.1363	fiddle	
Northleach (Glos.), Church of SS Peter and Paul	porch corbel	c.1500	rebec	
Norwich (Norfolk), Cathedral	cloister roof boss	early 14c.	fiddle	65
Norwich, Church of St. Peter Hungate (now a museum)	stained glass	15c.	fiddle	125
Nostell Priory (Yorks.)	Hans Holbein II (German) The More Family Group (? copy by Rowland Lockey)	16c.	Renaissance viol	147
Oakham Castle (Leics.)	Great Hall, figure above capital	1180–90	mediaeval viol	24
Oakham (Leics.), Church of All Saints	capital	14c.	rebec	

Location	Description	Date	Instrument	
Peterborough (Cambs.), Cathedral	roof painting	13c., but 'restored'	fiddle turned into violin	31
Ringland (Norfolk), Church of St. Peter	stained glass roundel	c.1310–25	fiddle	74
Rome, Museo Vaticano	Lateran Cope	1340–60	fiddle	
Romsey (Hants.), Abbey	south side corbel, exterior	c.1120–40	fiddle or rebec	12
St. Bertrand de Comminges (France), Cathedral	Cope of the Virgin	1300–20	fiddle	
Saxlingham Nethergate (Norfolk), Church of St. Mary	stained glass roundel	c.1420–50	fiddle	116
Shrewsbury (Salop.), Church of St. Mary	roof angel	late 15c.	crowd	134
South Molton (Devon.), Church of St. Mary Magdalene	capital	15c.	rebec	
Stamford (Lincs.), Church of St. John	roof angel	15c.	rebec	128
Stow Maries (Essex), Church of St. Mary and St. Margaret	window corbels, exterior	15c.	rebec	
Tewkesbury (Glos.), Abbey	roof boss	14c.	fiddle	97
Topcliffe (N. Yorks.) Church of St. Columba	Topcliffe brass (Flemish)	c.1391	rebec / fiddle	
Warwick, Church of St. Mary	Beauchamp Chapel, stained glass by John Prudde	c.1447	2 rebecs / 2 crowds / ?trumpet marine	122 / 123 / 124
Wells (Som.), Cathedral	misericord	c.1330–40	fiddle	88
Winchester (Hants.), Cathedral	misericords	c.1305	fiddle / rebec	54 / 55

Place	Detail	Date	Instrument	Plate ref.
Worcester, Cathedral	misericords	c.1397	crowd	108
			rebec	109
York, Church of All Saints, North Street	stained glass	15c.	fiddle	
	roof angel	15c.	rebec	121
York, Minster	south aisle, stained glass	c.1414	fiddle	113
	south-east transept, stained glass	after 1443	2 fiddles	119
	screen	c.1475–1500	fiddle	
			?trumpet marine	136
			bow skit	
			arrow skit	
	tower sculpture, interior	before 1472	fiddle	129
York, St. Mary's Abbey Museum	corbel	14c.	fiddle	

Representations of Bowed Instruments in Groups

❦⁘❧

The following list gives sample groups in which bowed instruments appear. It includes
(a) groups of ordinary human beings;
(b) any group, regardless of the nature of its performers, which could be regarded as musically realistic;
(c) performers spaced (i) around the side of a page, or (ii) in an architectural design, if, in spite of being artificially separated, they nevertheless represent an artistic unity.
The list does not include the less realistic groups of Apocalyptic Elders, or large numbers of angels spaced far apart in churches.

The cues below indicate the nature of the performers in each case.

A.	Animal(s)
Ang.	Angel(s)
Ap. & Mus.	Apollo and the Muses
D.	David
D. & M.	David and his Minstrel(s)
Dev.	Devil
E.	Elder(s)
G.	Grotesque
J.T.	King(s) or Prophet(s) in Jesse Tree
M.	Minstrel(s) (human)

Miscellaneous points:
(a) only one example is given of each instrumental combination;
(b) the pipe-and-tabor combination is listed here as one instrument, as is also the combination of tabor and small bells when sounded by one person;
(c) in certain cases, singers are included among the musicians;
(d) minstrels in disguise are listed under what they may represent, e.g. angels, animals, etc.
The system of numbering is as follows:
(a) the first number represents the number of musicians involved;
(b) the second number indicates the century of the representation;
(c) the third number shows its order in the relevant section,

e.g. 2.11.1 = two musicians, eleventh century, first example.

TWO MUSICIANS

Century	Instruments	Performers	Location	Reference no.	Plate no.
11c.	rebec and harp (D.)	D. & M.	Cambridge, Trinity College, MS B. 5. 26, fo.1	2.11.1	4
12c.	rebec and shawm (but see p. 40)	Dev. & A.	Canterbury Cathedral, Crypt capital	2.12.1	13
13c.	rebec and panpipes	A. & G.	Bristol Cathedral, Elder Lady Chapel, spandrel	2.13.1	32
	mediaeval viol and harp	Ang.	Cambridge, Trinity College, MS B. 11. 4, fo. 85	2.13.2	34
	mediaeval viol and fiddle	M.	BL Add. MS 28681, fo. 100	2.13.3	50
	fiddle and harp	M.	Cambridge, Trinity College MS R. 16. 2, fo. 22	2.13.4	41
	fiddle and gittern (citole)	M.	BL MS Egerton 1151, fo. 47	2.13.5	44
	fiddle (or rebec) and triple pipe	A.	Hawkchurch, capital	2.13.6	
	fiddle and chimebells	D. & M.	BL Add. MS 38116, fo. 89	2.13.7	47
14c.	rebec and psaltery	G.	Worcester Cathedral, misericord	2.14.1	109
	rebec and double shawm	M.	Winchester Cathedral, misericord	2.14.2	55
	fiddle and psaltery	G.	BL MS Royal 2 B. vii, fo. 193	2.14.3	

	Instruments		Source	Ref.	No.
14c.	fiddle and mandora (gittern)	A.	Hereford Cathedral, misericord	2.14.4	64
	fiddle and portative organ	M.	Oxford, Christ Church MS 92, fo. 29	2.14.5	79
	fiddle and double pipe	M.	Oxford, Bodl. MS Douce 366, fo. 45	2.14.6	82
	fiddle and pipe-and-tabor	G.	BL MS Cott. Domitian A. ii, fo. 8	2.14.7	91
	fiddle and shawm	A.	Oxford, Bodl. MS Douce 131, fo. 20	2.14.8	54
	fiddle and double shawm	A.	Winchester Cathedral, misericord	2.14.9	
	fiddle and trumpet	M.	New York, Public Library, Spencer Collection, MS 26, fo. 64ᵛ	2.14.10	60
15c.	rebec and lute	M.	Besthorpe, stained glass	2.15.1	126
	rebec and rebec	M.	Stow Maries, window corbels, exterior	2.15.2	
	rebec and pipe	M.	BL MS Harley 2838, fo. 45	2.15.3	133
	rebec and pipe-and-tabor(?)	M.	Cambridge, University Library MS Dd. viii. 18, fo. 110	2.15.4	135
	fiddle and lute	Ang.	BL MS Harley 2838, fo. 44ᵛ	2.15.5	132
	fiddle and fiddle	M. or Ang.	York Minster, south-east transept, St. Cuthbert window	2.15.6	119
	fiddle and bagpipes	Ang.	Norwich, St. Peter Hungate Museum, glass	2.15.7	125
16c.	Renaissance viol and lute	Not played	Nostell Priory, Holbein, *The More Family Group* (Although these two instruments are not being played, their adjacent positions suggest that they were sometimes used together.)		147

153

THREE MUSICIANS

Century	Instruments	Performers	Location	Reference no.	Plate no.
12c.	rebec, harp (D.) and horn	D. & M.	BL MS Royal 1 C. vii, fo. 92	3.12.1	14
	rebec, harp, tabor, with bells on clothes	M. & A.	BL MS Lansdowne 383, fo. 15^v	3.12.2	15
13c.	rebec and two singers	M.	Venice, Biblioteca Nazionale Marciana, MS Lat. I. 77, fo. 115	3.13.1	45
	mediaeval viol, harp (D.) and psaltery	D. & M.	Cambridge, Fitzwilliam Museum MS 330, leaf 5.	3.13.2	37
	fiddle (or rebec), harp and psaltery (D., who conducts)	M.	Venice, Biblioteca Nazionale Marciana, MS Lat. I. 77, f. 26^v	3.13.3	
	fiddle, harp and trumpet	M.	Oxford, Bodl. MS Douce 180, p. 37	3.13.4	
	fiddle, shawm and handbells	M.	Oxford, Bodl., New College MS 7, fo. 145	3.13.5	
	fiddle, bagpipes and gong	M. & A.	BL Add. MS 24686, fo. 17^v	3.13.6	48
14c.	rebec, pipe and horn	M.	Lawford, window carving (interior)	3.14.1	
	fiddle, harp and psaltery	M.	Cambridge, Trinity College MS B. 10. 2, fo. 30	3.14.2	107
	fiddle, harp (D.) and gittern (citole)	D. & M.	Brussels, Bibliothèque Royale Albert Ier, MS 9961–2, fo. 14	3.14.3	56
	fiddle, psaltery and mandora (gittern)	Ang.	BL MS Egerton 3277, fo. 160	3.14.4	103
	fiddle, chimebells (D.) and bagpipes	D. & M.	BL MS Arundel 83, fo. 55^v	3.14.5	69

FOUR MUSICIANS

Century	Instruments	Performers	Location	Reference no.	Plate no.
11c.	rebec, harp (D.), horn and other wind instrument	D. & M.	BL MS Cott. Tiberius C. vi, fo. 30v	4.11.1	2
12c.	rebec, mediaeval viol, harp and psaltery (D.)	D. & M.	Paris, Bibliothèque Nationale, MS Lat. 8846, fo. 54v	4.12.1	23
	rebec, harp and two horns	M. & A.	Vienna, Österreichische Nationalbibliothek, Cod. 1100, fo. 1	4.12.2	5
13c.	two rebecs, harp and horn	A.	New York, Pierpont Morgan Library, MS G. 25, fo. 57	4.13.1	
	mediaeval viol, organistrum, harp (D.) and psaltery	D. & M.	Cambridge, Fitzwilliam Museum MS 330, leaf 6	4.13.2	
	rebec, mediaeval viol, harp (D.), psaltery	D. & M.	Edinburgh, National Library of Scotland, MS Accession 3141, fo. 7	4.13.3	
	rebec, mediaeval viol, harp (D.) and double pipe	D. & M.	Cambridge, St. John's College, MS K.30, fo. 86	4.13.4	26
14c.	fiddle, harp, gittern (citole) and double pipe	Ang.	Oxford, Christ Church MS 92, fo.18v	4.14.1	
	fiddle, harp, gittern (citole) and trumpet	M.	BL MS Royal 2 B. vii, fo. 125v	4.14.2	
	fiddle and three singers	M.	London, Lambeth Palace, MS 233, fo. 145v	4.14.3	
16c.	two violins and two violas	M.	Hatfield House, Hoefnagel, A Fête at Bermondsey	4.16.1	152–3

FIVE MUSICIANS

Century	Instruments	Performers	Location	Reference no.	Plate no.
12c.	rebec, harp (D.), double pipe and cymbals	D. & M.	Lunel, Bibliothèque Municipale, MS I, ff. 5ᵛ–6	5.12.1	
	rebec, harp (D.), two horns, chimebells	D. & M.	Dublin, Trinity College, MS 53, fo. 151	5.12.2	16
	rebec, mediaeval viol, harp, pipe and panpipes	M. & A.	Barfrestone, south doorway	5.12.3	27
13c.	rebec, mediaeval viol, psaltery, harp and horn	M.	BL MS Arundel 157, fo. 71ᵛ	5.13.1	29
	mediaeval viol, fiddle, organistrum, harp (D.) and psaltery	D. & M.	London, Society of Antiquaries, MS 59, fo. 38ᵛ	5.13.2	33
	mediaeval viol, organistrum, harp (D.), psaltery and double pipe	D. & M.	London, Lambeth Palace, MS 563, fo. 20	5.13.3	
	mediaeval viol, fiddle, harp (D.), psaltery and chimebells	D. & M.	BL Add. MS 44874, fo. 7ᵛ	5.13.4	
14c.	fiddle, harp (D.), gittern (citole), portative organ and trumpet	D., M. & G.	Oxford, All Souls College, MS 7, fo. 7	5.14.1	
	fiddle, psaltery, pipe-and-tabor, trumpet and singer	M.	Oxford, Bodl. MS Ashmole 1523, fo. 99	5.14.2	
	fiddle, mandora (gittern), gittern (citole), two wind instruments (damaged)	M.	Lincoln Cathedral, north transept stained glass	5.14.3	
16c.	rebec, lute? pipe-and-tabor, shawm, broken instrument?	M.	Beverley, St. Mary's, Minstrels' Pillar	5.16.1	145

SIX MUSICIANS

Century	Instruments	Performers	Location	Reference no.	Plate no.
12c.	two fiddles (or rebec and fiddle), mediaeval viol, harp, psaltery and horn	*Ang.*	Florence, Biblioteca Medicea Laurenziana, MS Pluteus xii. 17, fo. 2ᵛ	6.12.1	9
	rebec, mediaeval viol, harp (D.), psaltery, double pipe and handbells	*D. & M.*	Oxford, Bodl. MS Gough Liturg. 2, fo. 32	6.12.2	28
13c.	rebec, mediaeval viol, harp, psaltery, double pipe and chimebells (David conducts, but does not play)	*D. & M.*	New York, Pierpont Morgan Library, MS G. 25, fo. 5ᵛ	6.13.1	
	rebec, harp (D.), psaltery, symphony, organ and chimebells	*J.T.*	BL Add. MS 21926, fo. 25ᵛ	6.13.2	
	mediaeval viol, fiddle, harp, psaltery, two triple pipes	*Ang.*	Lisbon, Gulbenkian Collection, MS L. A. 139, fo.41ᵛ	6.13.3	
14c.	two fiddles, harp, psaltery, gittern (citole) and double trumpet	*E.*	Dublin, Trinity College, MS K. 4. 31, p. vi	6.14.1	

SEVEN MUSICIANS

Century	Instruments	Performers	Location	Reference no.	Plate no.
12c.	two horns-and-gongs, two harps, mediaeval viol (D.), two chimebell players	*D. & A.*	Hildesheim, St. Godehard, St. Albans Psalter, p. 417	7.12.1	11
13c.	rebec, mediaeval viol, harp (D.), harp, psaltery, panpipes and cymbals	*D. & A.*	BL MS Lansdowne 420, fo. 12^v	7.13.1	36
14c.	rebec, fiddle, harp, gittern (citole), portative organ, pipe-and-tabor and trumpet	*M. & Ang.*	Brussels, Bibliothèque Royale Albert Ier, MS 9961–2, fo. 74	7.14.1	58
	fiddle, harp (D.), psaltery, gittern (citole), portative organ, trumpet and timbrel	*D. & M.*	BL Add. MS 49622, fo. 107^v	7.14.2	71

158

EIGHT MUSICIANS

Century	Instruments	Performers	Location	Reference no.	Plate no.
14c.	fiddle, psaltery, portative organ, two trumpets, timbrel, clappers and chimebells	D., M. & Ang.	Brussels, Bibliothèque Royale Albert Iᵉʳ, MS 9961–2, fo. 57	8.14.1	57
	rebec, fiddle, two psalteries, mandora (gittern), portative organ, trumpet, tabor	Ang.	Topcliffe, brass	8.14.2	
	two rebecs, fiddle, gittern (citole), four trumpets	M.	New York, Public Library, Spencer Collection MS 26, fo. 17	8.14.3	61
15c.	rebec, fiddle, two harps, two lutes, two portative organs	Ang.	Hillesden, east end frieze, interior. These instruments are divided into two groups of four, one on each side of the altar. Each group has a harp, lute, portative organ and a bowed instrument, suggesting antiphonal performance.	8.15.1	137–8

NINE MUSICIANS

Century	Instruments	Performers	Location	Reference no.	Plate no.
12c.	rebec, mediaeval viol, organistrum, harp (D.), psaltery, triple pipe, bladder pipe, handbells and chimebells	D. & M.	Glasgow University Library, MS Hunter 229, fo. 21ᵛ	9.12.1	21–2

159

TEN MUSICIANS

Century	Instruments	Performers	Location	Reference no.	Plate no.
14c.	portative organ, timbrel, bagpipes, symphony, psaltery, harp, fiddle, wind instrument (broken), nakers and trumpet (?)	M.	Adderbury, north side frieze, exterior	10.14.1	
16c.	fiddle, harp (Ap.) lute, pipe-and-tabor, crumhorn, triangle and four singers	Ap. & Mus.	Berlin, Staatliche Museen. Hans Holbein, sketch of a Triumphal Arch for the Coronation Celebration of Anne Boleyn in 1533	10.16.1	149

TWELVE MUSICIANS

Century	Instruments	Performers	Location	Reference no.	Plate no.
14c.	crowd, fiddle, harp, gittern (citole), portative organ, positive organ, double pipe, pipe-and-tabor, shawm, bagpipes, timbrel and gong	M.	Oxford, Christ Church, MS 92, fo. 43	12.14.1	78
15c.	portative organ, psaltery, symphony, gittern (citole), fiddle, harp, rebec, mandora (gittern), lute, triangle, (?)psaltery and timbrel (in that order)	Ang.	Alnwick Castle, Sherborne Missal, p. 276	12.15.1	114

THIRTEEN MUSICIANS

Century	Instruments	Performers	Location	Reference no.	Plate no.
14c.	trumpet, gittern (citole), fiddle, mediaeval viol, harp, trumpet, chimebells, trumpet, psaltery, clappers, two trumpets, horn	*Ang.*	Bologna, Museo Civico, Bologna Cope	13.14.1	77

161

Bibliography

❧

MEDIAEVAL AND RENAISSANCE TREATISES
(CHRONOLOGICAL)

JEROME OF MORAVIA, *Tractatus de Musica* (*c.*1280–1300)

(a) ed. S. M. Cserba, OP (Regensburg, 1935).

(b) Anna Puccianti, 'La Descrizione della *Viella* e della *Rubeba* in Girolamo di Moravia', *Collectanea Historicae Musicae* iv (1966), 227–37.

(c) Christopher Page, 'Jerome of Moravia on the *Rubeba* and *Viella*', *The Galpin Society Journal* xxxii (1979), 77–98.

JEAN VAILLANT?

Christopher Page, 'Fourteenth-century Instruments and Tunings: a Treatise by Jean Vaillant? (Berkeley, MS 744)', *The Galpin Society Journal* xxxiii (1980), 17–35.

JOHANNES DE GROCHEO, *De Musica* (*c.*1300)

(a) ed. E. Rohloff, *Der Musiktraktat des Johannes de Grocheo* (Leipzig, 1943).

(b) Albert Seay, *Johannes de Grocheo: Concerning Music (De Musica)* (2nd edn., Colorado Springs, 1973).

JOHANNES TINCTORIS, *De Inventione et Usu Musicae* (*c.*1487)

Anthony Baines, 'Fifteenth-century Instruments in Tinctoris's *De Inventione et Usu Musicae*', *The Galpin Society Journal* iii (1950), 19–25.

SEBASTIAN VIRDUNG, *Musica getutscht* (Basel, 1511, Berlin, 1882, Kassel, 1931, 1970).

MARTIN AGRICOLA, *Musica Instrumentalis Deudsch* (Wittemberg, 1528, rev. edn. 1545. Both edns. Leipzig, 1896, New York, 1966).

HANS GERLE, *Musica Teusch* (Nuremberg, 1532).

SILVESTRO GANASSI, *Regola Rubertina* (Venice, 1542–3, Leipzig, 1924).

POST-RENAISSANCE BOOKS AND ARTICLES

Abbott, Djilda, and Segerman, Ephraim, 'Gut strings', *Early Music* iv. 4 (Oct. 1976), 430–7.

—— 'Strings in the 16th and 17th Centuries', *N.R.I. Research Report* ii (Manchester, 1974).

Alexander, J. J. G. (ed.), *A Survey of Manuscripts illuminated in the British Isles* (London, 1975–).

Anderson, M. D., *Drama and Imagery in English Medieval Churches* (Cambridge, 1963).

—— *Misericords* (Harmondsworth, 1954).

—— *The Medieval Carver* (Cambridge, 1935).

Andersson, Otto, *The Bowed Harp*, ed. Kathleen Schlesinger (London, 1930).

—— 'The Bowed Harp in Trondheim Cathedral and Related Instruments in East and West', *The Galpin Society Journal* xxiii (1970), 4–34.

—— *The Shetland Gue, the Welsh Crwth, and the Northern Bowed Harp* (Budkavlen, 1954).

Anglés, Higinio, *La Música de las Cantigas de Santa Maria del Rey Alfonso el Sabio*, 3 vols. (Barcelona, 1943–64).

Bachmann, Werner, *The Origins of Bowing*, trans. Norma Deane (London, 1969), from *Die Anfänge des Streichinstrumentenspiels* (Leipzig, 1964).

Backhouse, Janet, *The Illuminated Manuscript* (Oxford, 1979).

Baines, Anthony, *European and American Musical Instruments* (London, 1966, 1983).

—— 'Fifteenth-century Instruments in Tinctoris's *De Inventione et Usu Musicae*', *The Galpin Society Journal* iii (1950), 19–25.

—— 'Jerome of Moravia', *FoMRHI Quarterly* vii (Apr. 1977), 24–5.

—— (ed.), *Musical Instruments through the Ages* (3rd edn., Harmondsworth, 1969).

Baltzer, Rebecca A., 'Music in the Life and Times of Eleanor of Aquitaine', *Eleanor of Aquitaine, Patron and Politican*, ed. William W. Kibler (Austin, Texas, 1976), 61–80.

Barrington, Daines, 'Some Account of Two Musical Instruments used in Wales', *Archaeologia* iii (1775), 30–4.

Bentley, William, 'Notes on the Musical Instruments figured in the Windows of the Beauchamp Chapel, St. Mary's, Warwick', *Birmingham Archaeological Society: Transactions for the year 1928*, liii (Oxford, 1931), 167–72.

Bessaraboff, Nicholas, *Ancient European Musical Instruments* (New York, 1941).

Besseler, Heinrich, *Die Musik des Mittelalters und der Renaissance*, 10 vols. (Wildpark-Potsdam, 1931–4).

Bevil, J. Marshall, 'The Welsh Crwth: its History and its Genealogy' (dissertation, North Texas State University, 1973).

Boase, T. S. R., *The Oxford History of English Art* (Oxford, 1949–   ), vol. iii, *English Art, 1100–1216* (1953).

Bowles, Edmund A., 'Haut and bas; the grouping of musical instruments in the Middle Ages', *Musica Disciplina* viii (1954), 115 ff.

—— 'La hierarchie des instruments de musique dans l'Europe féodale', *Revue de Musicologie* xlii (1958), 155 ff.

—— 'Musical Instruments at the Medieval Banquet', *Revue Belge de Musicologie* xii (1958), 41–51.

—— 'Musical Instruments in Civic Processions during the Middle Ages', *Acta Musicologica* xxxiii. 2–4 (1961), 147–61.

—— 'Musical Instruments in the Medieval Corpus Christi Procession', *Journal of the American Musicological Society* xvii (1964), 251–60.

—— 'The Role of Musical Instruments in Medieval Sacred Drama', *The Musical Quarterly* xlv (Jan. 1959), 67–84.

—— 'Were Musical Instruments used in the Liturgical Service during the Middle Ages?', *The Galpin Society Journal* x (1957), 40–56.

Boyden, David D., *The Hill Collection* (London, 1969).

—— *The History of Violin Playing* (London, 1965).

Bragard, Roger, and de Hen, Ferdinand, *Musical Instruments in Art and History*, trans. Bill Hopkins (London, 1968).

Brewer, J., *et al.* (eds.), *Calendar of Letters and Papers for the Reign of Henry VIII*, 21 vols. (London, 1862–1910).

Brown, Howard Mayer, *Music in the French Secular Theater, 1400–1550* (Cambridge, Mass., 1963).

—— and Lascelle, Joan, *Musical Iconography: A Manual for cataloguing Musical Subjects in Western Art before 1800* (Cambridge, Mass., 1972).

Bruce-Mitford, Rupert and Myrtle, 'The Sutton Hoo Lyre, *Beowulf*, and the Origins of the Frame Harp', *Antiquity* xliv (1970), 7–13.

Bullock-Davies, Constance, *Menestrellorum Multitudo* (Cardiff, 1978).

—— 'Welsh Minstrels at the Courts of Edward I and Edward II', *Transactions of the Hon. Society of Cymmrodorion* (London, 1974), 114 f.

Caldwell, John, *Medieval Music* (London, 1978).

Carpenter, Nan C., 'A Song for All Seasons: Sir Thomas More and Music', *Comparative Literature* xxxiii. 2 (Spring 1981), 113–36.

Carter, Henry Holland, *A Dictionary of Middle English Musical Terms* (Indiana, 1961).

Cave, C. J. P., *Medieval Carvings in Exeter Cathedral* (London, 1953).

—— *Roof Bosses in Medieval Churches* (Cambridge, 1948).

—— 'The Wooden Roof Bosses in the Fitzalan Chapel, Arundel, and in Poling Church', *Sussex Archaeological Collections* lxxiii (1932), 1.

—— and Borenius, Tancred, 'The Painted Ceiling in the Nave of Peterborough Cathedral', *Archaeologia* lxxxvii (1937), 279 f.

—— and Tanner, L. E., 'A Thirteenth-Century Choir of Angels in the North Transept of Westminster Abbey and the Adjacent Figures of Two Kings', *Archaeologia* lxxxiv (1935), 63–7.

Cervelli, Luisa, *Contributi alla Storia degli Strumenti Musicali in Italia: Rinascimento e Barocco* (Antiquae Musicae Italicae Subsidia Didascalica, Bologna, 1967).

Chambers, E. K., *The Mediaeval Stage*, 2 vols. (Oxford, 1903).

Chaytor, Henry John, *The Troubadours and England* (Cambridge, 1923).

Cosman, Madeleine Pelner, *Fabulous Feasts* (New York, 1976).

Coulton, G. G., *Social Life in Britain from the Conquest to the Reformation* (Cambridge, 1956).

Coussemaker, Edmond de, *Scriptorum de musica medii aevi* (Paris, 1864–76).

Craig, Hardin, *English Religious Drama of the Middle Ages* (Oxford, 1955).

Craik, T. W., *The Tudor Interlude* (Leicester, 1958).

Craik, T. W. (ed.), *The Revels History of Drama in English: vol. ii, 1500–1576* (London, 1980), vol. i forthcoming.

Crane, Frederick, *Extant Medieval Musical Instruments* (Iowa City, 1972).

—— *Materials for the Study of the Fifteenth Century Basse Danse*, (Brooklyn, 1968).

Crossley-Holland, Peter (ed.), *Music in Wales* (London, 1948).

Davidson, Clifford, *Drama and Art* (Kalamazoo, Michigan, 1977).

Davison, Archibald T. and Apel, Willi, *Historical Anthology of Music*, 2 vols. (Cambridge, Mass., 1946–50), i.

Disertori, Benvenuto, 'Il piu antico exemplare esistente di strumente ad arco', *Rivista Musicale Italiana* xlii (1938), 294 f.

Dobson, E. J., and Harrison, F. Ll., *Medieval English Songs* (London, 1979).

Dodwell, C. R., *The Canterbury School of Illumination 1066–1200* (Cambridge, 1954).

—— *The Great Lambeth Bible* (London, 1959).

Dolmetsch, Mabel, *Dances of England and France, 1450–1600* (London, 1949, New York, 1976).

—— 'The History of the Viol', *The Consort* vi (1949), 1 ff.

Dolmetsch, Nathalie, 'Of the Sizes of Viols', *The Galpin Society Journal* xvii (1964), 24–7.

Downie, Margaret, 'The Rebec: an Orthographic and Iconographic Study' (diss., University of West Virginia, Morgantown, 1981).

—— 'Rebec in French Literary Sources from 1379–1780', *JVdGSA* xix (1982), 71.

Du Cange, Domino, *Glossarium ad Scriptores mediae et infiniae Latinitatis*, 6 vols. (Paris, 1733).

Edmunds, Martin, 'Venetian Viols of the Sixteenth-century', *The Galpin Society Journal* xxxiii (1980), 74–91.

Edmunds, Martin and Harwood, Ian, 'Reconstructing 16th-century Venetian viols', *Early Music* vi. 4 (Oct. 1978), 519–25.

Emsheimer, Ernst, 'Die Streichleier von Danczk', *Svensk Tidskrift for Musikforskning* xliii (1961), 190 ff.

Engel, Carl, *Researches into the Early History of the Violin Family* (London, 1883).

Eras, Rudolf, 'Von Fiedeln, Geigen und Violen', *Instrumentenbau-Zeitschrift* v (1951), 107 f.

Evans, Joan, *English Art 1307–1461* (*The Oxford History of English Art* v, Oxford, 1949).

Felton, Herbert, and Harvey, John, *The English Cathedrals* (London, 1950).

Galpin, Francis W., *Old English Instruments of Music* (London, 1910; rev. Thurston Dart, London, 1965).

—— 'Old English Instruments of Music portrayed in the Ecclesiastical Art of Essex', *Transactions of the Essex Archaeological Society* xx (1933), 17–32.

Gardner, Arthur, *English Mediaeval Sculpture* (Cambridge, 1951).

Geiser, Brigitte, *Studien zur Fruehgeschichte der Violine* (Bern, 1974).

Gerbert, Martin, *De Cantu et Musica Sacra*, 2 vols. (St. Blasius, 1774, reprinted Graz, 1968).

Gerboth, Walther, *An Index to Musical Festschriften* (London, 1969).

Glasenapp, Franzgeorg v., *Varia/Rara/Curiosa* (Göttingen, 1971).

Gushee, Lawrence, 'Two Central Places: Paris and the French Court in the Early Fourteenth Century', *Bericht über den Internationalen Musikwissenschaftlichen Kongress* (Berlin, 1974).

Hammerstein, Reinhold, *Die Musik der Engel* (Munich, 1962).

Harris, Clement Antrobus, 'Musical Animals in Ornament', *The Musical Quarterly* vi (1920), 417–25.

Harrison, Frank, *Music in Medieval Britain* (London, 1958).

—— 'Tradition and Innovation in Instrumental Usage 1100–1450', *Aspects of Medieval and Renaissance Music*, ed. Jan La Rue (London, 1967), pp. 319–35.

—— and Rimmer, Joan, *European Musical Instruments* (London, 1964).

Harvey, John, *Gothic England* (London, 1947).

—— *The Plantagenets* (London, 1948).

Harwood, Ian, 'An introduction to renaissance viols', *Early Music* ii. 4 (Oct. 1974), 234–46.

Hassall, A. G. and W. O., *The Douce Apocalypse* (London, 1961).

Hassall, W. O., *Who's Who in History: vol. i, 55 B.C. to 1485* (Oxford, 1960).

Hayes, Gerald R., *The King's Music* (London, 1937).

—— *The Viols, and other Bowed Instruments* (London, 1930, New York, 1969).

Heartz, Daniel, 'The Basse Dance', *Annales Musicologiques* vi (1958–63), 287–340.

—— *Pierre Attaingnant Royal Printer of Music* (Berkeley and Los Angeles, 1969).

Heron-Allen, Ed., *Violin-making as it was, and is* (2nd edn., London, 1885).

Holman, Peter, 'The English Royal Violin Consort in the Sixteenth Century', *Proceedings of the Royal Musical Association* 109 (1983), 39–59.

Holmes, Urban T., 'The Mediaeval Minstrel', *Mediaeval and Renaissance Studies* (Durham, 1968).

Hope, R. C., 'Notes on the Minstrels' Pillar, St. Mary's Church, Beverley', *Transactions of the East Riding Antiquarian Society* iii (1895), 67–8.

Hughes, Andrew, 'Viella: facere non possumus', *IMS: Report of the Eleventh Congress, Copenhagen, 1972* (Copenhagen, 1974), i. 453–6.

Hughes, Dom Anselm (ed.), *Early Medieval Music up to 1300* (*The New Oxford History of Music* ii, London, 1954).

Hughes, Dom Anselm, and Abraham, Gerald, *Ars Nova and the Renaissance, 1300–1540* (*The New Oxford History of Music* iii, London, 1960).

James, Montagu Rhodes, *The Apocalypse in Latin and French (Bodleian MS Douce 180)* (Oxford, 1922).

Jusserand, Jean Adrien A. J., *English Wayfaring Life in the Middle Ages*, trans. Lucy Toulmin Smith, (4th edn., rev. London, 1950).

Jones, Edward, *Musical and Poetical Relicks of the Welsh Bards* (London, 1794).

Kauffmann, C. M., *Romanesque Manuscripts 1066–1190* (*SMIBI*, iii, London, 1975).

Lafontaine, Henry Cart de (ed.), *The King's Musick* (London, 1909, New York, 1973).

La Rue, Jan (ed.), *Aspects of Medieval and Renaissance Music* (London, 1967).

Lewi, Angela, *The Thomas More Family Group* (The National Portrait Gallery, London, 1974).

Liber Usualis, ed. the Benedictines of Solesmes (Tournai, 1953).

López-Calo, José, 'El Portico de la Gloria: Sus Instrumentos Musicales', *La Catedral de Santiago de Compostela* (IX Centenario de la Catedral de Santiago de Compostela, 1976).

—— *La Musica Medieval en Galicia* (La Coruña, 1982).

Marcuse, Sibyl, *A Survey of Musical Instruments* (Newton Abbot, 1975).

—— *Musical Instruments: A Comprehensive Dictionary* (Garden City, New York, 1964; London, 1966).

Marks, Richard, and Morgan, Nigel, *The Golden Age of English Manuscript Painting, 1200–1500* (London, 1981).

Mead, William Edward, *The English Mediaeval Feast* (2nd edn., London, 1967).

Meoli Toulmin, Rachel, 'Origini e data di un codice inglese della Marciana', *Saggi e Memorie di Storia dell'Arte* viii (1972), 45–65.

Meyer, Ernst H., *Early English Chamber Music* (2nd edn., rev. by the author and Diana Poulton, London, 1982).

Meyer-Baer, Kathi, *Music of the Spheres and the Dance of Death* (Princeton, 1970).

Montagu, Gwen and Jeremy, 'Beverley Minster reconsidered', *Early Music* vi. 3 (July, 1978), 401–15.

Montagu, Jeremy, *The World of Medieval & Renaissance Musical Instruments* (Newton Abbot, 1976).

Morgan, Nigel, *Early Gothic Manuscripts* (*SMIBI* iv. 1, London, 1982).

Morris, Meredith, 'The Crwth' (holograph, 1920, kept at the Welsh Folk Museum, St. Fagan's Castle, Cardiff).

Nagel, Willibald, *Annalen der Englischen Hofmusik, 1509–1649* (Leipzig, 1894).

Nelson, Philip, *Ancient Painted Glass in England* (London, 1913).

New Oxford History of Music, see Dom Anselm Hughes and Gerald Abraham.

Norrington, Ruth, *In the Shadow of a Saint: Lady Alice More* (Waddesdon, 1983).

—— *The Household of Sir Thomas More* (Waddesdon, 1985).

Pächt, Otto, and Alexander, J. J. G., *Illuminated Manuscripts in the Bodleian Library, Oxford*, 3 vols. (Oxford 1966–73), iii, British, Irish, and Icelandic Schools.

Page, Christopher, 'Biblical instruments in medieval manuscript illustration' *Early Music* v. 3 (July 1977), 299–309.

—— 'Fourteenth-century Instruments and Tunings: a Treatise by Jean Vaillant? (Berkeley, MS 744)', *The Galpin Society Journal* xxxiii (1980), 17–35.

—— 'German musicians and their instruments. A 14th-century account by Konrad of Megenberg', *Early Music* x. 2 (Apr. 1982), 192–200.

—— 'Jerome of Moravia on the *Rubeba* and *Viella*', *The Galpin Society Journal* xxxii (1979), 77–98.

—— 'Medieval fiddle construction', *Early Music* ii. 3 (July, 1974), 166–7.

—— 'The Medieval *Organistrum* and *Symphonia* 1: A Legacy from the East?' *Galpin Society Journal* xxxv (1982), 37–44.

—— 'The Medieval *Organistrum* and *Symphonia* 2: Terminology', *Galpin Society Journal* xxxvi (1983), 71–87.

—— 'References to String Materials in some Medieval Texts, *c*.1050–*c*.1430', *FoMRHI Quarterly* iii (Apr. 1976), 33–41.

—— 'String-Instrument making in Medieval England and some Oxford Harpmakers 1380–1466', *The Galpin Society Journal* xxxi (1978), 44–67.

Page-Phillips, John, and Dart, Thurston, 'The Peacock Feast', *The Galpin Society Journal* vi (1953), 95–8.

Palmer, Frances, 'Musical instruments from the *Mary Rose*', *Early Music* xi. 1 (Jan. 1983), 53–9.

Panum, Hortense, *Stringed Instruments of the Middle Ages*, trans. Jeffrey Pulver (London, 1941).

Pevsner, Nikolaus (ed.), *The Buildings of England* (London, 1951–).

Pirro, André, *La Musique de la fin du XIVe Siècle à la fin du XVIe* (Paris, 1940).

Praetorius, Michael, *Syntagma Musicum*, ii *De Organographia* and *Theatrum Instrumentorum* (Wolfenbuttel, 1619–20, Basel, 1958). Partial trans. by Harold Blumenfeld (New York, 1962).

—— *Syntagma Musicum II, De organographia Parts I and II*, edited and translated from the editions of 1618 and 1619 by David Z. Crookes (Oxford, 1986).

Price, David, *Patrons and Musicians of the English Renaissance* (Cambridge, 1981).

Prideaux, Edith K., *The Carvings of Mediaeval Musical Instruments in Exeter Cathedral Church* (Exeter, 1915).

Puccianti, Anna, 'La Descrizione della *Viella* e della *Rubeba* in Girolamo di Moravia', *Collectanea Historicae Musicae* iv (1966), 227–37.

Pulver, Jeffrey, *A Dictionary of Old English Music and Musical Instruments* (London, 1923).

—— 'The Viols in England', *Proceedings of the Royal Musical Association* (1921), 1–21.

Randall, Lillian M. C., *Images in the Margins of Gothic Manuscripts* (Berkeley, 1966).

Rastall, George Richard, 'Secular Musicians in late Medieval England' (unpublished thesis, University of Manchester, 1968).

Rastall, Richard, 'Minstrelsy, Church and Clergy in Medieval England', *Proceedings of the Royal Musical Association* xcvii (1971), 83–98.

—— 'Some English Consort-groupings of the Late Middle Ages', *Music and Letters* lv (Apr. 1974), 179–202.

—— 'The Minstrels of the English Royal Households', *R.M.A. Research Chronicle* iv (1964), 1–41.

—— 'The Minstrel Court in Medieval England', *A Medieval Miscellany in honour of Professor John Le Patourel*, ed. R. L. Thomson, *Proceedings of the Leeds Philosophical and Literary Society* xviii. i (Apr. 1982), 96–105.

Ravenel, Bernard, 'Vièles à Archets et Rebecs en Europe au Moyen Age (Fin Xe siècle, début XVIe siècle)', (unpublished doctoral thesis, Université des Sciences Humaines, Strasbourg, 1983).

Reese, Gustave, *Music in the Middle Ages* (New York, 1940).

—— *Music in the Renaissance* (rev. edn., London, 1954).

Reaney, Gilbert, 'The Musician in Medieval England', *Monthly Musical Record* (Jan.–Feb. 1959), 3–8.

Remnant, G. L., *A Catalogue of Misericords in Great Britain* (Oxford, 1969).

Remnant, Mary, 'Bowed Instruments in England up to the Reformation' (unpublished D.Phil. thesis, University of Oxford, 1972).

—— 'Bowed Instruments of the Middle Ages and their Use in Consort with Keyboard Instruments', *Journal of the Brockport Keyboard Festival* ii (1979), 1–15.

—— 'Fiddle', *Grove 6*.

—— 'Kit', *Grove 6*.

—— *Musical Instruments of the West* (London, 1978).

—— 'Opus Anglicanum', *The Galpin Society Journal* xvii (1964), 111–13.

—— 'Rebec', *Grove 6*.

—— 'Rebec, Fiddle and Crowd in England', *Proceedings of the Royal Musical Association* xcv (1969), 15–27.

—— 'Rebec, Fiddle and Crowd: Some Further Observations', *Proceedings of the Royal Musical Association* xcvi (1970), 149–50.

—— 'The diversity of medieval fiddles', *Early Music* iii. 1 (Jan. 1975), 47–51.

—— 'The Gittern in English Mediaeval Art', *The Galpin Society Journal* xviii (1965), 104–9.

—— 'The Use of Frets on Rebecs and Mediaeval Fiddles', *The Galpin Society Journal* xxi (1968), 146–51.

—— and Marks, Richard, 'A Medieval "Gittern"', *Music and Civilisation* (*The British Museum Yearbook* iv, London, 1980), 83–134.

Reynolds, E. E., *The Life and Death of St. Thomas More* (London, 1968).

Rickert, Margaret, *Painting in Britain in the Middle Ages* (Pelican History of Art, London, 1954).

Rimmer, Joan, 'Crwth', *Grove 6*.

Ritson, Joseph (ed.), *Ancient Engleish Metrical Romanceës*, 3 vols. (London, 1802).

Rittmeyer-Iselin, Dora, 'Das Rebec', *Festschrift Karl Nef zum 60 Geburtstag* (Zurich, 1933).

Robinson, F. N. (ed.), *The Works of Geoffrey Chaucer* (2nd edn., Boston, 1961).

Rooley, Anthony, 'The Problem of Double Bridges on 15th Century Illustrations of Rebecs', *FoMRHI Communications*, no. 2 (Nov. 1975), 2–3.

Sachs, Curt, *Handbuch der Musikinstrumentenkunde* (2nd edn., Leipzig, 1930).

—— *Real-Lexikon der Musikinstrumente* (Berlin, 1913).

—— *The History of Musical Instruments* (New York, 1940).

Saer, D. Roy, *The Harp in Tudor Wales* (National Museum of Wales, Welsh Folk Museum, forthcoming).

Safford, E. W., 'An Account of the Expenses of Eleanor, sister of Edward III, on the occasion of her marriage to Reynauld, Count of Guelders', *Archaeologia* lxxvii (1927), 111–40.

Sandler, Lucy Freeman, *The Peterborough Psalter in Brussels & other Fenland Manuscripts* (London, 1974).

Segerman, Ephraim, 'Some Thoughts on Gut String History before 1600', *FoMRHI Quarterly* x (Jan. 1978), 22–4.

—— 'Speculations on the Renaissance viol, the ubiquity of soundholes bracketed by bars, and the history of the soundpost', *FoMRHI Quarterly* xii (July 1978), 20–9.

—— and Abbott, Djilda, 'Historical Background to the Strings used by Catgut-Scrapers', *FoMRHI Quarterly* iii (Apr. 1976), 42–7.

—— and Abbott, Djilda, 'Jerome of Moravia and bridge curvature in the medieval fiddle', *FoMRHI Quarterly* vi (Jan. 1977), 34–6.

—— and Abbott, Djilda, 'Some speculations on mediaeval fiddle technique', *FoMRHI Quarterly* vi (Jan. 1977), 36–7.

Selfridge-Field, Eleanor, 'Venetian Instrumentalists in England: A Bassano Chronicle (1538–1660)', *Studi Musicali* viii (1979), 173–221.

Smith, Edwin, Cook, Olive, and Hutton, Graham, *English Parish Churches* (London, 1976).

Smoldon, W. L., 'Mediaeval Music-drama', *The Musical Times* xciv (Dec. 1953), 557 ff.

Southern, R. W., *The Making of the Middle Ages* (London, 1953).

Southern, Richard, *The Medieval Theatre in the Round* (London, 1957).

—— *The Staging of Plays before Shakespeare* (London, 1973).

Stauder, Wilhelm, *Alte Musikinstrumente* (Braunschweig, 1973).

Steger, Hugo, *Philologia Musica* (Munchen, 1971).

Sternfeld, F. W. (ed.), *Music from the Middle Ages to the Renaissance* (*A History of Western Music* i, London, 1973).

Stevens, John, *Mediaeval Carols, Musica Britannica* iv. (2nd edn., 1958).

—— *Music and Poetry at the Early Tudor Court* (London, 1961).

—— (ed.), *Music at the Court of Henry VIII, Musica Britannica* xviii (rev. edn., London, 1969).

—— 'Music in Mediaeval Drama', *Proceedings of the Royal Musical Association* lxxxiv (1958), 81 ff.

Stone, Lawrence, *Sculpture in Britain: The Middle Ages* (*The Pelican History of Art*, Harmondsworth, 1955).

Straeten, Edmund van der, *The History of the Violin*, 2 vols. (London, 1933).

Stratmann, Francis Henry, *A Middle-English Dictionary* (rev. J. H. Bradley, Oxford, 1891).

Strutt, Joseph, *The Sports and Pastimes of the People of England* (London, 1898).

Tanner, Lawrence E., and Howgrave-Graham, R. P., *Unknown Westminster Abbey* (Harmondsworth, 1948).

Temple, Elzbieta, *Anglo-Saxon Manuscripts 900–1066* (*SMIBI* ii, London, 1976).

Tiella, Marco, 'The Violeta of S.Caterina de' Vigri', *The Galpin Society Journal* xxviii (1975), 60–70.

Trapp, J. B., and Herbrüggen, Hubertus Schulte, *The King's Good Servant Sir Thomas More 1477/8–1535*, Catalogue of the National Portrait Gallery exhibition, 1977–8 (Ipswich, 1977).

—— *see*: Catalogue, National Portrait Gallery, 1977.

Tydeman, William, *The Theatre in the Middle Ages* (Cambridge, 1978).

Wangermée, Robert, *Flemish Music and Society in the Fifteenth and Sixteenth Centuries* (New York, 1968).

Ward, John M., 'The maner of dauncying', *Early Music* iv. 2 (Apr. 1976), 127–42.

Wickham, Glynne, *Early English Stages* (London, 1959, 3rd imp. 1966), i.

Wiltshire, Jacqueline, 'Medieval Fiddles at Hardham', *The Galpin Society Journal* xxxiv (1981), 142–6.

Winternitz, Emanuel, *Gaudenzio Ferrari, his School and the Early History of the Violin* (Varallo Sesia, 1967).

—— *Musical Instruments and their Symbolism in Western Art* (London, 1967).

—— *Musical Instruments of the Western World* (London, 1966).

Withington, Robert, *English Pageantry*, 2 vols. (Cambridge, Mass., 1918–20).

Witten, Laurence C. II, 'Apollo, Orpheus and David', *Journal of the American Musical Instrument Society* i (1975), 5–55.

Woodfield, Ian, *The Early History of the Viol* (Cambridge, 1984).

——'The Early History of the Viol', *Proceedings of the Royal Musical Association* ciii (1977), 141–57.

—— 'The Origins of the Viol' (unpublished Ph.D. thesis, University of London, 1977).

—— 'Viol', *Grove 6*.

—— 'Viol playing techniques in the mid-16th century: a survey of Ganassi's fingering instructions', *Early Music* vi. 4 (Oct. 1978), 544–9.

Woodfill, Walter L., *Musicians in English Society from Elizabeth to Charles I* (Princeton, 1953).

Woodforde, Christopher, *The Norwich School of Glass-Painting in the Fifteenth Century* (London, 1950).

Wooldridge, H. E. (ed.), *Early English Harmony*, 2 vols. (London, Plainsong and Mediaeval Music Society, 1897, 1913), i (facsimiles).

Wright, Laurence, 'Medieval Carvings of Musical Instruments at St. Mary's Church, Shrewsbury', *FoMRHI Bulletin* viii (July, 1977), 73.

—— 'Sculptures of Medieval Fiddles at Gargilesse', *The Galpin Society Journal* xxxii (1979), 66–76.

—— 'The Medieval Gittern and Citole: A case of mistaken identity', *The Galpin Society Journal* xxx (1977), 8–42.

Wright, Thomas, *History of Domestic Manners and Sentiments* (London, 1862).

—— A volume of vocabularies (2nd edn., privately printed, 1882).

—— ed. Wülcker, Richard, *Anglo-Saxon and Old-English Vocabularies*, 2 vols. (London, 1883–4).

Young, Carl, *Drama of the Mediaeval Church*, 2 vols. (Oxford, 1933, 1967).

Zarnecki, George, *English Romanesque Sculpture 1066–1140* (London, 1951).

—— *Later English Romanesque Sculpture 1140–1210* (London, 1953).

MUSEUM CATALOGUES, ETC

Brussels, Bibliothèque Royale Albert Ier, *La Librairie de Philippe le Bon* (Brussels, 1967).

Brussels, Bibliothèque Royale Albert Ier, *Trésors des Bibliothèques d'Ecosse* (Brussels, 1963).

Cambridge, Fitzwilliam Museum, *Illuminated Manuscripts in the Fitzwilliam Museum* (Cambridge, 1966).

Edinburgh, National Library of Scotland, *Treasures of Belgian Libraries* (Edinburgh, 1963).

Edinburgh, Reid School of Music, *European Musical Instruments* (Galpin Society exhibition, Edinburgh, 1968).

London, British Museum, *Catalogue of Manuscript Music in the British Museum*, 3 vols. (London, 1909, reprinted 1965), iii.

London, British Museum, *Illuminated Manuscripts in the Grenville Library* (London, 1967).

London, British Museum, *Romanesque Illuminated Manuscripts in the British Museum* (London, 1966).

London, British Museum, *The Golden Age of Anglo-Saxon Art* (London, 1984).

London, Burlington House, *Treasures from Trinity College Dublin* (London, 1961).

London, Hayward Gallery (Arts Council of Great Britain), *English Romanesque Art 1066–1200* (London, 1984).

London, Public Record Office, *Catalogue of Seals in the Public Record Office: Personal Seals*, i, compiled by Roger H. Ellis (London, 1978).

London, Victoria and Albert Museum, *Catalogue of Musical Instruments*, 2 vols. (London, 1968).

London, Victoria and Albert Museum, *Opus Anglicanum* (London, 1963).

London, National Portrait Gallery, *'The King's Good Servant' Sir Thomas More 1477/8–1535* (Ipswich, 1977).

Manchester, City Art Gallery, *Romanesque Art c.1050–1200* (Manchester, 1959).

Montpellier, Musée Fabre, *Miniatures Médiévales en Languedoc Mediterranean* (Montpellier, 1963).

New York, Pierpont Morgan Library, *The Glazier Collection of Illuminated Manuscripts* (New York, 1968).

Oxford, Bodleian Library, *English Illumination of the Thirteenth and Fourteenth Centuries* (Oxford, 1954).

Oxford, Bodleian Library, *Illuminated Manuscripts in the Bodleian Library*, 3 vols. (Oxford, 1966–73), iii, *British, Irish and Icelandic Schools*.

Oxford, Bodleian Library, *English Romanesque Illumination* (Oxford, 1951).

Oxford, Ashmolean Museum, *The Hill Collection* (London, 1969).

Norwich, Norwich Castle Museum, *Medieval Art in East Anglia 1300–1520*, ed. P. Lasko and N. J. Morgan (Norwich, 1973).

Paris, Louvre, *L'Europe Gothique* (Paris, 1968).

Index

❧❦❧